I APPEARED UNTO YOU

2035 Month of May... the End of Age

2020 Edition Fully Revised and Updated

THOMAS BAYO

Edited by Olubukola Omotoso

New Angels Press

1

I Appeared Unto You
By Thomas Bayo

Published by New-Angels Press/ Thomas Bayo Books

ISBN: 9788895024-26-4

www.thomasbayo.com

First Printed in 2014

Unless otherwise indicated, Bible quotations are taken from the King James Version. Copyright © 1979, Holman Bible Publishers.

Printed in Great Britain

Thomas Bayo

Thanks And Glory To The Lord For His

Wonderful Love

This Book Is Dedicated To My Angel

I Appeared Unto You

TABLE OF CONTENTS

Introduction

The Greatest Scriptural Prophecy of All Time

The generation of Noah knew the year, month, week, day, or hour when they would perish by flood. Going by common sense, the people saw the Ark and they knew the reason for the Ark. They were so blind that they did not take any action to prevent their destruction; because they were not capable of belief.

If, for example I see someone making an Ark in the middle of the city, not even close to the sea side, I may ask, "hello man, your work is fascinating; what are you doing with this stuff here?" Noah never lied, the motive of the Ark was published. The question remains, why did they not believe?

We all know that man has talent, and the ability to create extraordinary wonders such as submarine, spacecraft, strange equipments. Even if man is hedged around with iron in captivity, he still has the ability to escape, but the flood in Noah's time came rapidly and massively with strong tempest and there was no time for man to escape the flood.

As the flood came, means of transportation, communications, all kinds of energy were all destroyed. That flood was designed to kill anything that had breath; all loop holes to escape were blocked.

Man is one of the most dangerous creature and the Creator knows the capabilities of man. He knows how evil the heart of man is, and the Creator has sworn that He will not destroy the world by flood again. This time, He will shake the heavens and the earth and things under the earth.

Those who will be left behind on this earth shall wail in that day and their pains will seem endless. Those who are left behind, God will rebuke them and establish them.

The world refused to repent, men deliberately killed Christ and they knew He was the Son of God. He came doing good, blessing and healing people, yet the world tortured Him, gave Him pains and He was nailed to the Cross. The Europeans had the power to set Him free, yet He was handover to be killed. His apostles were killed in Europe, some were killed in Asia and in Africa. These is the works of men. Man continues to do evil up to this hour.

The wicked and your forefathers are guilty of all the blood of the prophets killed and slaughtered, the Creator as sworn as written in the bible that, starting from Abel to the last prophet killed, their blood shall be required if this generation.

In the time of Noah, they were informed that they would perish. This is same information that has been passed to this present world by the old prophets.

Wise men who are sent from the Lord God, who go to and fro in all the earth have been giving the world the message of the end, but the same problem remains. The ability to believe is not in them that dwell on this earth.

Jesus used the time of Noah as an example in His teachings to the people about the end. Noah was the core of His teachings, while healing and miracles are another aspect that carried heavy weight in His teachings.

One important point, which you need to remember as a believer is that you have many enemies that you may not even know of, many of these enemies live with you and lie within you.

At the time of Noah, the people chose to live in ways that seemed good to their eyes, they did their will, but that day and that hour that was programmed in heaven by God came, and that was their end; they all perished. So shall it be in this generation. There is nothing to hide, God will not hide anything.

It is a foolish person who loves to sleep and slumber thinking inside his heart that the year, month, week and the interval of days when the world will end will not be revealed because they love to sleep, and slumber. You think in your heart that the warning you have been hearing of the end since ages is fiction?

John 3:11 – is the greatest scriptural prophecy of all time, spoken by Jesus and written by John: regarding the ability of man to believe "Verily, verily, I say unto thee, We speak that we do know, and testify that we have seen; and ye receive not our witness."

This is one of the reasons why I was not willing to answer my calling, because I knew it may be a waste of energy to preach to an evil generation, people who refuse to believe. As you read ahead, you will see that I wrote this book with tears, pains, mourning and sufferings and I never wrote this book in mirth. A Biblical language saying 'bring forth the head stone' meaning to announce the date of the end; this is not easy, I paid a high price to write this book.

The truth is that the world did not accept any prophet from the God of heaven, not even one. Biblical history shows that no single human being believed any one of them. If the world had left one of the apostles alive, there may be a process of forgiveness or a table of talk. The apostles were killed, Christ was killed. The destruction of this world is an action of holiness taken by our heavenly Father. They saw Noah and his project, and to them it was nonsense, the world refused to accept.

In all the four corners of the earth, the prophet that is accepted is not a prophet sent from the God of heaven. Those who are sent from God of heaven have been afflicted so sore.

In the book of Revelations, the Creator warned that the last prophet that He will send to announce the date of the end. The Creator put it into law, which He had not done before. He said that anyone who hurts the last prophets must be killed. The Creator used the word "must" and as you read ahead, you will see more of it in this book.

I explored John 3:11, the greatest prophecy of all time, and I gave up my faith in man. I concluded in my judgment that the best way to deal with man is to rule mankind with a rod of iron, because his heart is too hard. The peaceful ones who believe shall live in peace and live a life of paradise as promised by God. The Father in heaven has His own judgment on all the beings He created, He has the power to judge, kill the body, soul, the spirit and cast into hell.

The message of the end has been spoken by the ancients before we were born. This is the same message the modern world is still telling. Finally, God has revealed the date of the end exactly as written in the bible. God is not hiding anything. Why would God hide the date of the end? Tell me, why? Is it because you will escape, or what?

All the prophets have one mission. Nineveh repented when they were told that God was coming to destroy them. God selected one specific person (Jonas) that had a hidden talent, but did want to develop this gift and use it to the glory of God.

But Jonah saw the power of God; God strengthened him to no longer be ashamed, but go and rightly divide the word of truth for the citizens of Nineveh so that they would be saved.

The mission of Jonah as a preacher was a success as they believed, if not Nineveh would had been another Gomorrah.

God uses situations to deal with situations, if you are rebellious man God will use a radical to give you a message for you to understand and know that He is the Creator of the heavens and the earth and everything inside them. If you are a peaceful person, God will also use a peaceful person to give you a message for you to understand. God gives understanding to those who lack understanding because lack of understanding makes people perish.

This book is a complete guide for anyone who believes in the second coming of the Lord Jesus Christ and everything written inside this book, I, (Thomas Bayo) was inspired to write this book in this way; this book is eyewitness account. In writing this book, I do not have any strength of my own. This book came to life by the strength of God Almighty.

Any who believe that I have written this book with my strength and by my wisdom has made an error. However, God has made me a child who will not lie. "For he said, Surely they are my people, children that will not lie: so he was their Saviour". (Isaiah 63:8.)

As for me, my faith is based on what I see I do not believe what I do not see. A lot of information is loaded in this book, with physical evidence for you to believe. As you read, you will understand that there are multitude of eye witness accounts around the world. These folks are still living up to this day. They saw face to face in the physical realm how biblical prophecy was fulfilled, but this was kept as a secret that was not told and all is revealed now regarding the mysteries of the end.

You need power in this world to reveal any secret, or you die a mysterious death of no profit. Because the beings you are revealing are the ones that sit in power in this earth, God gave me power to stand as His witness, and I see this power everyday and it is confirmed. I am using this power that has been given to me to reveal secrets to write this book.

Why do you need to expose those in power when there is no power in your hands? Revealing the secrets of those in power in this world when there is no power in your hands is as self destruction. Many have died tragic deaths trying to unveil secrets and many are awaiting their death for revealing those in power or to attack religion. The wise will seal their tongues and let the righteous justice of God intervene.

This power that has been given to me to write the date of the end is boldly written in the holy bible that even a weak thing can read and understand.

Prophet Zechariah, Isaiah and Apostle John spoke about who would inherit this power to reveal the date of the end; power is needed to make such an announcement. This power has been given to a Gentile, as stated in the bible; it will not go to a Jew. Those who have given a false date of the end, how was their end?

This power will only go to a nation that brings forth fruits to the kingdom of God exactly as written in the bible. This has been fulfilled, and as you read ahead in the second chapter, you will see the evidence of how this power went to a Nigerian citizen; seeing is believing. I don't complete a project that I can't finish; this has been my practice from my youth, even before I heard my calling from the Creator. All my friends knows me, if I say a word, I will do it, I don't say anything that I cannot not do. So, I, Thomas Bayo have already inherited this power. It has been given to me, I am a Gentile.

You cannot understand the words of prophets except there is a wisdom in you, that is why many read the bible, but they cannot understand. The rapture is simple as ABC which is now revealed.

Many generations in the past, wise men and all categories of human beings were thirsty and hungry to know when the Lord Jesus would come back to the earth a second time. They wanted to experience the return of Jesus. They knew the blessings behind seeing the Redeemer coming to the earth in His glory.

Great prophets of the past wanted to know even the year of the end. But it was not their time to know when Jesus will appear to take away the chosen. Words are not enough to describe this present generation that will see that glorious day of God. Our generation is a blessed one. The end of the world is revealed in our generation.

If Jesus is not coming in your generation what is the use in knowing the end? In the past, they only heard the message of the end but the mystery was not given to them.

Do you really need a revelation that you will not witness? Information about the date of the end that you will not see?

The generation that will witness the rapture are the ones that are qualified to know the date of the end. The ancient people were not qualified to know the end because it was not their time. It is our generation that is qualified.

God is holy, and He will not do things that are unholy. God will not give a revelation of what you will not witness regarding the end of age, the testimony of a prophet must be based on true facts, not what you will not see. This is a revelation that came from God, that the earth shall now witness what is written in the bible in reality and in action.

Introduction

Even if you do not believe the date in this book, do not sleep but watch for the coming of the Lord Jesus, do not sleep and slumber like the five foolish virgins and be left behind. Even though you call yourself born again, if you sleep and refuse to watch, you will not be taken. Jesus said you must not sleep but watch, why did He say that? Heaven and earth shall be shaken, and every unshakable shall be shaken; watch the glorious day of God.

There is nowhere in the bible that God commanded any man or woman to sleep and slumber when Jesus will come back. The warning has already be given to you, do not sleep, but watch. You may have mighty faith that moves mountains, your name may sound in the four corners of the earth, but if you sleep and refuse to watch as Christ commanded you to do, this is your fault and not the fault of God neither is the fault of any prophet or the fault of any of the heavenly angels.

The rapture will take place in a twinkle of an eye. Angels will not wake you up, neither will I, Thomas Bayo, wake you up; keep your eyes wide open.

The other five biblical virgins were foolish, because to them, revelation had no meaning. The wise will not sleep but watch because the wise will not take anything for granted and will regard this revelation with a meaning. Slow down their mind with a second thought while the unwise will respond without reasoning. Idle words do not exist in the face of the wise.

The undecided may even say, "well, let us see and we may not sleep, if this man (Thomas Bayo) is even saying the truth". As you read this book, you will see how this revelation came to me and you will be astonished by the wonders of God. The wise will take action, but not with a double mind. A double minded person cannot receive the things of God.

The greatest calamity that can befall a believer, is for him not watch, but sleep in that year, month, week and interval of days.

The bible describe such a person as a fool. The revelation in this book, is not indicating only the year like the way those "foxes in the desert" gave you their revelation that did not come to pass. The date of the end is revealed.

The fool says this revelation has no factor, and will sleep and slumber while the rapture happens. This is a revelation that must be fulfilled. My vision is to strengthen believers to be wise. The Lord Jesus said, "But I have prayed for thee, that thy faith fail not: and when thou art converted, strengthen thy brethren" (Luke 22: 32.)

Jesus Christ cannot make mistakes, and He cannot lie, His speeches were so perfect and no error was found in any of His words. All His speech regarding the end time was pinpointing to: day and hour. But He did not mention year, month, or week. I recommend that you study the bible very well.

So that you do not mislead yourself and others. The bible says, "Watch therefore, for ye know neither the day nor the hour wherein the Son of man cometh" (Matthew 25:13.) What did you see in the above verse? Did you see year, month or week? If you say you did not see year, month and week, you have made a righteous judgment.

However, if you say, what you are seeing here as written in the above verse is day and hour but not year, month and week, then, you have made a righteous judgment. This book will give a perfect understanding of the words of Jesus.

"And what I say unto you I say
unto all, Watch" (Matthew 25:13.)

The word "Watch" here, was written in capitals.

With wisdom, you will know that Jesus will not tell you to watch for His coming all the days of your life and not sleep. The Holy bible did give you a counsel that if you do not have wisdom, ask God to give you wisdom in prayers. It is impossible for Christ to tell anyone to watch without a date framework.

We all know the nature of Jesus, all His words have meaning. If you do not understand He will make you understand.

If you do not believe, then, you may go and sleep and do not watch for the coming of the Lord Jesus in the year 2035, accurate date of His coming revealed in my book.

A wise man, or any person that has great experience in life will tell you that forty years from today is like four months away from now. They that lack knowledge will always say forty or thirty years is too far from now.

The wise will regard thirty years very short and will prepare to stand strong in the judgment of the living God. The coming judgment is very terrible, I tell you the truth.

Time passes and if you do not put your ear to the ground, you may never know that time runs fast like the airplane. This year 2014, people of age of 75 and above may not see the rapture. But we who are alive shall see the rapture. And we cannot contain the joy in the glorious day of God and of partaking in the marriage of the Lamb.

A man cannot wake up from his bed in the morning and say the world will end in 2035; except power is given to a man, he cannot announce the date of the end. Power has been given to me by God the Father. I am revealing the end of the world with power exactly as it is written: Re:11:3: And I will give power unto my two witnesses, and they shall prophesy a thousand two hundred and threescore days, clothed in sackcloth.

Even though I was not willing to be a preacher of the gospel due to my lack of faith when I was an unbeliever, I have no choice, but to strengthen and encourage myself like Jonas to fulfil my calling.

God has no pleasure in death of the wicked. This is about power, not me. You cannot challenge power when power is not given to you.

Bear it in mind that there are many dark forces against me, big military that are fighting against me so that this revelation will not be known to the world but God is my Saviour, and He is your Saviour. When the bible says God is a Saviour, definitely He is a Saviour. They who have experienced the wonders of God know the meaning: God is a Saviour. But the Lord Jesus said, "Verily I say unto you, There be some standing here, which shall not taste of death, till they see the Son of man coming in his kingdom" (Matthew 16:28.)

Jesus wept? Why did Jesus weep when He knew He had the power to raise Lazarus from death? 90% of the world population is unwise. This is a big problem. When pain is beyond what you cannot bear, what comes next is tears. It was so painful to Jesus.

Here is the question, there is recorded biblical evidence that the people `tempting Jesus asked Him for the sign of the end. The word tempting means to do something that is bad, wrong, or unwise. Let us be truthful to ourselves, if somebody temptingly asks you a question, what will you do? You would do same thing Jesus did. Jesus brushed that question aside by telling them He did not know the date of the end, what He knows is that He is coming back again, period. And He departed from them. The Creator never said He would not reveal the date of the end.

There is no place where it is written in the bible that God does not know the date of the end.

There is nowhere in the bible that says, "I, the Creator will not reveal the date of the end."

Because, for the question, 'when is the date of the end?' The answer has been in the bible since the days of the prophets. Nobody can fool Jesus.

In this fact, the date of the end is written on a tree in the bible, this tree is located near mountain Ararat in the geographical location where the second life began after the flood of Noah, where eight people came down from the Ark that survived the first world destruction.

The category of people who asked Jesus were recorded in the bible as teachers, they were genii. If a genius can be proved unwise, what about the ordinary man? Ignorance is very catastrophic. We depend on geniuses to teach us the truth. Since time past, false teachers that claimed they were genius have given to us false dates of the end, some of them said the world would end in the year 2000, 2005, 2012, 2013 and much more, but the world has not ended.

In the bible, the date when the world will end is clearly written in code, but no one has been able to crack it, not even the brightest scholar; Mission Impossible. It is that tree in the garden that gave man knowledge that we can be wise and create like God Himself, and same tree that the date of the end is located. Knowledge is hidden in the tree.

Spoken by prophet Isaiah, "O LORD, be gracious unto us; we have waited for thee: be thou their arm every morning, our salvation also in the time of trouble" (Isaiah 13:2.) Terrorist hitting the world so hard, people dying and in fear, diseases that cannot be cured and people dying every day. How many can escape that terrible day of the end?

My book is a revelation, I have included my car accident in this book as you can see the image, a car accident that happened in Sweden, you can see a mystery in the background of my car accident, boldly written THE END, that was the shopping paper bag that I shopped with in Italy, a well known brand in Italy called, THE END. As you read ahead in the forth chapter, if you look carefully in the image you will see the bible on the ground, between my car and the fire fighters.

I drove from Italy to my home in Sweden, when I was in school and you will see the bible on the ground that fell from the boot compartment of the car due to the impact of the car accident, the car boot pulled out and flew in another direction, But nothing hurt me.

The car turned upside down and there was no way I could come out, the doors were pressed and sized, the only way out was I crept out of the car boot compartment safe and unharmed, to the extent that my clothes were not stained and the car was destroyed.

The nation of Sweden praised God when they saw the car accident and it was published nationwide in the famous newspaper known in Sweden as Expressen. Everybody told me, "please give us the revelation you have".

To become a biblical revelation genius is not the work of academics; bible prophecies come with code or sealed-lock. And the mystery behind the book of Revelations is that the ancient prophet who wrote down the prophesies was not even given the keys of the revelations, the evidence of this is written in the book of Revelations, when Apostle John was instructed to take a pen and write down his message, it was a dictation. It shows clearly that the revelations were given to the prophets, and the codes were not given to them. That is why many people stumble to know revelations, and some even give the opposite.

Bible prophesies have the highest security on this planet, because if prophecies do not have a code, false prophets will take advantage of a non-secured revelation to deceive men.

When a person opens the book of Revelations, how does he or she feel? Many pastors don't even open the book of Revelations, because they do not know how. I once heard a pastor condemning some bible revelations, because he did not understand them I laughed. Prophecies always come with code, since it's a high scale project.

To crack and decode a revelation, this is how it works: you can only use your own revelation to decode another revelation.

To reveal the date of the end is a top class project on this earth, and nothing can compete with it.

When I wrote a book that Pope Benedict XVI Ratzinger should resign, he resigned in February, 2013; this prophecy came to pass. I had physical proof against him. Titled, Vatican Pope A Liar A Defrauder.

I want you to understand that somebody gave a prophecy in 2008 that the Vatican Pope should quit; people demonized the author of this work, and claimed that it was not in line with their beliefs, so they ignored it.

But in February 2013, the Vatican Pope resigned, and that

shocked the entire world; they had never seen a Pope resign. This prophecy came to pass. I wrote a mocking letter to the Gibson Square Books LTD47 Lonsdale Square London UK-N1 1EWUK, and told them that, "now that you refused my works, what if this prophecy comes to truth?" Who will be the liar? You can see clearly that God did not make me a lair.

How do you feel when you tell people the truth and yet they do not want to accept? do you feel good? This was what made Jesus weep as recorded in the bible. He knew He could raise Lazarus from the dead, and yet He wept. Because, the ability to believe was not with the people. Ignorance is very destructive; this is how the people ignore important projects in their lives.

God Himself gave me three prophecies: one has been accomplished; the one of the Pope that publishers rejected. The second prophecy is the date that God gave to me when the world will end, this date is boldly written in the bible, and the same date written on a tree located in Europe, as recorded in the bible.

HEADSTONE: The bible is well known as the holiest book in heaven and in the earth, considered perfect and blessed; there is no error found inside. They that have wisdom know very well that the holy bible is very precise in all of its words, except many do not understand what the bible is saying. Such people who do not understand what the bible is saying need help and guidance from a third party to understand what the holy book is saying.

For example the bible says,

"Saying to the sixth angel which had the trumpet,
Loose the four angels which are bound in the great
river Euphrates. And the four angels were loosed,
which were prepared for an hour,and a day, and a
month, and a year, for to slay the
third part of men" (Revelation 9:14,15.)

The focus here is the dates. And you can clearly see it as written in these verses that the year, month, week, day and hour were mentioned here very precisely.

There is a difference between the sound of the sixth angel and the sound of the seventh angel. They have different duties.

In the dates regarding the loosing of the four angels bounded in river Euphrates, the bible indicates the hour, day, month and the year. These dates were not written for you not to know, the scriptures must be fulfilled, these dates are something that you have to know, that is why they were written. God did not see any reasons why you should not know these dates.

When the seventh angel sounds, it is the end of the world. This is when our joy will come and our tears will be wiped away.

We have been afflicted so sore and we have waited so long in this world of conflicts.

Let us see what is written in the holy bible, by comparing the sixth angel's sound to the sound of the seventh angel. The sixth angel's sound is when salvation will end, and the seventh angel's sound is the end of the world. People do not know what the sixth sound of the angels means.

"But in the days of the voice of the seventh angel, when he shall begin to sound, the mystery of God should be finished, as he hath declared to his servants the prophets. And the seventh angel sounded; and there were great voices in heaven, saying, The kingdoms of this world are become the kingdoms of our Lord, and of his Christ; and he shall reign forever and ever" (Revelation 8: 2,3.)

In the verses above, we shall look at the seventh trumpet. It will sound before the kingdom of our Christ is established and these present kingdom of this world of darkness and their government of evil and wickedness shall be taken from them and given to the Saints. We shall rule forever and ever with Christ.

Introduction

The world needs to know the year, month, week, day and the hour that the sixth angel sounded. When you survey the mystery or the revelation behind the sixth trumpet you will find out that God has nothing to hide when it comes to the seventh trumpets.

However, in regards to when the world will end, the Lord said, "But of that day and that hour knoweth no man, no, not the angels which are in heaven, neither the Son, but the Father" (Mark 13:32.)

My mission is to persuade human beings and continue to testify at any level that Jesus never mentioned year, month and week. What He pointed specifically was day and hour, a perfect and wonderful speech. The Holy bible is so precise and the judgment of God is holy; there are no errors.

You are not going to see the sixth angel, neither will you hear the sound of his trumpet; the sounding of the sixth angel's trumpet has nothing to do with the end of the world. This sound is not for you; you are not chained, if you are waiting or expecting to hear this sound, you will not hear anything. The sixth angel is designed to loose the four angels that were bound in river Euphrates, and there was a specific reason why these four angels were bound in river Euphrates.

The reason why the four angels were bound in river Euphrates is another topic.

Those four angels bound in river Euphrates means hell (prison.) Except you are in hell (prison) you cannot see how these four angels were in the prison.

The witness who will testify to this revelation, such a prophet must be in hell to see by himself what is happening, and his testimony will be based on what he has seen, as a truthful testimony. The sixth sound is not something a person will testify of based what he has read.

You must enter hell and see what is going on there and testify of what you have seen so that your testimony is true.

Except power is given to a man by God, he cannot see these angels. these four angels are very powerful and they are killers. Loosed to kill. It is the man who has seen these angels that will testify about what he has seen and quote the dates, which is the year, month, day and hour.

The bible described these four angels as killers. You cannot see these angels and live, except power has been given to you by God Himself. If you believe you can see these angels and live, you have lied.

The sixth angel sounded already, which was published in my first book, titled What Do You Want? The date the seventh angel will sound is written in the bible, which I also wrote in my book. Jesus never said nobody knows the date when the sixth angel will sound. The date is revealed.

The bible is precise about its word when it says nobody knoweth the day and the hour when the world will end. This is a perfect spoken word that is recorded in the bible.

I will always encourage people and I do not discourage anyone. "But I have prayed for thee, that thy faith fail not: and when thou art converted, strengthen thy brethren" (Luke 22: 32.) You can see the reason why it's a prophet's duty to encourage believers after he has repented?

You must repent first before you can encourage a brother; if you have not repented while you are preaching to a brother, your preaching has an error. Repent first. Think this word twice and re study the spoken word of the Lord.

"and when thou art converted,
strengthen thy brethren"
(Luke 22:32.)

Believers have areas in their ministries, but I am blessed by God when it comes to revelations.

Not everyone has the capacity to teach the book of Revelations. Revelation is what that has been covered and later revealed, and you cannot interpret revelation when you do not have revelation.

A revelation is what you have seen that you are testifying of. It is an error to testify to what you did not see. If you use academic knowledge to interpret the book of Revelations, it may seem sweet in the mouth, but if you did not see anything, there is no truth in that testimony.

A blind man cannot teach revelation. It is he that revelation has been given, such a soul is competent to testify of what he has seen.

What I am teaching in the bible is not based on academic knowledge, my teaching is to testify to what I have seen face to face. This is exactly the ministry of the all the prophets: they all testified of what they had seen, and none of them testified of what they did not see or touch with their hands. What they touched with their two hands, they told the people.

Any man who has seen God the Father face to face in this generation, the revelation will be given to him; it is good news that will encourage the believers. Because what everyone is waiting for, is the end of the world. All of us are waiting for the end. And God cannot appear to a man in this generation without telling him when the world will end. God does not keep secrets from His friends exactly as written in the bible,

"The secret of the Lord is with them that fear him; and he will shew them his covenant" (Psalm 25:14.)

In the bible, God called and made man His friend. For example, if God appears to you today, would your first question not be, "Father, when shall the world end"

Everyone asked Christ this question of the end. Even His own disciples asked Him. Jesus let them know that only God the Father knows it. The question regarding the end of the world is so important.

People tell lies that God appeared to them. If you are truly the friend of God, He will tell you His secrets because friends do not keep secrets from each other. God did appear to His prophets. Joseph Smith of Mormon movement did not see God not even Jesus, including Benny Hinn, they lied. This is impossible for the Creator to pay a divine visit to a person in New York, God's divine visits are always in the capital city of any nation. There was no biblical proofs of Joseph Smith statement, not even

Benny Hinn. This is impossible for Jesus to appear to a person that is holy, so what is Benny Hinn talking about?

A bible prophesy genius will tell you that God cannot go to New-York city. Why? New-York is located on east part of the United States, which is the left hand of God. There are a lot of biblical evidence that the Creator has no dealing with the east.

All false religion in the world are all positive to the east exception of one religion that is not positive to the east which is Christianity; which many Christians do not know this. The Creator allowed Satan to exist for now but on the east side, so if Satan is coming to any country it will be on the east part but cannot proceed to the north part. The comprehensive explanation of this will be on my next coming book, titled, Vatican Pope A Liar A Defrauder.

Prophet Micaiah saw the Lord God and he said the truth, "I saw the Lord sitting on his throne" (1 Kings 22:19.)

If you are saying that your friend appeared to you and he did not tell you his mind, there is no friendship there. The God of heaven does not appear to servants; masters don't show servants secrets. He appears to men whom He made His friends, and reveals secrets to them.

For example, God appeared to king Solomon. What Solomon requested from God was wisdom, and He gave wisdom to Solomon. Solomon never asked for the end of the world from God.

If king Solomon had asked God to tell him when the world would end, God would have definitely told him. This is for sure. Solomon was a very wise man, so wise that he believed there was no point asking God about the end when Christ was not even yet born in his time.

Christ is the author of the end; He came a first time by virgin birth, which was a fulfilment of the words spoken by the prophets, and He is coming again a second time. But this time, not by birth but with power and ten thousands of His saints to execute what is called judgment, which you also have read about in the holy bible.

Jesus does not want to know when the world will end. He

is same as God the Father, but the point is, He only submitted some of His rights to God the Father according to His will, which includes not knowing the day and the hour of the end.

What makes my faith like a rock today is what I have seen face to face. It is the Holy Ghost that makes a revelation truthful. God is light; in Him there is no darkness. I remain strong despite the fact that we have been afflicted so sore by the wickedness of this world.

To be a pastor does not mean that you have wisdom; there are many pastors who have wisdom in them. I have surveyed them; there is pride in their lives, they refuse to repent, refuse to obey, refuse to listen and they are self esteemed. All my spoken words are with power that has been given to me; my words are not mere words. Living in this physical world is a tough task and God is helping me by His grace and I am taking the challenges.

How do you define the wisdom of God? People mistake the academic wisdom of this world for the wisdom of God. Academic wisdom is a tradition of men, and the impact of this has affected the church of God which makes the works of God of no effect.

Be a pastor with patience, positive communication and ready to reason with God.

Saying to a learned man that the world is going to end, such a learned man will ask you, when will the world end? You blink or roll your eyes in another direction and you tell him that you do not know.

Such a man will tell you that you are ignorant and anyone that believes you is foolish, your testimony is based on what you do not know, Jesus knew that He was dealing with people who were blind, and any question Jesus answered regarding the end of the world was based on their blindness, the answer He gave, is for blind people who actually have eyes, but cannot see with it. Jesus never said that the year, month, week, interval of days of the end will not be revealed, He said nobody knows the day and the hour.

The bible used the word 'Headstone' to label the date of the end, the Father Himself never said that I, the Lord will not reveal the date of the end of the world, God said He will reveal it (since only He knows it) prophet Zechariah described how the date of the end will be revealed, a term or a word that matches the subject of discussion: the end of age: this is eternal death. The bible was telling you that somebody will bring forth the headstone. Look at the verse below.

> "and he shall bring forth
> the headstone thereof
> with shoutings, crying,
> Grace, grace unto it."
> (Zechariah 4:7.)

Headstone is a gravestone or tombstone. This is a question of mourning and remembrance. And the right word used by the bible actually matches the subject of discussion. Headstones must always carry a date: day, month, year, and hour. If you have wisdom, ask yourself, which headstone in the entire world that does not carry a date? Or which headstone have you seen that has no date?

In the verse above, that is the date of the end that includes the day, hour, month and year, that is written in the bible, and the people asking a question that has already been answered, Jesus knew that these people were fooling themselves. The wicked shall continue to fool themselves, this is your headstone.

When the bible used the word "headstone", the false prophets will tremble over it because, this is the date of their end, the headstone.

Somebody will bring forth the date of the end. Zechariah mentioned the person's name who would bring forth this date.

A headstone is to commemorate a famous event or placed by a statue or over a grave in memory of the dead. If the bible is pointing you to a headstone, this is eternal death. This is the doomsday.

If you believe that a headstone does not carry dates, then, you remain ignorant and your knowledge is behind the clock.

Except your heart is hard – the bible already told you "...he shall bring forth the headstone..." It is only through the headstone that you will know the date of the end and nothing more. As you read on, you will see how the date was revealed.

An ignorant person does not succumb to wisdom, no matter the length, that is why you have to treat an ignorant man according to his ignorance. It will be at your own risk to fully engage the ignorant, because you will heavily be contaminated. So take care of yourself.

This is the only advice a prophet can give to you, he may not give you money. Be careful with the ignorant or beware of them. They chose to go backward.

We are living in the mist of the ignorant, so life is not easy. Exactly why Jesus told His disciples that they should beware of the Pharisees. Pharisees are religious people that include the so called Christians that chose to backward, Muslims, Buddhist, Jewish leaders and much more. These are ignorant people.

I, Thomas Bayo, the author of this book, what pains me mostly is that, these ignorant are the pastors who are controlling millions of believers around the globe. Can you imagine this? What made prophet Hosea write that my people are destroyed for lack of knowledge. Who are his people here? These are the ones that called themselves Christians and pastors who rejected knowledge. Even the apostles wrote it down for you in the holy book that the righteous are scarcely saved. Because of ignorance.

Look at what the Creator is saying here, "My people are destroyed for lack of knowledge: because thou hast rejected knowledge, I will also reject thee, that thou shalt be no priest to me: seeing thou hast forgotten the law of thy God, I will also forget thy children" (Hosea 4:6.) This verse, you are a rejected pastor because you rejected knowledge, you rejected the headstone, your members who are your children are rejected people and they are not children of God. The greatest prophecy of all time is: (John 3:11.)

There is a difference between dealing with a blind man and dealing with a man that sees; if you are dealing with a blind man as if you are dealing with a man that sees, then you need a physician yourself. Deal with a blind man on the basis of his blindness.

What do the scriptures says about the ways of God? He speaks once, Jesus is the invisible image of God, and in the book of Zechariah He has spoken to the world that to know the date of the end, it will come from Zerubbabel.

It is now left for the world to find out who Zerubbabel is, that will bring forth this headstone (the date of the doomsday.) And what do you understand when the bible says "crying, shouting Grace, grace", on this subject of the headstone? This is something to do with salvation regarding the topic of the headstone.

The name Zerubbabel is a biblical code name for strong safety measures to protect this date of the end. And if these names are not coded, a liar will say I am Zerbbabel, just like what some have done before by giving fake doomsday date to the world and many were deceived, sold their houses and properties expecting to arrive in heaven but at the end, it was a fake date.

Example of code names and how it functions: a code name is designed for a high profile project, and the code name can only be revealed at the appointed time or when the project is successful.

The world has been trying to crack the date of the end, but it has been a mission impossible. Many have come out with lies that the world end would end in 2012, 2011, many wrong dates. If you cannot crack the code name of this great prophecy, the date of the end, there is no way you can even crack the name of the man that will reveal the date of the end.

Zerubbabel here is Adebayo from Nigeria, records did show that Nigeria is the greatest religious country on this planet, which BBC did broadcast that the country that believes in God is Nigeria, more of this is in the book as you read on. The Creator has spoken that it is only the country that brings forth fruit that He will chose Zerubbabel from.

Introduction

The world's high profile people who are men of note, presidents of nations, world super powers do have code names, such code names are very confidential, and it is only the military and secret service personnel who know any code name, except the names are revealed. Example of the United States former president, George W. Bush, his codename was Trailblazer.

Code names are for safety measures, for example if a military personnel or a secret service agent working in the United Sates White House and mention Renegade, you who are an ordinary man will not know whom they are talking about. But if the name is revealed to the public, this is when you will know that they are talking about George W. Bush.

All this explanation is to define to you what a code name means. It has been existing in the bible and there is a codename for a signet of God.

Jesus Christ Himself, His name was coded as Emmanuel, and when He was born, He was named Jesus. For example, if anyone had be born at that time and claimed that his name was Emmanuel and that he was the Christ because the prophets mentioned that His name would be called Emmanuel he would have lied. Before Emmanuel was revealed, it was only the prophets and heavenly citizens who know Emmanuel was a code name for Jesus.

Any person who knows how to use code names for a project or people has taken the key of knowledge. Code names originated from garden Eden or from the bible, the knowledge of code name is from the tree of knowledge, and the bible came from the tree of knowledge, if not for the Tree of knowledge, there is no way bible would be in existence.

This is the name that was given to me by my parents, but only heaven knows my code name, which is Zerubbabel, but now it's revealed.

If you meet a man who has taken or been given the key of wisdom and ask him of Zerubbabel, he will tell you that such a name is only given by tradition based on the actual time of birth, and only a royal descent bears such a name, not everyone. If you track the prophecy of Zechariah, the witness of God who will bring forth the headstone is of royal descent, internationally connected with a trace of captivity, not just anyone who will say "God, send me".

The holy bible does not use names to identify prophets; revelations were given to various prophets, and is our duty to crack its code and unveil it to the world. Adebayo, abbreviated to 'Bayo, is a Yoruba Christian name. If you Google the meaning of Adebayo, it is well defined in the dictionary.

Something motivates parents to name a child. Parents don't gives name to a child for naming sakes, and names have meaning. A question you should ask yourself is, "what does my name stands for?" Or "why was this name given to me?"

Why was I named Bayo? And what does it mean? This is originally a Nigerian native Yoruba name, which means a child that is born into power, wealth and joy, in accordance to the bible, "and he shall bring forth the headstone thereof with shoutings, crying, Grace, graceunto it. (Zechariah 4:7.)

In the time of my birth my father got a great wealth, my uncle was crowned as a king and I lived in his palace. The king was very nice with me, my father was given the highest chief title in my land because he was rich and powerful, and he was called the greatest man in my land. Today the Creator gave me power, so you can see that my name is in accordance to what the bible says.

Meanwhile, if you base your hope or expectation on academic works in this book, this book will definitely fail you. This book is not an academic work, at all, this book is a matter of eternal death that affects your life: the Headstone.

They that see with look at the headstone. The Lord speaks only once and if you do not take it, your heart becomes hardened. If you are dealing with people that are blind, it may result in disaster except God intervenes.

Some blind people who have eyes think that they see with their eyes; these are lairs, you are a blind man. These are like the foxes in the desert that do not see anything.

However, the revelation of the date of the end remains solid.

Why? Because it came with the package of grace, Grace. My eyes were full of tears. People may not know the meaning of grace, the word Grace here is, freely given, unmerited favour and love of God. The word grace is written in the bible twice in this specific verse, this is to tell you the weight or the capacity of a revelation that has been given to you, a special grace marked in capital letters.

As written in the bible with capital letter Grace, grace, twin: the English defines twice as: in doubled quantity or degree. The grace written in capital is, approval, satisfaction or delight. This is a love without condition. To challenge this date written in this book carries eternal punishment.

For example, if a person has cancer and he or she knows the day of death, such a person can prepare his or her headstone, write his or her name, short life story, date, engraved or cast on the gravestone, awaiting.

There are people who buy their coffins before they die. Why do you think headstone has been engraved and cast? It carries a topic and dates. So, the year, month, day and hour of the end is already revealed based on His GRACE. So, when Jesus says nobody knows the hour and the day it has a meaning: this is what this book all about. Keep on reading and enjoy your book. God bless you. Amen.

Biblical truth clearly show that Jacob saw God face to face. Secondly, he wrestled with God, so if you engage in any kind of activities with the Creator either in physical or spiritual, and touch the Creator with your hand, and the Creator touches you with His hand, there must be an evidence of His DNA in your behavioural and molecular genetics.

For a person to bring forth the date of the end, there must be a genetic evidence of his relationship with the Creator, because such a date is the greatest project on earth. I use the opportunity to testify of my relationship and activities with the Creator. To publish the result of my DNA, and information about the end is embedded on my DNA. So, the date of the end has a genetic evidence, secondly a date found in the bible on the tree.

The result of my DNA was given to me by forensic technicians. The end of the world embedded on my DNA by the Creator exactly as spoken by prophet Zechariah, Apostle John, as you read ahead you see more of it.

For a person to give the date of the end, one of the most important projects in this world, it would be impossible for his biography not to appear in the bible. All the prophets who fulfilled great prophesies have their biographies written in the bible. Prophet Zechariah revealed in the bible that the two end time witnesses of God are a man and a woman, and also revealed the DNA of the two witnesses which I published in my book titled, What Do You Want?

Kings College, London and Case Western Reserve University in Ohio, carried out a research study recently about, How Entrepreneurship Might Be Genetic. Their study revealed that your genes can affect your tendency to be an entrepreneur by influencing the type of personality you develop. I personally contacted, Lesley Nott, Kings College, London and discussed with some of the scientists and I told them of my project exactly on, How a Prophet Might Be Genetic. They agreed to assist me on this study in their laboratory.

In this book, I hereby donate my DNA in this book, and any scientists is free to use it for research, including institutions, medical laboratories, media houses, churches, religious ministries, police, judges, law firm, judiciary courts, journalists, government, students, teachers, researchers to use it for any projects that includes, educational, publications and much more. If you need sample hair or saliva and a proper consent letter, you are free to email me. 2035project@gmail.com. Please, just let me know the name of laboratory or the institution or whatever. Thank you and God bless you.

Many false prophets who are like foxes in the desert, did not see anything, they have told you in the past that the world will end. But nothing happened, but my revelation is genuine with a physical data: my DNA proves it.

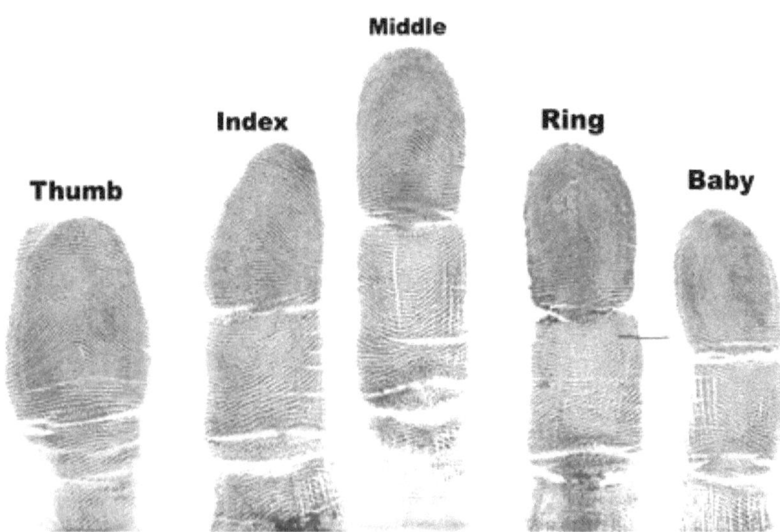

Thumb
Index
Middle
Ring
Baby
Right Hand

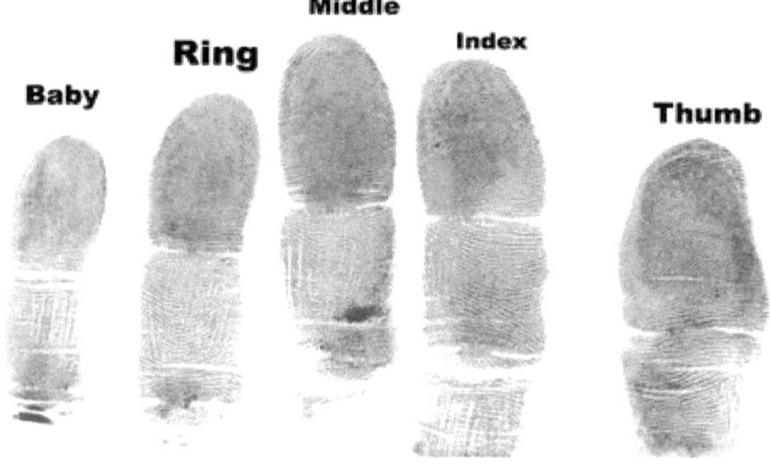
Baby
Ring
Middle
Index
Thumb
Left Hand

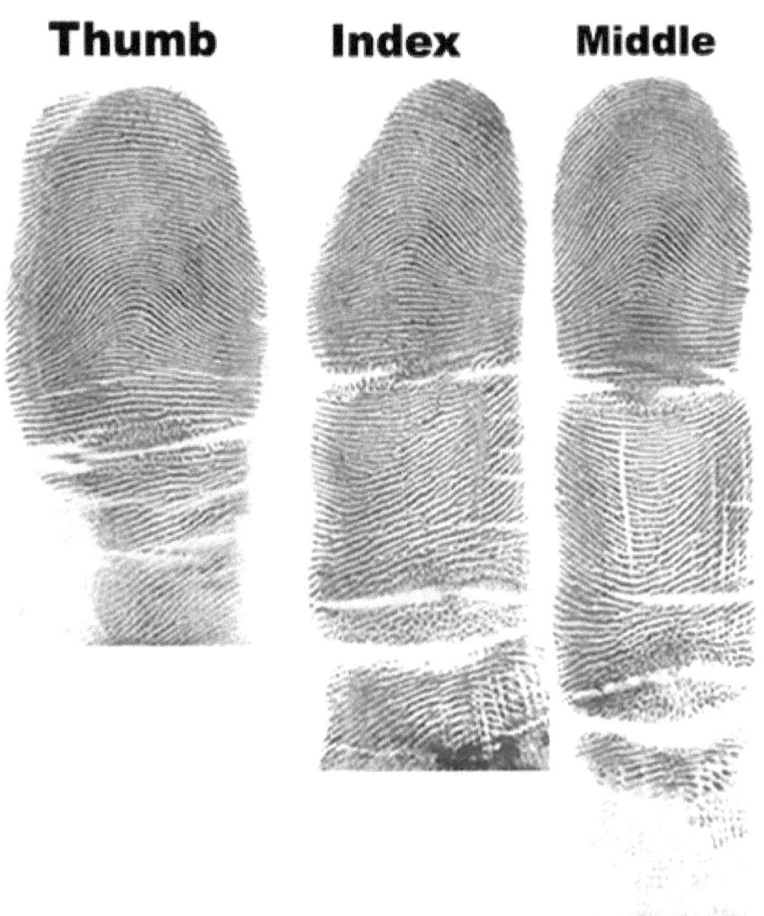

Thumb
Index
Middle

Ring

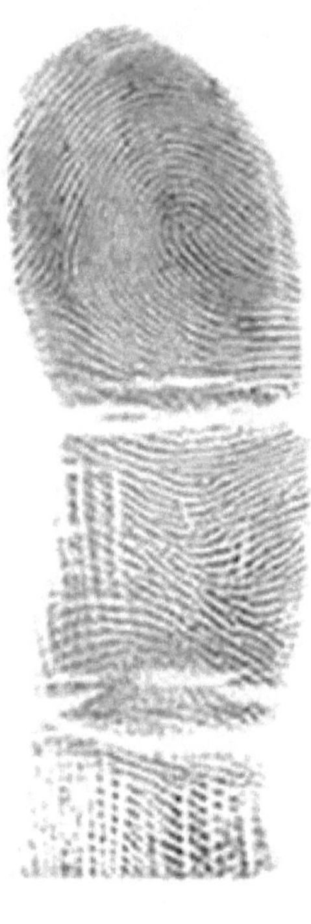
Baby

I Appeared Unto You

Chapter One

The Antichrist

In history, April 4th 1998, the Antichrist was revealed physically and seen by thousands of people, but these April fools did not know; they are still expecting the Antichrist.

Folks from the four corners of the earth, Africans, Americans, Europeans, Asians and the Islands saw the Antichrist face to face in the physical realm, it was the Antichrist that was written in the holy bible and he has come and gone, this prophecy was fulfilled in the year 1998. But this remain an untold story.

The late Archbishop Bishop Benson Idahosa, was a Charismatic Pentecostal preacher, and founder of the Church of God Mission International, that had 6 million followers worldwide. His burial ceremony took place in a national stadium in Nigeria, where all the world's greatest preachers attended including Osborn of Oklahoma, Reinhard Bonnke and many other great preachers from different countries including Asia. The day of Idahosa's burial in the stadium Satan was revealed and seen by many.

People saw the Antichrist face to face bodily as he revealed himself, and this was kept a secret. Many of the "big fish" preachers in all the earth who control millions of people in congregations were present on that day, with a physical proof including a video record, yet they kept it secret.

The huge congregation of people saw Satan, who is also called Lucifer the devil, also called the beast, face to face in the physical realm as he revealed himself, and he has been worshiped as God standing in the holy place. The Antichrist has come and gone but the April fools are still expecting the Antichrist up to this day.

With patience, carefully read below what is taken from the

BBC with a meaning and with wisdom, with a question and with an answer. The Antichrist is a religious belief, but not a political matter and this is not entertainment, this is an issue of life and death, that is why I have to draw the attention of people to what is happening in the entire world.

The issue of the Antichrist has a role to play in a nation that leads in religious belief worldwide.

Conducted by ICM poll for the BBC. Independent Communications and Marketing, a member of the British Polling Council (BPC.)

BBC is a news media which many African depend on. It has good credibility compared to many other news agencies, BBC has an ear to the ground, things happening in the land and things happening in the air when you stay connected to them.

As written by British Broadcasting Cooperation below.

NIGERIA LEADS IN RELIGIOUS BELIEF

A survey of people's religious beliefs carried out in 10 countries this year suggests that Nigeria is the most religious nation in the world. Ten thousand people were questioned in the ICM poll for the BBC programme What The World Thinks Of God.

Over 90% of Nigerians said they believed in God, prayed regularly and would die for their belief.

The highest levels of belief were found in some of the world's poorer countries, as well as in the US.

The countries polled were the US, the UK, Israel, India, South Korea, Indonesia, Nigeria, Russia, Mexico and Lebanon. The interviews were carried out in January 2004. India and Indonesia were also recorded as countries with a high level of belief in God.

But the results of the poll showed that levels of belief and religious activity in the UK, Russia and South Korea were consistently lower than in most of the other countries polled.

In Lebanon and the US, 71% said they were willing to die for their God or their beliefs. In most of the countries covered, well over 80% said they believed in God or a higher power. In Nigeria the figure was 100% and in the US 91%, with the

UK scoring lowest at 67%.

In Nigeria 91% of people said they regularly attended a religious service, contrasting with 21% in the UK and only 7% of Russians. The average across the 10 countries was 46%.

In most countries well over 80% of the sample agreed that a belief in God or a higher power made people better human beings, with only 56% agreeing in the UK - by far the lowest figure.

The subject of prayer found 95% of Nigerians and 67% in the US claiming to pray regularly. Those saying they never prayed included 29% of Israelis and 25% of Britons. But across the entire sample, almost 30% of all atheists surveyed said they sometimes prayed.

The world has conducted its survey on the nation that leads in religious belief. Heaven did not deny this result. No one can cover the truth. Can heaven deny this result? No way. Heaven will not lie.

Before the earth conducted its poll, heaven had already conducted it polls on the nation that leads in religious belief. Heaven and the earth arrived at same result: that Nigeria leads in religious belief in the entire world.

The big question is, the nation that leads in religious belief, what role does it have to play in the end time?

The second big question is, the nation that leads in religious beliefs, what is the spiritual impact on it?

The third question is, what is the interest of Satan in a nation that lead in religious belief?

This result has triggered the invitation of the ultimate killer onto Nigeria. And why was this religious belief poll conducted by ICM poll for the BBC? People who have wisdom and understanding will learn from all corners. BBC is doing its work and it has done a wonderful job as evidence that they can be able to deliver astonishing news.

So, heaven and the earth know who leads in religious belief, and a biblical prophecy will be fulfilled in a nation that leads in religious belief, heaven and earth recognise such a nation and what are the benefits and the shortcomings?

The world gave us the answer already: people who have faith, how many people will have this knowledge and understanding that heaven has conducted its survey to find out the nation that lead in religious belief.

People may say there is no data to prove a result from heaven regarding the nation that leads in religious belief compared to ICM poll for BBC. But now there is data from heaven with strong physical evidence as to how this prophecy was fulfilled in a nation that leads in religious belief.

Nigeria, which leads in religious belief worldwide has a great role to play in the end time events. Secondly, the Antichrist was revealed in Nigeria, and people from all parts of the world were present on that day. And there is no data greater than this. You will see how the ultimate killer (Satan) was revealed in Nigeria, seen by thousands of people who are still living witnesses up to this day as you read on.

I believe what the BBC said is exactly what is written in the holy bible, God said He would give the kingdom to a nation that brings forth fruit, so, Israel is totally ruled out in this case.

Do not expect any revelation from Israel regarding the end time and not even Rome. If you are expecting any revelation from these zones, then, you are behind the clock. The date of the end will come from Nigeria. All the preachers in the entire world who have trade mark names are keeping their eyes on Nigeria, all of them have visited Nigeria. Look at what the bible says here about Nigeria.

"Therefore say I unto you, The kingdom of God shall be taken from you, and given to a nation bringing forth the fruits thereof" (Matthew 21:43.)

The bible says a nation, not nations. This is a specific nation.
When you have knowledge and understanding and take time to survey this spoken word of God, then, believe that Israel is not a nation that brings forth fruit to the kingdom. That

does not mean Israel is not qualified for salvation. Israel has everlasting salvation but with a definition. (As written by prophet Isaiah). Salvation is of three packages. The complete details of this teaching are already explained in another of my book titled, What Do You Want?

Nigeria is a key factor in fulfilling the end time prophecy for its religious recognition and spiritual position in heaven and on earth. So, look to Nigeria when talking about the end time. Tribal and ethnic conflicts, ransom kidnapping and many troubles at the exact time of Christ's coming as spoken by the prophets. False preachers will rise everywhere and many shall be deceived. They shall be fooled.

I was deeply touched in the heart when I heard from ABC news in USA that, Nigeria is well known for its religious and loving people, but missionaries are been kidnapped for ransom. Isaiah plainly said of the end time that our salvation is in the time of trouble.

"O LORD, be gracious unto us; we have waited for thee: be thou their arm every morning, our salvation also in the time of trouble. (Isaiah 33:2.)

In the bible, Daniel did foretell of the "419" phenomenon that is happening in Nigeria today, and the full teaching of this is already in the book titled, What Do You Want? At 18 years old, my younger sister Rachael joined the police force, and as she finished her training, she started full duty as a police officer. One day, I saw her arrest some folks and I asked her, "why are you arresting these folks?" She said that they were 419 people. And I asked her what 419 is. She replied, "have you not heard of 419?" I said to her, "no", this is my first time of hearing about this 419", she explained that 419 is a criminal code in the Nigerian law for fraud.

The people were so eager to find out from Jesus the exact year, month and week when the world will end. Jesus did not tell them for a reason, and He pointed and named a prophet, another Jonas shall come which is me, Thomas Bayo.

Jesus pointed plainly in the bible that the prophet who will reveal the date of the end, his life style and characteristics will be exactly like that of prophet Jonas, and you will see a wonder in his life as a sign of the prophet, which manifested in Sweden and it was national news. The full testimony of this is in the book titled, What Do You Want?

For God to chose a man, the outside looks do not matter; God does not look at the outward appearance of a man He looks at the inside of a man. Your colour is not important to God and the Holy Ghost does not look at your colour; He is interested in your heart since, He has power to forgive.

Does the Creator have an interest in any nation that lacks religious belief? Will God pass over a nation that leads in religious beliefs?

There is no way the Creator will skip over a nation that leads in religious belief and chose a prophet from another country. He said He would give the kingdom to a nation that brings forth fruit. God did chose me, Thomas Bayo to reveal the end of the world.

When God the Father came from His throne in heaven, visited me on this earth and showed me Himself from hair to His toe and showed me His glory face to face, He spoke to me with His mighty voice.

The inspiring question is, what is so important that the Creator has to visit me by Himself and not send an angel? Yes, I will testify of Him, my testimony will be based on what I have seen, so when I tell you I have seen the Creator face to face, this is based on truth and any message that come from me is from Him, and by challenging this book is to challenge the Creator because He sent me and I do not send myself.

This book is of a mighty message or a date that will affect every life on the planet, and will affect the unborn children. A snare that is coming on a massive scale that is greater than that of the flood of Noah, Nineveh, Sodom and Gomorrah, in the wilderness, the plague of Egypt, the wall of Jericho that fell.

The Author is God and the announcer is man, then God paid a visit to the man who will make the announcement to the entire world so that his witness will not be based on second hand information or what he has read.

The revelation of the Antichrist is based on eyewitness account. A true life story. I ran away from my calling like Jonas. When Jonas was kept in a belly of a fish for three days and three nights, he saw the power of God.

Jonah repented under captivity in the belly of a fish, repented with great sorrow, tears and lamentation and said, "yes, LORD, I will tell Nineveh to repent or they will be destroyed".

Any nation on this earth that says they have more religious belief than Nigeria has to reason twice. God entered the earth from His throne in heaven and visited Nigeria only to see His friend, Thomas Bayo, this is the testimony I have and I have good news for you. However, another being also visited Nigeria to see his children and who is that? In history, April 4th, 1998, the Antichrist was revealed, visited Nigeria to see his children.

Here is the deal: God the Father revealed Himself to the Jews at river Jordan when John baptized Jesus, the people saw the Holy Ghost in the form of a Dove. This was a Bird but not actually a bird. It was power descended from heaven.

The people saw the Holy Ghost in the physical realm face to face in river Jordan not by dream, and whoever has seen the Holy Ghost has seen God the Father and whoever has seen Jesus has seen God the Father. The Holy Ghost is the Spirit of God. And He is God.

In this early month of April, 1998 the Antichrist manifested in the physical realm and took the shape of a bird, white eagle. And he flew into the congregation of people that came from all over the world, he flew around and around so low, near to the ground that the preacher who was on the pulpit preaching told everyone to make sure they concentrate and look at the eagle. The preacher made a remark, in my book titled, What Do You Want, this is in comprehensive explanation.

Before the preacher started to preach, he told the congregation that a white eagle would come, and it came and went.

This is something that happened in our world. The greatest preachers in the entire world, Africa, America, Europe, Asia, the Islands, and the seven churches were present and represented on that day. All colours of human race were present on that day. Even the Asians attended this historic ceremony with their native costumes in honour of the Antichrist; it astonished Africans that the Americans and Europeans dressed in their own native apparel to mark this a day that has been established. This is a historic day that was put on record. But it remains an untold story.

All religions were present and represented and all kinds of renown men, top governmental officials, ministers, even the head of state paid his homage on that day. These are members of the alliance of the Beast worldwide, group by group and category by category.

One preacher alone in that ceremony is influential enough to echo that Satan had been revealed, and the Christians in their respective nations would have known that the Antichrist had been revealed. Meaning that you should not expect a second Antichrist; he has come and gone.

These preachers have the financial resources and the metal ability to make sure their congregation hear how the Scriptures are fulfilled but they refused to say it and kept it secret.

No man can manipulate the word of God except some will allow others to fool them. So, do not allow others to fool you; Satan has been revealed and we are in the end of the world.

The Holy Ghost appeared on one occasion as a bird and not on two occasions. The Holy Ghost is the Spirit of God which came to river Jordan.

Many people in the entire world are still expecting the Antichrist, but Satan has come and gone and he is not going to come back again. The same foolishness of the Jews: up to this day they're expecting the Messiah but Christ has come and gone. Elias has come and gone.

Whoever has seen that white eagle has seen Satan. The false

prophets did keep this a secret and refuse to say it.

But Satan has been revealed but the world did not know. We are at the end, expecting the seventh angel to sound.

God gave me the authority to interpret the white eagle and its mission to the world; you have been deceived. Who has bewitched you that you should not obey the truth?

Many have been fooled, chained by the power of Satan. Many do not know the meaning of the eagle that revealed itself in a holy place. Dove means peace, while eagle means pride; a dangerous bird an ultimate killer. The killer visited the people. Not like the Dove who came to the world. God brought peace to you.

> "And these are they which ye shall have in
> abomination among the fowls; they shall
> not be eaten, they are an abomination:
> the eagle, and the ossifrage, and the ospray"
> (Leviticus 11:13.)

The Antichrist that manifested and revealed himself as a white eagle in the congregation of mass worshipers is the beast, the antichrist, 666, the abomination. You can see how it was revealed in the Holy bible that the eagle is an abomination, such a bird is not supposed to show itself in the holy place.

Why did Satan chose to reveal himself to the world in Nigeria? The devil is interested in that nation that is bringing forth fruit to the kingdom of God.

The Father in heaven has proposed in His mind that such nation will be rewarded. And Satan himself is interested in such a nation to deceive them. Satan will not even skip a nation that brings forth fruit to the kingdom because he knows that if he overlooks such a nation, many will find their way to heaven and he is losing. Satan has vowed to knock many out of the race and he chose to reveal himself in Nigeria.

Who will Satan desire to deceive? If you say he is interested in deceiving the believers, you have judge righteously.

The Antichrist is a spirit, not a human being. The Antichrist has been existing since the time of the apostles.

Are the April fools expecting the Antichrist to manifest as a human being? If you expect the Antichrist to manifest as a human being in the Arab land or anywhere else in the world, then your wisdom is behind the clock. The Antichrist has been in existence but he has been operating spiritually, not physically. The things of God are spiritual, not physical.

"Therefore when you see the 'abomination of desolation,' spoken of by Daniel the prophet, standing in the holy place" (whoever reads, let him understand:") (Matthew 24:15.)

Chapter Two
Genius

"Jesus answered and said unto him,
Art thou a master in Israel, and
knowest not these things?" (JOHN 3:10.)

The word "master" here is a genius.

There are humans who have extraordinary intellect and talents, people with skill and ability and originality, strange intellectual power specially manifested in creative activity. These geniuses are the people you see in the spotlight, they are in politics, sports, economics, justice, science, academics, music, entertainment and much more.

When it comes into the field of different kinds of religion in the earth that includes Islam, Hindu, Buddhism, Paganism, Atheism, Christianity and more, there are people who are geniuses. People who have extraordinary intellect and talent. These are people in the society that are well known because of their knowledge and wisdom that even President of nations pay homage to them.

Think about the founders of a religious groups, sects, movements and confraternities, if these founders are not genius, they cannot penetrate the mind of the people and recruit them, these geniuses are men who know what to say just by looking at your face. Jesus described some of these geniuses; they are people who have taken the key of knowledge.

After I checked the bible properly and surveyed the spoken words of the living God, I checked my spiritual life and faith. And I measured my faith against that of others, asking myself why I became a Christian, and why my faith is strong. I got an answer.

Now, the Lord Jesus discussed with all kinds of people when He was on the earth, He discussed with these geniuses and told them that they needed salvation from Him. No matter the kind of religion you belong to, you need salvation from Jesus Himself, whether you are a Muslim, Buddhist, Hindu or any other religion on the planet.

This made me remember when I was in Austria; I asked a Muslim guy in Austria a very simple question;, between Jesus and Mohammed, who is greater? He said Jesus is greater than Mohammed. Then, I loved him.

A genius does not have the power to show you the way of salvation. Jesus is greater than a genius and He knows the ability of a genius, He knows the thoughts of all geniuses.

A genius is so expert that he knows how to hinder you from entering into the kingdom of heaven, he knows the techniques.

But surprisingly, the world loves a geniuses. God is God and the difference between God and a human being is very clear.

I came to find out myself with my biblical knowledge that even geniuses are trying to enter into the kingdom of heaven with their mental power, without doing the will of God, but Jesus will stop them. It is when you engage in the will of God and humble yourself even though you are a genius then, this is for sure that you will inherit the kingdom of heaven.

If God were a man, believe me geniuses will enter heaven, they will go there and mess it up like they messed this world up with Satan, but God is not a man; He is wiser than a genius.

Geniuses cannot be faulted. That is why they are geniuses. A genius does not go jail, and you cannot capture a genius, because they always know what to do, and how to make themselves seem innocent. Anyone who has been to jail, such person is not a genius

The young rich man whose story was written in the bible, whom Jesus told to sell all what he had and give them to the poor.

If you survey the life style of that young rich man, the holy bible states very clearly that this man is not a fornicator adulterer, no fraudulent act was found in him. What he lacked was the mystery of God. This man knew the philosophy of life and knew how to make money. He knew which button to press and the money would come; he was a genius. Jesus knew where this man was going

You cannot have the mystery of God by attending Church or in any kind of temple. Today, if you ask some people why do you attend church? They may not have the right answer. But a genius will give you a pass mark when it comes to religion.

The English define the word "genius" as a person endowed with transcendent mental superiority; specifically a person with a very high intelligence quotient. Or A strong natural talent, aptitude, or inclination.

Worldwide, the people you are dealing with in the name of religion are masters or genius. If you trace their academic record, it is beyond belief; they are bright.

These religious genius are so talented that they know how to form a kind of ecstasy in the mind of a human, and such a human will act as if he or she knows God.

One category of these masters, by name Nicodemus saw the works of Jesus and he came to meet the Lord.

After I surveyed the words of Jesus and His discussion with such a genius, what came to my mind was: has this man (Nicodemus) committed a sin?

I carefully picked the words in these verses in each section as I read over and over again, to really see where the faults of such a genius lie.

I clearly saw the fault: the ability to receive and believe was not in these genius.

They refused to believe. The righteous have wept for these kinds of people. Some time I remain silent for a few minutes when I am on my own, seeing all kinds of people who just refuse to believe.

The knowledge to believe Jesus as the Son of God is not

in them and they went to form their own religion, leaving the One that used His own blood to save them from the coming eternal fire 'For all have sinned, and come short of the glory of God' The word "all" here means every human being that exists on the face of this earth.

The Lord Jesus designed and prepared salvation for all to come and take freely, and named it the bread of life. As for me, I called salvation a yummy lolly from heaven.

You are invited to come and eat this bread of life, this yummy thing and your joy will be full. Many tasted it and they are not able to bear the joy, and it remains sweet in their lives.

Jesus has departed from this earth to His throne in heaven with resurrection power, with many witnesses. The ones who came after Christ as wolves designed counterfeited salvation.

With all the knowledge and wisdom they have, these geniuses they end up designing counterfeit salvation. This is a ruin to the soul of mankind, at the end of this world many will submit their salvation at the judgment throne of God, but they will be told "depart from me, you that worketh iniquity" because of counterfeit salvation.

The English define counterfeit as, "made in imitation of what is genuine with the intent to defraud". If you are not a genius, you cannot do this. These defrauders, you can never catch them. These are people that even seduce we the very elects.

If you have been caught, you are not a genius.

"Now when they saw the boldness of Peter and John, and perceived that they were unlearned and ignorant men, they marvelled; and they took knowledge of them, that they had been with Jesus" (Acts 4:13.) God will not use a genius of this world, flesh and blood to do His work.

The apostles, they all knew how to read and write. Matthew was working in the ministry of finance. John had wealthy parents and much more.

Peter himself had his own personal business and he was not working as a slave for anyone. They did had normal education, and the educational qualification they held was not enough to regard them as masters in Israel.

The people weighed the brain capacity of Peter and John, and it resulted that they were unlearned and ignorant men, meaning that their mental faculty as they were rated by the people was not enough to influence any person.

With common sense, we know that they were not genius, because the people described them as written in the holy bible as unlearned and ignorant men. And this is true.

The people knew the reality, that Peter and John and the rest of disciples did not have that skill or mental power to pull any crowd. It was power given to them, which they saw that made them marvel. The Holy Ghost was doing the work in the lives of all the apostles and the people marvelled. Humans like Nicodemus were genius.

The prophets and apostles were not directly famous people, but, either their earthly fathers were prominent or they had royal blood line on earth. If you study the bible very well, if you survey some of the writers of the books, they were always making reference to the generations of the prophets, their last names.

These kings of the ancient times were married with many wives, their families extended to many generations.

So do not be surprised that many of the apostles, some of the biblical writers were always mentioning their fathers names.

Some of the apostles did had direct access to kings' palaces in foreign lands, and preached the gospel directly to them. And there was no hindrance.

Those kings had the policy that, if you are not of royal blood, you cannot even pass a night in their palace, or dine on same plate with the king, this was not a hindrance to the gospel, most of the apostles were from royal families. God provided all means for all category of humans to hear the gospel.

God gave the right of dignity to royal families for ever. This is not pride, it is their right. If you fight against a royal family, nature will fight against you.

Moses was among the prophets raised in the king palace. On Moses' side, there were no qualms. Entering the gate of the palace was not a new thing, Moses already had a strong identity from birth. Moses was not a slave, and Joseph was not a slave despite the fact that he was sold.

Joseph was chosen by God, he took a blessing from his father Jacob, so the twelve tribes of Israel had the king's blood line injected into them.

The family background of the apostles were not written in the bible. Jude was one of the disciples who went to a foreign land (the land of the gentiles) to preach the gospel and he went to kings palaces to preach to them. The bible mentioned his last name, Thaddaeus. This is believed that Thaddaeus should be a famous name during his generation.

Before the apostles were called, they lived normal lives, spending most of their time working for a living, they never thought that one day they would be chosen as apostles. The God of heaven was happy to chose them.

A man can be a genius without holding a university degree. To be chosen as a prophet is not based on university degrees it doesn't work this way.

Imitation has been in existence in all areas of life, not only in religion, even in the fashion industry, medication and cosmetics, and much more.

For example, at a time the people of the world were fed up with equipments or things that were counterfeited, including machineries, currencies, electronics, religion, and many high techs.

After buying some of these things like electrical equipments, they never last long, after some time they don't function, compared to the original product. There are people who only have the ability to produce counterfeit products. Let us use currency as an example, there are many people who do not have the eyes to detect a counterfeited currency note; they do not know whether what they are holding is genuine or not.

While some humans know how to detect a counterfeited product with the ordinary eyes. A high percentage of human beings on this earth cannot detect an original product with their physical eyes, of anything whether money, materials, religion, people and much more. We do know that there are fake people living among us, invented people.

Fake things have been in existence for many years, and many have been falling victims of counterfeited products, men with knowledge successfully developed a machine. An example of this kind of machine is the one that detects fake currency.

Original producers of the products give you a guarantee that what you are buying is an original product, and you do not need to be afraid that what you are holding is counterfeit; they give you a certificate. That certificate is your physical evidence that you have the guarantee of the original products.

The wise God knows that there will be religious fraud and these geniuses will be involved in it. The Creator put inside the original people, the mechanism to detect fake people through feelings and contact.

This religious fraud has overtaken the earth right now, humans continue to produce counterfeit salvation.

Some can even back up their counterfeit salvation with signs and wonders. Then, the Almighty God of heaven came with a solution to help those that believe Jesus as the only begotten Son of God, giving them genuine salvation. And the Holy Ghost serves as guarantee that what you are holding is genuine salvation.

The biblical prophets and the apostles did preach about this Holy Ghost, but no one in this generation knows about this Holy Ghost, including this present generation of pastors; they only hear of Him and read about Him in the bible, but have not see Him at anytime. "The wind bloweth where it listeth, and thou hearest the sound thereof, but canst not tell whence it cometh, and whither it goeth" (John 3:8.)

There are two ways to check if your salvation is genuine or not, and you will see as you read this book.

There are two types of Christians: The Called Christians and the Freelance Christians, these are equal. The Holy Ghost is the only guarantee for the called and the freelance Christians.

Geniuses doesn't know who s the Holy Ghost is; they do not know Him and they have not seen the Holy Ghost at any time.

The "manifestation" of the Holy Ghost is like as a physical certificate of guarantee. The Holy Ghost is a fire that manifests in the physical realm. The Holy Ghost will lead Christians in the right direction if they accept the truth.

Because when a man has fallen into the hands of a genius, he needs grace and prayer according to the will of God to pull him out. Alternatively, you have to break the tradition of man and escape.

In the past, the ancient brethren in the early church did not receive the Holy Ghost immediately, first they used their real eyes to detect and chose the original salvation: you have your free will to chose, this is what God allowed you to do, He will not decide for you; salvation is something you need to work out by yourself.

Another way is, a new guarantee has come to protect your salvation as original: "Blessed are they which do hunger and thirst after righteousness: for they shall be filled" (Matthew 5:6.) If you follow the spoken word of Jesus, your salvation is protected. If you are thirsty and hungry after righteousness, God will fill you, and you have the guarantee already.

The Lord Jesus knew that by leaving His throne in heaven and coming down to this earth to establish salvation on earth, and depart to His throne in heaven, counterfeit salvation will expand, He made a comment, "do not be afraid in anything you hear and in anything you read; I will be with you to the end". The Holy Ghost is same as Jesus present in the physical realm, there are no differences.

The man Nicodemus, a genius with all his wisdom and knowledge, he was given a lesson as he faced the Lord Jesus, to understand what is known as a newness of life, that is, to be born again.

"That which we have seen and heard declare we unto you, that ye also may have fellowship with us: and truly our fellowship is with the Father, and with his Son Jesus Christ. And these things write we unto you, that your joy may be full." (1 John 1:3, 4.)

There is no guarantee greater than this. No matter who you are in any nation of the earth, even you are a genius, if you say what you do not know and testify about what you have not seen, there is no guarantee here.

God is Spirit, all the key prophets in the bible all saw God the Father.

Although you have the biblical right to preach the gospel in according to the will of God, not according to your will,

if you testify about what you did not see with your eyes and what you did not touch with your hands, there is no guarantee in such a sermon.

Although, blessed are they that have not seen, but yet they believed, this spoken word needs comprehensive explanation, you will see more of this as you read.

To believe without seeing is a blessing, but it does not give you the guarantee of heaven. Jesus did not say you will enter heaven.

There are many believers who are called by God, many ministers of the gospel in this present earth. All these have testimonies. Even though you have not seen Jesus now, the bible says you will see Him later. Jesus is the perfect Man and His speech is perfect and no mistakes were made in any of His sermons.

In the Biblical ministries, there is a division of labour in the vineyard of God. Jesus is the Master sketcher of all things and He is the owner of the vineyard. Each person in the ministry has his own office and duties to do, all cannot be an apostles or a prophets at the same time, "And God hath set some in the church, first apostles, secondarily prophets, thirdly teachers, after that miracles, then gifts of healings, helps, governments, diversities of tongues."

This was the question Apostle Paul put forward to all, "Are all apostles? Are all prophets? Are all teachers? Are all workers of miracles?" If you are a bible teacher and you jump into prophecy, it will not be possible if you are a miracle worker, gifted with healings and you jump into bible prophecy, it will not work. Jack of all trades is not in the vineyard of the living

God. You cannot be a miracle worker and at the same time become a prophet.

Biblical prophecy is a potential ministry due to the personal relationships that prophets have with God the Father. This ministry is very potent; they hold the original manuscript from the heavenly Father, they do the translations and interpretation to the people. And the one you read is authenticated by the Holy Ghost same as original, purified and tried in the furnace of fire seven times, holy and full of truth, with a strong blessing, because those words are already authenticated by the Holy Ghost and with His fire. Those written words are full of truth, since these words are not from prophets, they are given by God.

Some preachers, are specialised in singing and wonders ministry, ministry of help, business, marriage and relationship, success, singing, teaching, children, counselling and much more.

My ministry is bible prophecy, exactly what the Father has given to me will I give out, and I will not add to His words and I will not take away, because I have no power to add to it because it is fire that is controlling my hands when writing physically either in the computer or with the ink, there is no chance to add to the word of God.

Those who will believe will l believe, and those who want to refuse and be disobedient to the commandments of God will still refuse, exactly what Daniel wrote in his book, the wise will understand while the wicked will continue to be wicked.

People do say the bible is contradicting. Humans may not know the mysteries of God the mysteries behind revelations.

The God of heaven gives revelations to prophets, and this revelations come in different forms and not at once. Much patience is needed to compile them, since it is a human being who writes the manuscripts. The whole bible was not written in one day, it took many years to complete. It is the oldest book on earth.

You can see the example of Jethro, Moses' father in law. He was an expert whom God used to guide Moses to make his work professional. Prophet Joshua was there at this time and some others were there in the wilderness, these are prophets who have their field of works. But yet the Lord God of heaven used Jethro to teach Moses how to govern the people. Jethro was a political genius.

However, among the fruits of the Holy Ghost is patience. When a prophet writes his book regarding the revelation he has seen, God will give wisdom to many to understand it. This is the reason why the apostle requested that you to seek wisdom from God if you don't have wisdom, and not to depend on others but depend on God to teach them His word.

A prophet of God may get a revelation from God today and start writing it, to be published. However, God will not rush His things and He will give revelations according to circumstances, according to events and according to His will, not according to the will of man. The God of heaven will do His things at the appointed time. God is not in rush like men.

Another revelation may flow in after a book is written and you need patience to start over. For example, an angel may be coming with a revelation and Satan may withstand such an angel for 21 days. What will the prophet do? He needs to be patient according to the will of God.

Some of the prophets wrote their books in captivity, under hard labour. Daniel stood on his feet all day on his job when he was in captivity, he was working. If a prophet sees a new revelation, he will add it to the previous ones and his job is complete. These are human beings. It is not easy for a prophet to compile a book.

And you should understand that in ancient times, there was no computer and no typing machine. They used to write their books by touching a dark liquid, something like a coffee to write a book.

However, it is what they saw that they all wrote down. The prophets used all their knowledge to write as they were inspired by the Holy Ghost. This explanation will give a perfect under-standing to them that say the bible is complicated. The bible is not complicated. The holy bible is the word of God and is life. The bible is accurate. This is the truthful judgment. Some, because of evil in their hearts are looking for any chance to accuse.

If you continue to say the bible is contradictory instead working out your salvation with fear and trembling, then, by saying such words, you are putting briars and thorns on the battle way of God. The bible is the holiest book on earth and everything the prophets wrote are true. There are no contradictions in the Holy bible.

Contradiction means denial, or to express the opposite of a statement. You cannot use such words in describing the word of the living God, who Created all mankind.

Moses wrote the book of Genesis and he was a prophet. Genesis is a fundamental book in the bible which many scholars today have gone through. And they have made comments about it.

Some of these scholars lack understanding and they are confused.

If only these scholars can understand that they are dealing with things that are spiritual but not physical; you cannot force spiritual things.

The nice and obedient people will always point to the spiritual aspect but not the physical aspect because the word of God is not targeting physical things. This is where they are confused and you cannot use academics to justify the holy bible that has its foundation based on spiritual things.

God said He would make their knowledge foolish and backward since they are not spiritually minded. If you continue to listen to these scholars and they sow a seed in your heart and you begin to think like them, then remember, "Thus saith the Lord, thy redeemer, and he that formed thee from the womb, I am the Lord that maketh all things; that stretcheth forth the heavens alone; that spreadeth abroad the earth by myself; That frustrateth the tokens of the liars, and maketh diviners mad; that turneth wise men backward, and maketh their knowledge foolish;" (Isaiah 44:24-25.)

Moses, who wrote the book of Genesis was not a professional when it came to organisation and government, but his heart was good and the true. God of heaven described Moses as, " Now the man Moses was very meek, above all the men which upon the face of the earth" (Number 12:3.)

So, you do not expect God to go and chose another man other than Moses, a man that was not meek, because he was a genius and use him as a prophet.

God has a way of doing His things, when Moses, as a strong man of God led the people in the wilderness, Jethro visited Moses, and Jethro gave Moses the code of organisation and government and Moses applied it as a meek man.

The truth remains that the world knows what the prophets are talking about; the heart of man is evil continually. Repentance is not a difficult language, this is just the message of all the prophets and the apostles in the bible and this is not complicated to understand. I am weary of hearing people saying the word of God is contradictory.

God already created a conscience in you, the truth is already sown in your heart and you know the difference between good and evil.

A person who is a miracle working pastor does not know anything about bible prophecy. There is no college or university where you study bible prophecy. God the Father who created the heaven and the earth, He pays divine visits to bible prophecy prophets and gives to them revelations, let them see His glory face to face. So that they will testify to what they have seen. This is the fact.

One of the major reasons why God will deal with bible prophecy teachers directly is because, He as the Father is revealing to the entire world the actions that He will take. And these kind of prophets are a warning alarm to the world. This requires seriousness.

The fact that you are a miracle worker is not guarantee of eternal life and is not a criteria to enter into the kingdom of

God and you can take it as an advantage that the kingdom belongs to you.

There are scriptural proofs indicating that in the time of the disciples with Jesus physically, there were non-followers of Jesus who performed signs and wonders and they healed people and cast out demons from them in the name of Jesus.

The disciples of Jesus saw these young guys laying hands on people and commanding demons and healing them with same name of Jesus; their ministries were moving fine and they were colleting offerings.

The disciples of Jesus acted right to take permission from Jesus and return to stop them, but Jesus did not ask His disciples to stop these guys. Can you deny this? All these powers you see manifesting in the places you are calling church, these are not proof of salvation.

What guarantees you entry into heaven is the will of God and you need to be thirsty and hunger after righteousness and God will fill you.

Bible prophecy preachers in all the earth are the ones capable of dealing and teaching the book of Isaiah, Jeremiah, Daniel, Revelations, Mathew, Zechariah, and more. When God gives us the message, then, we testify of what we have seen, and we do not have problems with any human being. It will be up to anyone to accept it or not, and we will always remind the world: it is a terrible thing to fall into the hands of the living God.

When you study the book of Isaiah, Daniel, John, and much more, they are like hammers that break rocks into pieces.

The words of God that came out of the mouths of the prophets are like bullets that strike the enemies, and like that stone that David use to strike Goliath. The word of God is life and will save you from the hands of the enemies. His word is our battle axe.

Any person who is a ruler in this world is a genius; the only difference is power.

When the God of heaven raises any nation to be great on this earth, you do not take the law into your own hands.

Meanwhile, God is not going to hold the president responsible for the act of invading Iraq, neither will He will hold the military responsible. No, the judgment of God does not go this way. Although the president will face his own eternal judgment.

God is holding the citizens responsible for the actions taken in Iraq. Because it is the people who voted the president into power; if you did not vote him into power, there is no way he could have done such a thing.

If you love yourself, your people your nation, be wise and chose a leader who will not put your nation into plague in the world to come. Even the voting you do in your own country can stand as judgment against you on the last day. God will judge every one, and no idle thing shall be left behind.

The people will be held responsible because the government is of the people and by the people, and any failure is still of the people.

Power is like a force that works on any person. But when you have Christ, the plague that is coming ahead of time will not affect you. Men who have wisdom will always say it is not profitable to gain the world and lose one's soul. With the Blood of Christ in your life, when the plague shall come it will pass over you in the destruction that is coming.

When king Pharaoh killed all the children in Egypt in the time of Moses, God did not kill Pharaoh, He had the power to take his life but He did not kill him. Pharaoh was a king and he held power.

Chapter Three

The Fading Flower

God revealed through apostle John in the bible, one particular woman, and upon her forehead was written. MYSTERY, BABYLON THE GREAT... Who actually is this woman?

I have personally seen an angel, face to face. A citizen of heaven, right now all angels are in their homes in heaven, and this is the place where God the Father lives.

Mankind needs to know that God does not use epicene angels to deliver messages to them that live on this earth, and no prophet has ever seen a epicene angel in the physical. Epicene angels do not have womb since there are no marriages in heaven. But we know that in this earth, females are with organs with all the capacities. But man angels have I seen in the physical realm face to face.

The ones who probably saw a epicene angels was Ezekiel and Zechariah, and they saw them in dark form, this is to say it was in form of revelations and they saw them with wings. Wings have a meaning.

Wings are a symbol of the heavens. Symbolically, angelic creatures with wings live higher than human creatures living on the land.

Biblically, wings are a message which the prophets understood.

Do angels have wings? In reality, angels do not have wings.

It was only apostle John who saw a epicene angel plainly and he was emotionally aroused. John was a human being with emotions like any other human. Since angels are divine, apostle John was absent in the body.

As written in the bible, Apostle John saw the complete shape of a epicene angel face to face. Angels have spiritual bodies which never die.

For example, I have seen Lucifer the devil in the physical realm face to face with my two naked eyes, not that I was sleeping, I was walking with my two legs in the physical realm and the spirit of God was with me and I saw Lucifer face to face.

Satan is an angel, but a fallen one from heaven. He still remains as he was created, at first he was created holy and there was no sin found in him, but later, he chose to sin. The bible called him the dragon. Satan is a dangerous being. And we need to be aware of him, and we need a Saviour to protect us from him, this Saviour is Jesus.

The woman upon whose forehead was written. MYSTERY, BABYLON THE GREAT... The word mystery here is defined as a religious truth that is incomprehensible to reason and knowable only through divine revelation. This woman is a mystery.

Her identity is unknown and she arouses curiosity. Personally, I have seen this angel who is a woman face to face in the spirit realm and she's one of these fallen angels who have no wings.

Epicene angels are extraordinary beings created by God, wellformed, extraordinarily beautiful. So much that when you see an angel face to face, you will have a feeling of delighted approval and liking. They are just too beautiful for us to see.

The way I saw my angel was different from the way I saw this woman. When I saw my angel, I was happy and I could not bear the joy and I gave glory to God of heaven, this was a great blessing.

But this woman of mystery, when, I saw her body and legs were exposed, but she was not naked. I saw her face, hands, legs, and eyes as I saw her I was having aroused and I was acting strange with surprise because of her beauty.

After I saw her, I was wondering for about thirty minutes, and I asked: what is this?

According to the bible, "for she saith in her heart, I sit a queen and am no widow, and shall see no sorrow."

We are created in the image of God, same as angels. God does not have wings, so angels do not have wings as we humans do not have wings. Angels have passions like us humans. They know what is good and what is evil, just the way we humans know what is good and what is evil.

The epicene angel looks like a human woman, the difference is that they do not have wombs. Their outward appearance is like that of 18 years old in our world today. The difference is that they maintain the same body shape and are never stricken with age; they do not die.

The question unbelievers are asking is if there are virgins in heaven, and is there sexual intercourse in heaven? What I will say is that, will God hide anything from His people? Jesus already gave this answer to us in the bible and told us the truth. Although some know the answer to their question, but still want to ask. I do not have any idea if there are virgins in heaven or anything like sexual intercourse, I cannot say what I do not know.

All the angels in heaven are not men. God did not create only man. He created he and she both in heaven and in the earth to live as twins forever.

Some may say I am using rude language to describe an angel. My response will be that, I am using the best of my ability to write this book, and I thank God for it. My greatest joy is that, the Holy Ghost has allowed me to write without being stopped by His fire. All the things I have written here in this book have been declared holy and truthful, tried with fire as many as seven times. The eyes and the mind of the Holy Ghost have seen it and this is pure heart.

Angels are greater than humans beings and they work for God, the Almighty is their Father in heaven and also our heavenly Father here on earth. These angels have powers from God, but they cannot give salvation, it is only Jesus that has the power to give salvation.

Some angels in heaven rebelled against God and these angels were many. However, they are now on this earth, but I do not know the actual number When you survey the Scripture by reading it, you find out that these fallen angels are many on this earth.

They had positions when they were in heaven, and after they were removed from heaven, their position became vacant.

God decided to select believers who are humans on this earth that will inherit the.

One day, I went to Rome, to my home country embassy to get a certificate of nationality because at this time, I did not have an International Passport. The immigration police asked me to get any document with a passport photograph on it from my embassy to show exactly where I came from. Then they can listen to me and process my residence permit.

I was at the embassy in Rome, on that day, we were up to 50 people applying for the same document.

We were asked to produce evidence that really we are from Nigeria before we could even enter into the embassy premises.

My case is even worse; I do not speak my father's language.

So the embassy needs evidence. If we do not have any type of document to prove ourselves, we would have to return to where we came from. The embassy is very strict on matters such as these.

As I arrived in Rome, we were able to sail through the process by various means, either you have a Nigeria driver's licence or a police report or by introduction and recommendation from somebody who knows the embassy staff to guarantee that you are Nigerian, a well documented and signed letter with the duplicate copy of your recommendation letter, or word of mouth identification by any Nigerian is acceptable.

We succeeded in entering into the premises. This document was so important to everyone that we were so desperate to get it. Many of us came from very far distances, some came from Verona, Padova, Venice, Florence, Torino, far north even Novara, some cities close to the Swiss border.

Some people among us took the night train to arrive in Rome in the morning, so they wanted to make sure that we rounded up everything on that day, so that they could go back same day.

As we were inside the embassy, after we had waited for hours to get the document, it was tough and some did not have enough money for a hotel. Moreover, we were asked to pay some amount of tax by the embassy for the processing fees. But something happened on this day.

A girl among us did not have money to pay and her name was announced in public.

When she was asked to pay the fees, the girl said she did not have enough money to pay. I turned and look at her. And I brought out my wallet and immediately gave her the complete amount to pay. She said to me that I should please give her my address, so she could send me the money. "I'll pay you back", she said.

I told her to forget it and take it as a gift. I did not really know what I had done. I gave her the money out of sympathy; when I saw the girl's face, I felt very sad for her.

The embassy staff who was in charge of issuing the document was astonished, the crowed marvelled when I gave her the money. The consulate staff kept silent for a while and left. Everybody's eyes were on me, watching the whole scenario. Not up to 30 minutes later, the embassy staff brought all the papers and all were signed with official mark were stamp in all. But it was very fast. And everybody got their documents the same hour, same day.

When we came out of the premises of the embassy, some of them called me and said, "it is because of you that we were given this document so easily. What you did for that young woman publicly amazed us all, even the embassy staff. It is hard to find a guy like you. What you did was great."

The experience above in Rome is the reason I said it can take a twinkle of an eye to know a person and for their character to be revealed. We who are children of God cannot hide. "Ye are the light of the world. A city that is set on an hill cannot be hid. Neither do men light a candle, and put it under a bushel, but on a candlestick; and it giveth light unto all that are in the house. Let your light so shine before men, that they may see your good works, and glorify your Father which is in heaven". (Mathew 5:14-16.)

One day, I was on my bicycle going to my house. But I was in a place called Calenzano, and this is a commune in Florence, towards Prato. As I was cycling, I looked forward and saw a woman waving at me to stop, then I stopped.

The young lady's face was very tired and she spoke a language I did not understand.

What was coming from her mouth was, French. I said to her "no French, but English or Italian". She switched to another language, Portugal. I told her I did not understand what you are saying, I was using both English and Italian to tell her that I did not understand what you are saying. But she continued to speak a language Portugese.

I wanted to leave her because I thought she was drunk. But I said to myself, Thomas, have patience and listen to this woman even though she is drunk. This is a human being. Then, I relaxed my mind and folded my hands.

When I was in the world I had girlfriends who could not speak a word of English, and I could not speak a word of their language, but we got along fine, we understood each other's needs. It was a great fun and experience. From my previous experience, I knew what to do. Language cannot stop communication between two people.

I started gesturing and drew closer to her. She smelt good and her clothes were not rumpled; this woman is not drunk.

As I listened to her, I came to understand that she missed her way. As she was speaking with me, she was crying.

She could not speak any Italian or even English language, anybody she stopped left her. She remained stuck.

But I was still wondering if this woman was genuine. She was deeply troubled, and she could not control it. I tried to calm her down. We were communicating with hands and I asked her of her identity card to know which country she came from.

She gave me her ID card, and I looked at it. She was

from Switzerland. This was when I was totally convinced that this woman needed help. Through feelings and gestures, I got to understand that she went shopping alone and got lost on her way back.

The only word she understood and could say is Swisspoo.

I asked her what is swisspoo? She could not pronounced it correctly. She was trying to say Swissport. Swissport is a company that is located in Prato, in industrial zone.

What she said was "zona Indusral". I knew she was saying industrial zone. And she remembered the area, a company called TNT that was close to this Swissport where her husband was waiting for her.

I gestured to her that I would take her there, but she was asking for a taxi. I told her that area was far from where you could get a taxi.

I asked her to get on my bicycle, and she could not wait to jump on of the carrier. I used my bicycle to take her to the industrial area. When we got there, it was late in the night. As we got to TNT, it was the wrong direction and it looked like would have to start afresh. I was riding my bike through a hill, taking her with me. I was almost fed up.

When we were talking, I saw an officer and I called him. I explained to this officer the problem of this woman, I let the officer understand that I had been using bicycle to transport this woman. The officer said that he could not help, and that I should call the police line. I knew that calling the police would be tedious for her, because they would have to take her to the station and do a lot of telephones about her. Taking her to my home and letting her rest t was another option.

Luckily for the woman, I was able to find a vehicle with Portuguese plate number. I got closer to the vehicle, and asked him if he spoke Portuguese, the man replied that he was from Portugal, and he man spoke good Italian. I told him the whole story. I brought the woman to him and they spoke Portuguese to each other.

I delivered her to her husband. She was very happy and

she brought out some money to give me. I told her it wasn't necessary. She said, thank you in French and I said goodbye and I left.

I know that the bible taught me to show kindness if I see my neighbour falling by the way.

People may say that I am nice, but my older brother Andrew is nicer than I am. But he died at the age of 28. That is why I am worried that nice people do not last long and the ones left behind are not so fortunate. It takes the grace of God for nice people to live and succeed. Andrew had a thrilling character.

Another of my best friends on earth, by name Joseph, was of the same age group as my late older brother. Joseph was my best friend, he slept in the Lord at the same age of 28, he was a man that had thrilling character.

Joseph was born and brought up in a strong Christian family home, he loved me very much and we were good friends. I was not born into a Christian family. Joseph would always tell me about hell fire since when we were young, I so much loved his stories, he was such a very nice guy.

The reason why he loved me was that, he knew that in my youth, I did not like to stay where there was trouble. Anywhere there is trouble, I would keep myself from that area entirely.

Nevertheless, let those who have good behaviour continue to do good and those who love to do bad, let them continue to do bad.

God will not chose a woman for a man, it is the man that will chose whom he loves, but, when there is tragedy beyond human control with every possibility that it can result into death in the name of looking for a wife, God will intervene and solve the situation and He will chose a woman and give her to a believer (man.) Only with this condition. God can use any means to save a man.

If you have the strength to provide for yourself a partner and you have one already, this is fine. It is those who do not have the strength to get a wife or a husband based on the fact that Satan is taking it as a duty to destroy or to manifest his evil on this category of believers that God has much interest in.

God of heaven has spoken, He will use His strength to get a partner for these ones and they will glorify His name. Satan destroys marriages and relationships.

For example, in my case, I almost died in the process of looking for a wife. My case was a nightmare; God intervened and I was blessed with one woman. If God had not intervened in my case, my life would have been a cinema.

If God is blessing you with a woman, God will not give you an earthly woman or earthly man for the woman. No. The blessing of God doesn't work this way. The blessing that God will give is different from the blessing man will give and is different from the blessing that angels will give to a man or a woman.

The gift of God is unique. Cannot be compared to any other kind. And no woman on this earth can be compared to her. The difference is very clear. A woman that is chosen by God Himself is a queen. And the man God will chose to bless a woman, this is also a king. The gift of God is of the highest quality. However, as beautiful as this earth is, it is the dust at the feet of God. What God will give is directly from heaven.

When God presents a gift to His child, what He will always say is, be patient, you are not alone; I am with you, I am Spirit.

Looking for true love and thinking you have not found any and refusing to marry are not the same, some just refuse to marry. If the decision is based on health reasons, this is another thing. This is not their fault, and God will still reward these ones.

Apostle Paul was not married, and the reason of this was revealed in the bible. The commandments of God sets you free on some certain ground regarding being unmarried: this is very tight.

So if you do not have a partner and you are a strong believing sister or a brother, and you are grieved every day in your heart because of this, you see people hanging around with their partners smiling, having fun together and people say all manner of words to hurt you because you are single, the Lord already said as written in the bible that you should rejoice, you will leap for joy; this is based on a special case to be set free in the commandments of God. And those who are happy now shall weep.

The prophets have great wisdom and their lives are an example to counsel you; it was written that, is better to go to the house of mourning, than to go to the house of feasting.

As the author of this book, when I was seeking for a wife and it was a disaster to me, a real war. At a time I headed into trouble and my case was so severe that nobody could help. I nearly died.

In that time, a husband and wife from the north of Sweden gave me an offer; they had a beautiful daughter at home. they wanted me to come and take her as a wife. By the time I was given this offer, I was already a troubled child, very confused. If you are in the state of confusion, the capacity to reason well is damaged. He promised that if I saw his, daughter I would like her.

I saw from this man's expression, that her daughter had a nice character, was loyal and respectful. A daughter that had trust for her family. There is no joy greater than trust; in it there is confidence and safety. Moreover, to trust someone is a blessing. A daughter who believed that her parents could not give to her evil.

The understanding between a parent and a child is very important, and it is a joy to see in such a home that there is unity. When there is a unity in any home, a daughter can be a present and a blessing. Any child you have is a blessing to you. When a home is not united, evil takes control and you can even fall into tragedy because of the child that you have given birth to. I have seen cases of people who fell into misfortune because of their children; no unity.

Friends do introduce friends to friends, even computers and the internet also introduces people to each other which is online dating, and sometimes the meetings end up in relationships, romance and marriage.

In all these explanations, if you have a love relationship that is not build on solid ground it becomes a horror. Trust is the dream of the good heart. If such a dream comes true, then the sky is your limit.

Even ghost people on the web do connect people;, there are billions of Euros in the business of dating worldwide.

A man whom I had never met before, came with his wife and offered me his daughter. They persuaded me to come to their home immediately to have their daughter as a wife. Is this not a wonder?

You find yourself in a situation where you are looking for a wife and along the line you were hurt, and the pains were severe and you carried such a great pain. It was in the middle of this pain that someone offered you his daughter for marriage, this offer is from heaven, not from man. It happened live in Sweden, this is for free and no single dime will be spent.

At this time, my life was already a disaster beyond control with severe depression, my soul was in agony and I did not follow this marriage offer up.

If the world had presented to me Miss universe for marriage, I would have rejected it because my heart was wounded so sore and the pain was grievous because of what another female did to me in the name of marriage.

I went to Sweden to study in the city of Uppsala where I had a lot of experiences, your character can be revealed within a twinkle of an eye and people will trust you even though it is their first time meeting you.

When it comes to the issue of choosing a wife, a man will chose a woman and God will bless them. And both of them will live together for eternity.

God will not chose a woman first and tell her to go and chose a man. God will always chose the man and make the man His friend and the man will agree with a woman on this earth as partner and the blessings will take place effectively.

In this time of the end, the bible says two witnesses from God will come. God will chose a man and give him power to announce the arrival of Jesus Christ.

God decided to chose a man and one woman to make His end time witnesses as revealed by the prophets.

God the Father has chosen me, the author of this book and He spoke to me and He gave me power which is the Holy Ghost and with fire. I am one of His witnesses. We who are believers, our faith is based on the word of God. He has spoken that He will give us the kingdom, a kingdom that belongs to Christ and we shall rule with Him, a kingdom that has no end.

Since the Creator has chosen me, it is now left to me to chose a woman as my eternal partner, then she will be blessed.

The Creator will give my partner a crown of glory.

This chosen woman, the second witness, shall be the glorious beauty in heaven and power will be given to her as I have mentioned above, since God has chosen me, it will be my spouse that God will use to fill this position. This is when I chose a woman called Maria Östergren, the other side of coin her name is now, Maria Oscarsson.

This is the revelation of the two end time witnesses as written by apostle John, God will give power to two of His witnesses. There is not enough space to treat this story in this book, the details of this revelation have been written in the book titled, What Do You Want?

I wrote previously in this chapter that a man requested to give to me his daughter for marriage but I abandoned it because of the pains I received; such a wonderful request. The woman who did evil to me, that gave me pains, her name is Maria Östergren, in Uppsala Sweden, shewas wicked to me. I would have died of AIDS; Satan used her as a tool to snare me, but God saved me. Because of her, I suffered captivity in Austria. My book titled, What Do You Want? I explained more of this.

Maria designed an evil in an attempt to make me to act in response to deny the Lord and lose my salvation, and that would have made me to have eternal death. I went through many tears that cannot be numbered. I told God something: that I will not deny Him, despite what Maria has done to me.

I told God that I love Him.

If not for the mustard seed faith that the Lord has blessed me with, I would have abandoned Christianity.

This is the question that some are asking: why does God allow suffering? It took me time, but not a day. I studied the whole system of the world, the nature of man and the nature of the earth, the cause of any pain and suffering on this earth shows that God did not allow suffering. Man is the problem and God is innocent and I stand as one of His witness, because I know Him and I have seen Him face to face.

His holy and Almighty love, God did save me from sexual disease, car accident, cold blooded murder, and death in captivity, racism and a killer. This was what Maria Östergren caused because I told her to be my wife. You see how God is involved in my case?

I believe that every human being on this earth is supposed to have a personal timetable or a schedule. When a timetable has been drafted and when an unknown person goes there and wipes it off, the human time table is disorganized.

And sometimes, various timetable are very sensitive and if anything changes, it will be a serious problem.

To choose a life partner, I made my timetable on spiritual grounds, meaning my timetable was scheduled for me to marry when I was in bible college. My spiritual faith told me that is good to chose a sister, not an unbeliever so as to build by house on the rock and when the storm comes, it cannot take it away.

Refusing affection is not great alarm, at least there are many fishes in the river. If you refuse someone's affection the rule is do not hurt him, go your way and the man will go his way and peace will reign. Maria held me to ransom.

The dictionary defines "hold to ransom" as to force someone to do something by putting them in a situation where something bad will happen to them. This is exactly what Maria did to me. Up to this day, I cannot figure out why she held me to ransom. We were both students in the bible college.

She was a snoop for the school. a snoop tries to track evil

men, but there was no wrong doing in me.

Maria went to betray me to my teachers Calle Lilja and Ingrid to kick me out of the bible college. This was where the problem began.

Because of a small thing, Cali Lija and Ingrid who anointed Maria as snoop, booted me out of school for a small thing. That made me a school dropout. And I made up my mind, I finally gave up education. This made me confused in life. I worked hard and saved money for my school, the school certificate I dreamed of having to fully follow my ministry, but my plans were destroyed. It affected me psychologically and I was lead in a wrong direction.

. I was depressed for many years because of Cali Lilja and Ingrid. But I am bearing it. I would have perished long ago.

If you aggressively kick a man from bible college because of a small thing that does not requires aggression, what do you expect such a man to do?

We have the biblical right to learn faith in anywhere on this earth whether Sweden, or elsewhere, any country because faith comes by hearing the word of God.

But the teachers you depend on to increase your faith, they are out to destroy you like the Pharisees. If you do not have proper wisdom, you may put the blame on God, meanwhile God is innocent. Our God is good; He does not send anyone to hurt any and kill any both physical and physiologically.

Normally, when I was supposed to finished from the bible college, my passion was to go into the evangelical ministry, but since my hope was destroyed by Maria, Calle Lilja and Ingrid, there was no certificate and no education. I went to involve myself in the world.

This made me confused and I ruled another school out of my life; I did not want to see another Maria, Calli Lilja and Ingrid.

I left for Austria, and established a company there. It was out of depression that i formed a company, because I did not know what to do anymore. What would I have done?

With this depression in me, I went deeply into fornication with dozens of girls, I cannot even remember how many, all with unprotected sex.

If you tell my mother that her son is fornicating, she will tell you that it is a lie. My mother has never seen me one day with a woman. She brought me up to run away from fornication.

When I was in bible college in Sweden, at the beginning when as I was admitted, God revealed to me that AIDS was coming to me. I did not take this revelation seriously, because I saw myself as going to marry to a Christian sister. One woman, one life, and one happiness.

Fornication was not even on my mind at the time of revelation, I did not even believe that I would do it, after Christ told me of it.

After Calle Lilja and Ingrid kicked me out of school, I forgot that HIV was in existence. I know that God is my Saviour, and that He stopped HIV/AIDS, and I was not infected even with HIV, I remain negative forever; it was the power of God, not my power.

Believing in God is one thing, and being a preacher is another thing. I have no strength to be a preacher. I encouraged myself to be a preacher by applying to a bible college in Sweden. God blessed me with finance, there was enough money. I was given a student visa and residence permit. If I had not been given the permit, I would have told God that, "you see, this is not my fault. I told You, I can't do this. But everything was complete, so I didn't have any excuse. I entered the school, Cali Lilja and Ingrid destroyed my courage, they spoiled it. Even sister Elisabeth who is my mother encouraged me to enroll in another school when I told her I was asked to pack my bags and leave her house.

This was the period I asked God not to let me see another Maria, Cali Lijla, and Ingrid. People who cannot forgive.

My depression was so strong that I ruled out any Christian female in my entire life. Are there no women in the disco night club? Are these not women?

I was worried that going to another bible college would be a disaster. My trust was totally destroyed.

The question I asked in my heart all the time was: what is so grievous that I have done that got me kicked out of bible college?

Christianity is not a physical thing. This is not a matter of flesh and blood. You are dealing with things that you do not see, yet you believe. In this world, you will find people who kill themselves over things they cannot see; there is a power behind these things. This will give you a good idea of spiritual warfare.

The influence of religion in this world is very high. This means that the invisible world has a role to play in the lives of the people. We live in a physical world, inside a world that cannot be spiritually seen.

All tribes and ethnic groups in the nations of the earth believe in the existence of a higher being, depending the one they are familiar with. This gives a perfect understanding that, in the spiritual realm, a decision can be made on your behalf of someone.

If unseen forces have influence in our lives, even unknowing to some, then, you have to play the game carefully, or it can backfire. For this reason, do not take life for granted.

If you cannot be a work man for God, it is better you do not come in, and if you want to be a work man, you have to do it perfectly and let no fault be found in you on the Judgment Day.

A man can hear the word of God and happily receive it, and later, this same man can be offended by the word of God. The outcome can be like the parable of the sower. Another person may not want to be a work man at all, because he has no strength to do it, not that he is offended by the word.

I do not have the strength to be a work man for God, because I know that I do not have the strength to be a prophet. He invited me to be a work man. God has done no evil in inviting me to be His witness. The Lord became the source of my strength because He called me to do it.

I know that some people are strong, but I am not that strong. A thing may be so small, but such a thing can kill a human being. I appealed to Calle Lilja and Ingrid to let me finish my studies at the bible college, so that I would have the zeal to continue the ministry somewhere. They rejected my appeal. It was terrifying.

The Lord asked a question in the bible. Who made His witness kicked out of the bible college as written by Zechariah?

What Calle Lijla and Ingrid did to me was physiological murder, but with the mustard seed of faith I have in me, I survived this death because there is no time when I denied the Lord.

Waiting for Mr. Right does not give you the prerogative to hurt others, as what Maria did to me made me a psychological child. I went to prison in Austria. She sold me out like Judas.

Be careful how you play the game. Do not use what God has given to you as a weapon to hurt others. Respect it and respect others. For God is a respecter of no person.

God has spoken, that He will give the kingdom to the ones you called harlots, stripteases and all kinds of X-rated women who know life, people who have the ability to repent. And you will not enter into the kingdom of heaven, neither will you taste of His supper.

He will remold the sinners perfectly and establish them like Himself. These are the ones that do not value their lives, but will gain it. If you value your life too much, you will lose it.

The bible already warned, do not hurt any of my two witnesses. These (two witnesses) have the power to shut heaven and have power over water, to turn it to blood. The word them here, as written in the bible, refers to people that dwell on this earth.

If a woman shows any sign of unwillingness to engage in a marriage relationship with a prophet, he will not be interested in such a woman in this world, and in the next. Even though the woman later be fully willing, a prophet of God will not be interested any more, but that does not mean she has sinned against the prophet.

A prophet will not impose his will on any, or force any

woman against her own wish. Even God the Father has never imposed His will on any since the foundation of this world. He only admonishes you to chose life, and it will be good for you. If you want to chose death, that is your decision to make. It will be as you want it.

It is the will of God for me to communicate with Maria, since my communication does not pose any danger to her life. I am not a murderer, I only gave her a simple message of love and joy. It is not a sin to be marriage minded. It is a good thing to look for a wife. If she is not interested, I have to leave her alone and say thank you. I did not hurt her, neither did I use harsh words against her, I gave Maria great respect, she knows all these things.

The message of prophets is to tell you to be established in righteousness.

Prophets are not violent people. If you are not interested in a relationship with a prophet, go your way and let peace reign, than to go and backbite or sell him out. God gave you grace in the name of Christ to live, but many have misused this grace entirely, and this is very bad.

The heavenly Father did not call His prophets servants, He called them friends.

Prophets are obedient to the Father in heaven. And they will never act against other humans' wills, children, the old and the young.

It is the guiding principle of a prophet to allow other humans exercise their will. However, prophets are very easy human beings, they have no qualms with anyone.

But the prophet gave very good advice in the bible, that you should not follow the thought of your heart. Follow the commandment of God, and fear Him.

However, the bible is saying, to execute such ministry, it involves a first lady, for she will give moral support to me, the prophet of God that will bring forth the headstone shouting, crying, Grace, grace unto it. And this is what makes us the two witnesses of the living God. Me and a woman.

The verse below is saying that such first lady, her biography must also appear in the bible and she will also be in the spotlight. These are the two end time witnesses of the heavenly God; the complete explanation of this is written in my book titled, What Do You Want?

If you are dealing with a prophet on a certain level, remain perfect. If you mess with a prophet, this is when you will become a fading flower. Maria messed up with me, a chosen material of God and heaven declared her a fading flower.

Maria was supposed to be the right woman destined to inherit this crown, but she became evil. Since Maria became a fading flower, God decided to give this position to one of His angels in heaven which is now my angel, read the complete details of this in my book, What Do You Want? When God blesses a man with a woman, He chooses the best of His creatures to give.

God revealed my angel to me, which is the second witness. God opened heaven for me to see. Zechariah spoke of the two witnesses, a prophet on earth and one angel in heaven that makes the two witnesses of God. Satan was resisting, until the Creator rebuked Satan and the storm was calmed as written in the book of Zechariah.

Prophet Isaiah revealed Maria, even Apostle John pointed in his revelations that two of us will meet in a court and a temple. This court is a school of academic institute in Sweden, and the temple is a church in Sweden and Apostle John also pointed directly that the two witnesses are Gentiles. So Maria is supposed or a supposer.

Below this is the autobiography of Maria as written by prophet Isaiah.

> "And the glorious beauty, which is
> on the head of the fat valley, shall be
> a fading flower, and as the hasty fruit

before the summer; which when he that
looketh upon it seeth, while it is yet in his
hand he eathet it up" (Isa:28:4.)

Glorious beauty here is full of glory, magnificent and worthy of high praise. A great honour, a queen. This is a woman which is Maria, "head of the fat valley" is the judgment throne of the saints; because it is revealed in the bible that the Father judgeth no man, it is the saints that will judge the world.

Maria had a crown that qualified her as chosen with the power to perform judgment on the judgment throne of the saints, which Isaiah pinpointed here, "And the glorious beauty, which is on the head of the fat valley." The word head here is: to be in the leading position.

For the Creator to use such a powerful language to identify a woman, you should know the kind of power this kind of human being should hold? For the Creator to describe you as a glorious beauty this shows clearly, this is a type of chosen that will sit with God in the last day to made decisions and judgment because you can see the magnitude of this prophecy. This is a key of heaven and the keys of hell, anything such a glorious beauty will bound on earth is bound in heaven and anything such a glorious beauty is lose on earth is loosed in heaven.

It is the saints that will decide where all the people of the world will spend their eternity, since we have been chosen by God.

In the above verse, is written "and the glorious beauty shall be a fading flower" this is eternal death penalty given to Maria, based on the evil she did to me.   Look at what Isaiah is saying here, "and as the hasty fruit before the summer", this is always in the case of some women in a rush to hustle for Mr. Right; what shall it profit a man to gain the whole world and lose his own soul? If you read my book, What Do You Want, I explained the details step by step.

When I met Maria, she was eating an apple in front of

the church, and the bible says that it is the apple fruit she was eating, this is how I identified her in front of the bible college immediately we resumed school.

Isaiah made it very plain that, when I, Thomas Bayo, will meet the second witness in the court, which is the bible college in the land of the Gentiles, I will see a girl, a glorious beauty eating fruit in front of the school, and that the second witness is Swedish. Before I got to the school admission, I knew her already.

The revelation is not saying that God chose Maria for me, no. The revelation is saying that this is the Christian sister that I have chosen to marry, and this is approved in heaven and she will be crowned as the glorious beauty.

Prophet Isaiah said here "and as the hasty fruit before the summer; which when he that looketh upon it seeth, while it is yet in his hand he eathet it up" (Isaiah 28:4.) An agriculture expert will tell you that this particular fruit written by prophet Isaiah, is an apple. So, biblically Maria's code name is Apple. This is where her autobiography is revealed. An expert who is a historian will tell you the meaning of "Apple".

Even a layman will tell you that apple is a hasty fruit before the summer.

However, there is something in this earth that also happens in heaven, when you involve yourself with a super star, two things will happen to you, first you will face what is called scrutiny, and secondly, you will be in the spotlight. This is exactly what happened to Maria.

Maria was appointed as a snoop by my bible college teachers, they trained her to follow me. She engaged in a fake relationship with me, I thought she was a genuine human being, so I gave her all my secrets. It was a false hope for marriage; she was faking all her smiles, the evidence of this is that she revealed my private life to my teachers, that made my teachers angry and I was sent out of school.

I am a man whom the Creator called His friend, paid me a divine visit on earth, yet, Maria the woman that I loved greatly, betrayed me. You can imagine, loving somebody with all your strength, with your mind, heart and soul. She even took me to her village to see her mother and father.

I find it difficult to believe that Maria betrayed me. She even defrauded me; the money she borrowed from me, she did not pay me back.

Heaven scrutinised Maria for policing a prophet. And you can see the result below. Apple means "child abuse". I met Maria when she was a matured girl, above 18 years. Maria was abused, she was raped by an Arab in Sweden before I met her. Maria was a virgin before the incident, after sexually assaulting her, this rapist escaped and he was not caught.

It was revealed already that Maria is an abused child, I knew she was an abused child, but I still loved her, and the question heaven asked was, did I want to marry her? I said yes. All depended on me.

Before I made the move to begin a relationship with Maria, I concluded that she had been raped and abused; if I chose her, God already chose her. In this case, her destiny can be changed by God to good, He is the Creator.

There was no fault found in me, but I was asked to leave the school that I paid for. I wept bitterly. With this grievous pain, will it be easy again to love?

I continue to tell people to beware of these geniuses, these teachers are geniuses, they know how to kill. They succeeded in slaughtering my trust, they attempted to kill my faith but they did not succeed. They believed they ejected me from bible college, I would abandon my faith by accusing an innocent God. They could not kill my revelations, it is the revelation that made my faith solid. I will continue to praise the God of heaven and worship Him.

The only question and answer that came out of me was, what have I done so bad that I was asked to quit the school? The answered was only tears.

When I was a student in Sweden, I left a historic record that the Swedish nation will not forget, the entire nation praised

God in Sweden, a sign of the prophet revealed by the prophets; this is my car plummet that happened that gave me nationwide news coverage that brought me to the spotlight. Maria saw the wonder of God in my life.

The heavenly Father gave me the keys of hell and the keys of heaven which I saw face to face and I was requested by the Creator to act on my will as written in the bible. There is no way Maria will survive the judgment day!

"These have power to shut heaven, that it rain not in the days of their prophecy: and have power over waters to turn them to blood, and to smite the earth with all plagues, as often as they will" (Re:11:6.)

Look at what the bible says in the above verse, it says power. Power is always designed for fulfilment of a ministry. This is exactly what the Creator is saying here as written in the bible.

The bible telling you here that, "and have power over waters to turn them to blood", this is key of hell.

Maria Östergren's salvation has been stripped off her. Anyone who tells her that her salvation is still valid is deceiving her. The bible stated clearly that she is a fading flower.

Who will support Maria? And who will support Cali Lilja and Ingrid? Such person has supported evil. These people are evil. They deserve their judgment.

Who will support a betrayer? It is God that delivered me from death. No one came to rescue me. Instead, I was hit more. With love, God with His compassion came to take me out of the pit. I knew how many times I wept.

A prophet cannot give you salvation, neither can an angel give you salvation. only Jesus has that power to give salvation and He does not take it back, no matter what. A man who has the Holy Ghost and with fire can take away your salvation when you hurt him as to say you have sinned against the Holy Ghost, especially the two witnesses of the living God.

If you do not have the Holy Ghost and power, you do not have the power to strip anyone of his or her salvation, because power is not given to you by God.

Human beings can be fished out of multitudes of people in this world with only one thing. One word the Lord God of heaven speaks of you, and only a word will reveal you, exactly in the case of Maria.

You do not need to be a musician, politician, model or a celebrated person to be known.

One thing that brought me out in the eye of millions of people in Sweden, the plummet that was spoken by prophet Zechariah, through this plummet, my brief biography was revealed to millions of eyes in Sweden.

In the bible, as written that the world will see the plummet in the hands of the prophet. This prophet will announce to the world the coming of Christ. Shouting Grace, grace unto it.

Those whose lives reflect in the bible cannot hide; your good will shine, your bad will smell.

In my school, I could not hide, at work, I could not hide. This is exactly what the Lord told me, the Lord God Himself personally commanded me that I should search the bible very well. I searched the bible as the Lord commanded me, and the many things that were written of me astonish me.

"Ye shall know them by their fruits", if Maria had listened to me, she would have be the chosen one but she is the hasty fruit before the summer, she became a fading flower.

Prophet Isaiah gave this revelation step by step and this is interpreted very simply for you to understand at any level of your education. Because the prophets in the bible wrote in the simplest grammar that even the unlearned will understand.

It was my spiritual time of training according the schedule of my time-table. I made a decision of marriage, and I went to a fellow student, Maria, and told her of my plans. I met her eating this apple fruit in front of the school, I approached her directly, and that day, I saw a great joy on Maria's face.

She took me straight to her bed room and showed me everything in her house, the kitchen, parlour, even the toilet, she showed me everything, even her father and mother, brothers and her only sister. I saw all of them. She prepared lunch for me with her own hands.

We drove the long distance to meet her parents, to introduce me to them, and her mother hugged me warmly. It was the teachers who brainwashed her in the beginning, she was genuine, but later she changed.

Before I met Maria, I prayed to the God of heaven. I had decided to chose a wife, my life partner, so I went to Maria. To hold such potential position in heaven, such a soul must be a person of faith.

In regards to women, it is only a queen that can have patience and tolerance, then, God will crown her. If you cannot control your temper, you can never be a queen. Trials must come to test your faith; if you are qualified to be a saint, you will be shaken by Satan. Because Satan has declared war on all who will inherit heaven. This is what is written in the bible. This war must affect all.

> The Lord said, "Behold, I come quickly:
> hold that fast which thou hast, that no
> man take thy crown" (Revelation 3:11.)

The God of heaven has warned Christians, in the above verse. Some have lost their crowns, Maria is an example. The date of the end has been revealed, Christ is coming quickly now. The word hast here as written in the above verse, means to tolerate or endure.

The salvation you now hold, do not eat it up. Just as salvation was in the hand of Maria, the bible says, she ate it up. If you eat up your salvation, your crown will go to someone else. God will perform His word. If you do not hold that fast which thou hast, believe me, it will go to another person.

Your spirit is holding a trophy of victory when you have the ability to forgive your neighbours when they ask for forgiveness. While the body suffer pains, God will surely reward. The body must suffer pains to achieve a triumph.

For example, Jesus Himself suffered pains to give us salvation. He wept. He suffered for us all. And His rising from death is our triumph today. And now, He enjoys our honour, praises, glory and thanks. And He is worthy to receive it.

Those who know the rules of physical body building (believe they need to undergo pains.) Suffer with pain to get what you want.

When I was a young boy in my early school, there is a saying we had: suffering before pleasure. We used this word to counsel ourselves to achieve success in planning our future. We would always say, "study hard, and one day you can become a chief judge, central bank manager, governor, dentist, doctor, politician, scientist, engineer, even the president. When I was in school, most of us would drink very thick coffee, so that we do not sleep, but always read books.

Some break the day reading books, we were known in this area, studying from evening until morning the next day, and what you would hear was, "suffer before pleasure." The explanation here was to give you a good understanding that even youths know that we must suffer before pleasure. If you want to become a master, first you must serve.

When believers come into the area of forgiveness, you must undergo pains physically and in the spirit before you get victory. This is our basic principle of faith.

This is exactly the lecture I was giving to some group of women in Lucca, Italy, although they were unbelievers, I told them that they must forgive no matter what. The message was so strong in their heart and they confessed to me, that it is difficult to forgive. Only a woman that is a queen can forgive.

It is easy to say "I am a Christian, I am a believer, I am a born again", but a real measure of our Christianity is the ability to forgive.

In the prophecy of Isaiah, he wrote about the glorious beauty, a fading flower as I explained above.

The woman, this fallen angel from heaven, as written in the Bible, "for she saith in her heart, I sit a queen and am no widow, and shall see no sorrow." on her forehead was written. MYSTERY BABYLON THE GREAT...

Satan killing Maria physically does not make her lose the crown. To kill her is to make her get the crown. What Satan did was to push her to another man, that is when she lost the crown.

The style of my preaching is a modern way; the ancient way of life is different from the 20th century way.

It is by the grace of Christ that we are operating in this modern way of life, if not, the ancient life would have remained. People may think that God has changed. No! God does not change. He remains as He is. Man changes, but God does not.

Human beings can never be satisfied, they will always murmur, if you give to them an ancient preaching they will still complain, even a modern preaching, they will still complain. But I know that they that have wisdom will understand. Those who want to live in wickedness will continue to do wickedness.

No human being on this earth can stand Satan except power is given to you by God. The only way to defeat Satan is by your faith.

In this world, if you want to become wise, then act like a fool. People may call you a fool, but you know what you are doing. This is why the God of heaven uses the foolish things of this world to speak to them that are wise and them that are mighty.

The calling of God, does not look to the academically brightest. Let me use an example of a school class room. If God wants to select a boy or a girl, He will look to that boy or that girl in the school class that took second to the last position in the examination, the one people called a failure. This is the one He loves. The one who has no strength.

That boy you see hanging around with girls that you say this is a sinner, I do not think that he is a good Christian. Such a man has no strength. The eyes of God are on this one. The power is with Him to strengthen such a man to be perfect like Himself. The reason why the God of heaven will choose the second to the last, the one the teacher and the people call a failure is that, He will reveal His power through the weak, and the world will be amazed. God is interested on them that need a physician, so that He can work on him.

One day, in the heart of Florence city, at my work, I met a girl and we were chatting. I asked her of her age and what school she attends. This girl was so cute, with a very sweet face. She was 19 years old. She told me she was in class three, in the secondary school.

I was shocked and I ask her why. She said she had failed three times in her school. Normally, she would have been in her final year in secondary school, ready to go to the university the next year. But she was still in the third year in the junior secondary school, hadn't even started the senior secondary level. I smiled and looked at her and I told her, "what I think of you is that, you are taking the first position in your school, the best school results are yours"

In my counselling to her, I said, you may see yourself as the last person in your school, but you are the first.

Such a girl has no strength in her, and if you hurt this kind of a soul, you may meet your destruction ahead of time; the God of heaven will let you to understand that it is He who created this girl, and He created the heavens and the earth. The Lord God has no pleasure in the wicked on the death of the wicked, and the wages of sin is death.

Whosoever blesses such a girl cannot lose their reward in this world and in the next world to come. These are the people that God uses to bless people.

Regarding me and Maria, this is what that has been written in the holy bible, this is not a secret thing that needs not to be told.

With all my strength, I persuaded Maria to accept me, since we had already stated our mission of love and romance, I was patient to the last minute; I did a good thing.

I didn't have problem with Maria, but since she didn't want me, she was running away from me. I tried to persuade her not to run. I never pursued her, it was the evil she was doing that made her run away from me. I did not want to quarrel with her, despite the fact that she was not interested, I just needed the last kiss from her, since I knew that I would be finally leaving Sweden, never to see her again, so that both of us could part in good faith, but she refused.

If I had requested the last kiss, and we had agreement on it, I would not have broken my agreement. I maintain my word and I don't change my word. But she did not give me the last kiss, so I went away with tears.

When I was in the building of her house, she did not even allow me enter her home, I was on the passageway with her cousin and her only sister. What I did to Maria was great, because we were in the same bible college students. I respected her to the last minute before I left Sweden.

God will not force anyone against their own will, she chose her life and the direction she wanted to go. She is free to go any direction she has chosen.

Those two teachers in the bible college in Uppsala, Calli Lilja and Ingrid, they can never run away when they are guilty in accordance to the bible, not in accordance to the will of man. Christianity is like a struggle, just as the fight, "I have fought a good fight, I have finished my course, I have kept the faith" (2 Timothy 4:7.)

I know completely well that a woman on this earth who will be the second witness, who will be the queen, with mighty power from heaven, it will not be easy for her, she is going to face terrible temptations. Satan knows that I am the chosen one, and he knows that my spouse will be the chosen one, and the enemies are ready for war, so do not be surprised that Maria was snared, because she loved to do evil more than good. When humans give themselves as instruments to the devil, Satan will use them.

We who believe, we walk by faith and not by sight. What you see in the physical is temporary, and what you do not see in the spiritual realm is eternal. If Maria had faith and did not walk by sight, it may be possible that she would have overcome.

Satan knows the nature of the man very well, and Satan extremely dislikes man. One of the devil's weapons is the woman. He uses them to accomplish his goals, because men are vulnerable to women, just as women are vulnerable to Satan.

When I used my God given spiritual eyes to survey Maria, I was grieved deeply in the heart that she ate up her crown. Maria, the glorious beauty in front of the fat valley is a fading flower. She was snared by the enemy.

To be a witness of the living God of heaven, you are going to have to withstand Satan. Exactly what the bible says about the two olive trees and candlesticks, two witnesses that will stand before the God of the whole earth.

"These are the two olive trees, and the two candlesticks standing before the God of the earth" (Re:11:4.)

The bible already told you that Satan is the God of the whole earth. For you to be the witness of the heavenly Father, to have this mighty crown, the bible pointed to you that you must stand Satan. Standing before the God of this earth, this is power to oppose the authority of the ruler of this world.

The God of heaven has already given me the eyes to see the devil. And, me and my angel are standing before him and his kingdom in this earth, for the weapons of our welfare are not canal, but mighty through God of heaven to the pulling down of strongholds.

When the bible says me and my second (two witnesses) will be standing before the God of the earth, you have to understand that this is not child's play, but God has made it easy for us with the power of the Holy Ghost, Satan cannot stand the fire of the Holy Ghost, evils are consumed with this fire, and they have been defeated by the Spirit of the Living God of heaven.

Zechariah also revealed to the world "Then said he, These are the two anointed ones, that stand by the LORD of the whole earth" (Zechariah 4:14.)

The interpretation of "stand" here is, pressure of the devil. For more understanding this is heat from the devil. Satan will continue to harass or annoy me and the second witness until the last day when Christ returns to this earth. The word "harass" means to wear out, exhaust. This is exactly what prophet Daniel revealed in the holy scriptures regarding the end time. The bible used the words "...shall wear out the saints of the most High". The words "Most High" here, refer to the God of heaven, the Almighty, the everlasting Father.

This is continuous harassment. Annoy, hassle, threat, oppress, stress, disturb; all these things are to put fear into my heart, and this is a concern to the second witness, my angel. God is my Saviour. My angel has faith, and she knows that as I live on this earth, I will walk through the narrow way, and this road is not easy. She has passion like I do, anytime I feel pains on earth, this doesn't bring her joy. When I am hurt, she's hurt. She is a believer, also waiting for the last day.

Satan uses fear in fighting believers, and this is his greatest weapon and to weaken people. If one avenue is closed to him, he uses another avenue. But I do not boast regarding this, I know whom I worship, that is able to deliver me from all the tricks and trap of the enemies.

Satan is the God of the earth, he is in total control of all the children of perdition in all the earth. It is easy for him to posses them and use them against the saints of the Almighty God. To harass and oppress the saints around the world, with different manifestations of problems.

"Shall wear out the saints of the most High." The questions is, can we the bear it to the end? Righteousness is the only key to heaven, and nothing more. When Christ comes back and He finds your body, soul and spirit in fault, your rapture is not a guaranteed.

I will frankly confess that I get grieved in my heart, and soul almost every day. I am really weary and worn out. But I have to follow the way of righteousness, this is not easy.

I know the sufferings I am going through. And I began to

come into knowledge, the reason why John the Baptist went to stay in the wilderness, he could not stay in the world with the people. The world if full of sin. Yet, sin is increasing every day. The wicked continue doing wickedness, they make it their tradition to hassle us the saints of the Most High. We are people who have no fault in Christ.

Despite John the Baptist ducking away not to offend man and not to see evil, born a holy prophet among all the humans in all the earth, he could not bear the evil of the people, because he knew the power that lived inside him, a holy fire.

John the Baptist went through human torture; he was beheaded. The saints shall wear out and may not bear it to the end. Many have fallen away, and also their love has waxed cold.

Some of the saints shall be prisoners with specific reasons as spoken by the prophets, and the detailed revelation is in the book title, What Do You Want?

Can a person who is hungry and thirsty after righteousness make one enemy? Or can he live in malice? Yet, I have to maintain the sweet commandments of God and I live without blame in the body and in the spirit. And continue to live a righteous life.

I was abandoned and I struggled with humans. I cursed the day I was born into this earth. This is exactly what Apostle Paul revealed, that the kingdom of God is not meat and drink. "For the kingdom of God is not meat and drink; but righteousness, and peace, and joy in the Holy Ghost" (Romans 14:17.)

I live in righteousness and in truth, perfect and without fault. I am thirsty and hungry not to offend anyone. And I know the road of righteousness, how narrow is it. This is the road all the righteous shall pass.

The kingdom of God is not meat and drink, but longsuffering which is the fruit of the Holy Ghost. My joy today is the Holy Ghost. Seeing the power of God, in me I gladly rejoice.

It was the Holy Ghost who made all the apostles rejoice, even in their time of suffering. Because they were seeing the power of God in action physically, every second in their lives.

The question remains: can a woman stand Satan, the God of the whole earth? When Satan harasses the woman, is there any spiritual ability to stand the devil? The devil will use all avenues to pursue. And remember, we all must pass this narrow way, and this is definitely a narrow way. Does the woman have the ability to take hurdles? Satan uses fear as a weapon.

When Satan brings harassment to the life of a believer, if he succeeds, there are always casualties. And some have given up the race. They can no longer walk the narrow path.

I have read stories of women, even had the chance to speak with some who were hit hard by Satan. It resulted frustration, and they started doubting that there is a God at all.

To doubt God is sin, and this is terrible. Anyone who doubts Him, such souls are not supposed to have been born. God is a respecter of no person. Satan has hit many very hard and they denied the Lord.

In the time of trouble, a man needs to stand strong and a man needs to maintain his faith and not to deny the Lord, always confess that Jesus is Lord. Continue loving your neighbour as yourself, and do no evil. Love the God of heaven with all your heart.

A real woman is a weak vessel, and it is easy for Satan to use her. If Satan is coming to war in a zone, he leaves the women and wars the men. Satan knows very well that women surrender easily. A woman cannot stand the devil, because women are captives of Satan. The cheapest thing for Satan is the woman. Look at what the bible says about the man.

"And when the dragon saw that he was cast unto the earth, he persecuted the woman which brought forth the man child" (Revelation 12:13.)

The great question I am going to ask here is, what has the woman done to the devil? Man is capable to stand Satan, himself knows. If God wants to deal with Satan, He will chose a man to deal with him, Angel Michael is a man. Michael and his angels bundled him out of heaven, including his angels.

Lucifer only comes to kill and to destroy. This is a spiritual fight! It will be an error if you think that this is a physical fight. For a woman to be the end time witness of the living God is to stand Satan, the god of the whole earth as the bible says.

The two witnesses are a man and a woman, which is me and my angel as; revealed. Satan cannot persecute an angel they are free.

It was easy as A, B, C, for Satan to take hold of the Eve. Eve was a woman like any other woman on this earth. Some may want to deny this, but you cannot deny the truth. This is not a discrimination against the woman, I do respect the woman.

If I want to be captured today, it is easy for a real woman to capture me. The power is in her to do it. But now, I have the Holy Ghost and fire and it will be hard for me to be captured by a woman. Adam did not have the Holy Ghost.

Satan used Eve as a weapon to destroy the man. Adam, who was the man, sinned against the living God who is the Almighty Father and this is the reason we are all suffering in the world today, the disobedience of one man affected all.

We sweat before we reap and eat. Terror, death, political woes, diseases, and many disasters now exist on the planet. In the beginning, it was not so. Man was created and placed in the garden of beauty, and everything was available. All kinds of enjoyment we can think of, any kind of fun was available, beautiful animals were living with man in peace. Eve spoiled the whole show, Adam followed the voice of his wife rather than the voice of God.

Power is still with Satan to penetrate the woman as revealed in the bible, "...he persecuted the woman which brought forth the man child. "The English define the word "persecute", as "to oppress or harass with ill-treatment, especially because of gender..."

When the woman gets to heaven, she is no more under the persecution of Satan, and no more a captive. This is the reasons a nice man of God will advice the woman to relax, and not be a priest in the altar.

A woman preaching on the altar is a liability to the church. Among the fruits of the Holy Ghost is patience. The sisters should wait until they get to heaven.

Sisters should implement their ideas at home regarding the gospel with the man as a helper. This is a great counsel for the woman, for their own security. So that at the end, they will not find themselves screwed up. Be patient.

This is a simple language to advice the woman, and nobody will stop you who is a woman. If you stick to acting as if you are a man by saying "I am a priest", you are doing this at your own risk.

You can attend a church where a woman is preaching, this is not a problem; she's only doing it at her own risk, it does not concern you who is a listener, you are only being obedient to the word of God.

A woman who says she is a priest, is not hundred percent safe, rapture will leave her behind, she will not inherit the kingdom of heaven. And this is the worst. Jesus did not command any woman to act as a pastor, He only commanded men to be the pastor of His church. We know that women have ideas, but it has a degree, compared to men; this is on the ground that when you search the bible very well.

The blessing of a man is more potent than that of a woman. Isaac blessed his son Jacob, not Rebecca. This up to anyone to choose if it's the blessing of Rebecca you need or the blessing of Isaac.

When you are in the congregation and a female pastor calls you and you let her pray for you, this is as the blessing of Rebecca. Let the man lay hands and let them pray for you. Women laying hands on men, I have never seen this in the bible.

Wise men in the church, they keep the women on the pulpit to keep the place busy and interesting, but in reality, a man is the architect of the whole thing because they know within themselves that there is nowhere in the bible that a woman is commanded to act as a pastor. Men are no fools. Men know what they are doing. If the women think that men are fools, they have made an error.

A woman acting as a pastor is not guaranteed to inherit the kingdom of heaven. The woman should not say, "because I am a pastor, this qualifies me to inherit the kingdom of heaven". Such a woman is making an error. This does not qualify you to enter into heaven; you are going to face judgment. And this judgment is very terrible.

God created the fruit of life and the fruit of evil, He created both. If you want to eat evil, He will not hold your hands because He gave you a free will to chose life or death, this is up to you. He sent the prophets to inform the world, choose good and do not choose evil.

God will not force any against his or her will. God is holy. Some group of men believe that if you are a woman and you want to be anointed as a bishop, these category of men will not insist so that you don't look at them as a sexist, they will even anoint you and give the bishop's crown and certificate, but within themselves, they know that such a woman is going to destroy herself.

Any man who anoints a woman as a priest it is the woman that destroy herself there is no fault from the man, women have eyes and they know where is written in the bible that woman should remain silent in the church. But yet they want to talk. "Let your women keep silence in the churches: for it is not permitted unto them to speak; but they are commanded to be under obedience as also saith the law" (Corinthians 14:34.) Look to what the bible says here, "the law", hope people know the meaning of this. The spirit of judgment is blind and does not know anyone.

A wise man will not argue with a woman who wants to preach as a minister if she insists that she has the right to do it, because this will bring a quarrel. Allow them. You can be tagged sexist. Or you can even receive insults. Do not deprive anyone of what she wants to do. We need peace. But grace will soon expire, because it has a time limit.

A woman is weak, but do not take it for granted; To be

violent with a woman and refuse to repent, such a man cannot enter into the kingdom of heaven. Check the bible very well; none of Jesus' friend was ever violent against a woman. None.

Bear the bad character of the woman, take it easy and remain calm with wisdom. Your Father in heaven will compensate you. Pains and suffering must surely come; this is the nature of life, if you do not have pains and sufferings on earth, how can your Father in heaven compensate you? Satan designed all these sufferings to shake the faith of them that believe.

God has spoken; He will pay all the damages caused in your life because of the love you have for Him, so do not be violent with a woman; let her live as she wants. Stay with her in peace and maintain her as your wife; do not divorce her because of a bad character, in accordance with the bible.

It is not in the holy bible that you should be brutal to a woman. If a woman uses harsh words, curses and violence with you, turn a deaf ear to her and do not touch her. Do not respond negatively to her. If she refuses to repent, she will fall in her own mischief.

That mustard seed of love that I had, to me it was a golden, special thing, I reserved it for a daughter of God but the woman (Maria) I wanted to give it to did not know the value of such a treasure, instead, she killed it.

A seriously wounded prophet of God married to a striptease. Is it a perfect match? Even on the day of our marriage as we celebrated, she stripped off her clothes. To add more insult to injury, the marriage ended in tears and in pains.

My wife said to me that there is a force behind the end of our marriage. That even resulted in the death of a lawyer. At the time of my marriage, the effect of my confusion caused by the pastors (bible school teachers) was still evident in my life. Jeremiah used the words in the bible, "scattered sheep". This is how I went in a wrong direction.

As a striptease, I did not condemn my wife or her life style; she was a treasure, for the short time in my marriage, my joy was full. I don't judge people based on religion, if you believe in Jesus as the Son of God, I am fine with you, I told her "don't go away stay with me".

When someone is confused, he is out of the track; this is a psychological issue, the only way out of this mess is to have a revelation.

In my case as the author of this book, my only hope today is the revelation that I have, Satan and those geniuses have no ability to kill my revelation, it is what I have seen that I testify of that makes me like a Lion of Judah. My revelation gave me great hope, I concluded that my revelation makes me a living stone.

They would have knocked me out of the heavenly race the way Maria was knocked out and the way my wife was knocked out of being the queen: look at what the bible says: the two chosen witnesses will stand before the God of the whole earth. My wife told me face to face that there is a satanic power behind the end of our marriage. Maria could not stand Satan, my wife could not stand Satan.

What Satan is saying, since he is the God of the whole earth, he has power over all women, exactly as written in the bible, "And when the dragon saw that he was cast unto the earth, he persecuted the woman which brought forth the man child" (Re:12:13.) The bible cannot lie. The word persecuted means mistreated. Power is still with Satan. And you can understand what it takes for a woman will be the second witness of God of heaven.

When the bible says, "these are the anointed ones the olive trees that stand before the God of the whole earth". If you have wisdom, you will get to figure out the spoken word of the Creator that, there will be history between me and the Dragon which prophet Zechariah revealed in the bible, the complete story of this is written in my book titled, What Do You Want? Satan is saying that he will give me, Thomas Bayo, a wife. Satan means it. When I saw the woman that Satan brought to me for marriage, this is when I knew more about who Satan is. The Dragon is bad to the core.

If Satan is coming to deceive you, he is not coming to tell you that he is Satan, he will transform into an angel of light. So when you see him, you will believe that he is from the God of heaven. This was the time the Dragon appeared to me in a revelation, he came like an angel of light, told me directly of one particular woman and I was wondering.

The woman that Satan brought to me for marriage, what I have to utter about her is not suitable to hear. This incident happened after my wife left me. When my wife left me, it became difficult for me to love. I was always thinking of her with many tears in my bed. But the woman that Satan brought to me, when I saw her, believe me I forgot my wife immediately, her eyes alone were wonderful. I fell in love with her and I was experiencing a new life altogether, but at this time, it had not be known to me that this woman was from Satan, because an angel appeared to me and told me of this girl, and I believed the whole thing.

The longest relationship that I had in life was when I was with this girl. She warned me that I could not leave her and I knew I could not leave. I came up with an option of leaving Europe to live in Australia with a another woman. It was a prison which was set for me, and I was arrested.

I was in prison and I stayed in prison for three years in Austria, she did not know where I was, she could not find me, the prison warders did not allow me to make a phone call for over a year. It was in the prison that God revealed everything about this girl to me and how Satan appeared to me like angel of light and seduced me that this girl was for me. Satan himself was even angry that I was in jail. When I saw the revelation, I was shocked. Many people in this world, including many who are in the church, you do not know whom you are married to.

If I ask some of you that you do not know the person you are married to, if you tell me you know him or her I will laugh over it. Most people do not even know the person that they are married to. Make Jesus the anchor of your life and you are safe from the hands of people you do not know.

My marriage only lasted for a month and she personally went to the court and file for separation, I insisted that I wanted to maintain my marriage. I will not separate from my wife.

I concluded that I am not under bondage of anyone; if she wants to leave, let her leave. "1Co:7:15: But if the unbelieving depart, let him depart." A brother or a sister is not under bondage in such cases: but God hath called us to peace".

The bible says if the wife or husband wants to leave, let her or him leave. My marriage happened immediately after Calle Lilja and Ingrid tampered with my faith and kicked me out of school. This was what they wanted; when I was falling, they were jubilant over my failure.

> "Woe be unto the pastors that destroy
> and scatter the sheep of my pasture!
> saith the LORD" (Jeremiah 23:1.)

The word "destroy" here as spoken by prophet Jeremiah is, to render useless or ineffective. You see how Calle Lilja and Ingrid they rendered me useless and infective? This is what that has been seen ahead of time. Another definition of destroy here in English language is, put an end to. Or to ruin completely; spoil. This is how my marriage life was slaughtered by the geniuses.

Do you know how many people in that school whose lives were ruined completely? The word scatter here is, to cause to separate and go in different directions. Those bible college students who were scattered by those teachers, God will gather these ones together when He comes back and take them home.

That is why God does not condemn anyone whose faith has been wrecked, He makes a perfect judgment. It is man that condemns, but not God. I persuaded my wife to stay and not leave. The complete story of this is written in the book titled., What Do You What?

None of the prophets had a history of separation or divorce and none of them taught about divorce, they wanted to teach about divorce, but God did not allow them to teach about it, because they would have made an error.

This error is in the sense that the prophets are truthful people, and no lie was found in their tongue, if they had taught about divorce, and they did not have a case of divorce, their testimony would not have been true, saying what they did not see, or saying what they did not know.

There is no truth to be compared to a minister that has seen a revelation of God face to face. Prophets are truthful people, and is what they saw and what they touched with their hands they taught the world and their testimony is true and remains truth forever.

In the days of the prophets, that was in the stone age, the commandment was written in stone. To break it, carried a death penalty. There was no room for mercy. So, if any woman committed fornication, the punishment was death, divorce was not common. Divorce did not even exist in the lives of the prophets. There was nothing like that. There was nothing to say about this. They knew the law; no mercy. They were commanded to re-write the law in front of their door post while the original manuscript remained in the stone. The word "divorce" did not even come from their tongue; it was not found in any of the apostles.

I will give you the wisdom of divorce, because of my experience as a prophet, because my wife told me that she would divorce me. This was her statement and I am writing what I know and testify of what I have seen.

If it were to be in the stone age, my wife would died by stoning. The whole city would have gathered together and stoned her to death by the law. This is an evil death, and such a soul will not even be buried in the city, such souls are buried far from the city in a wasteland. Children, the young and the old, they grew up with the knowledge of the stone to wipe away evil out of the land and so that no single curse should be found in the land, evil was not permitted to exist in the land.

The people in their various lands in the days of the ancient prophets knew well that they had to implement and execute what the commandment says, not to support any kind of evil at any level, and they were ready to lay down their lives to make sure the commandment written in the stone is implemented and accomplished since it is the glory of God.

They knew that if they did not implement the law and remove evil from the land, the destroyer would come like a tractor and make sure he makes the land clean of its dirt and take away any evil.

Those who refuse to support the commandments written in the stone and supported evil were not qualified to live in the days of the ancient prophets because the commandments came from the Creator.

In the biblical history of the entire world, nations, cities have been once wiped out, and no single soul was saved because of the wickedness of mankind. In this present time, the prayer of any person on earth is not to see the destroyer from the God of heaven, a destroyer's job is to remove and clean the land and give glory to God.

What is happening in our days did not happen in the days of the ancient prophets. Sin has increased rapidly in the entire world and now, we are expecting the end of the world because of the evil of men. If there was no wickedness, the world would not need to end; and it would continue. The fault is from man, and not from God, God is holy. He created us based on His love, if God were to be evil, He wouldn't have created us. Evil will not live as He has spoken.

On the issue of my wife, there is no room for divorce. "And he saith unto them, Whosoever shall put away his wife, and marry another, committed adultery against her" (M'r:10:11.)

"And if a woman shall put away her husband, and be married to another, she committeth adultery" (M'r:10:12.)

The issue of divorce is settled here. Let the people know, if you are married and you personally divorce, this is wrong. Like I told my wife, I will not divorce. Period. Even though you are a striptease, I don't divorce whom I have married.

God will put His anger on he or she that goes to divorce. And He will take away His anger from the other. The Father in heaven did not see any reason why He will put His anger on an innocent souls who say he or she will not divorce and love the wife or the husband.

If the anger of God is taken away from you, the definition of this is that, there is no blame on your side under these circumstances. Based on this, God will show His mercy, because this is not your fault, you did not divorce. Second marriage is unbiblical. If your wife divorces you or your husband divorces you and you decide to live together with another, the anger of God is not in you, there is mercy. If you are not a divorcee, do not teach about divorce because you are saying what you do not know, and testify of what you have not seen. Because you do not know what you are talking about.

He that is filled with the Holy Ghost will never teach about divorce, because the manifestation of the Holy Ghost is based on the truth, to testify what you know. Polygamous marriage look likes an old fashioned way of living, but some nations still practise it up to this day. If your nation allows it by law, God's judgment will be based on the heart: He will look to the heart to judge, not appearance. He wrote the law in the heart of mankind. "Which shew the work of the law written in their hearts, their conscience also bearing witness, and their thoughts the mean while accusing or else excusing one another;" (Ro:2:15.)

Based on my past life experience that involved me and a lesbian, this really gave me a truthful knowledge of same sex marriage. If I am writing anything about same sex marriage, I know what I am talking about. Sometimes, the Creator may allow some certain manifestations happen in your life, it will give a perfect experience so when you speak about it, it becomes a truth. Same sex marriage did come into effect because salvation has ended; in the beginning it was not so, see more of this in my book, What Do You Want?

Whether the marriage is done in the church or done in the

community hall or in native land, these are same. No room for divorce, must carry each other's pains, that is why two of you are one flesh.

My wife took up to three lawyers when she broke the marriage, but I took no lawyer. I stood for myself, in Italy separation/divorce is not a small journey, some even take up to ten years, some even abandon it and let him or her that wants divorce e fight for it.

My wife's statement against me in court was that I ran away from the marriage. She planned it with her lawyer.

Her statement before the judge, her charges against me was that, I left home without telling her, and she could not find me. She said that none of my clothes and property were in our home. That she could not even see me and there was no address for the court charges to be posted to. They did not even know how to get in touch with me. Both of us had same residence address.

This is a woman that I married, before I came home, she locked the house, she was angry with me because she went to perform an abortion at the hospital and I did not come with her to the hospital. To me, it is over my dead body to go and witness where an unborn child is being killed. I don't go to such hospitals.

Because I did not go with her to the hospital, she took all my belongings, kept some few of my clothes in a carton and threw it from the window to me. She changed the house keys. I was homeless.

I slept for almost a month inside my car; I thank God it was a summer. After a while, I got an apartment of my own, I called her many times on the phone, she refused to pick the calls. One day she was kind enough to come to know the house I lived, I bought pizza and we ate together. I asked that we both come back together, she refused. At this time, she had already filed separation papers in the court without telling me.

I went to the city hall to check the status of my marriage and the city hall told me that my wife had filed a separation case against me and they told me the court date.

On that exact date, a few minutes before the court proceedings, I appeared.

As they saw me appear, that was the beginning of their confusion. The question she and her lawyer asked me as they saw me unexpectedly was that, how did you know that there is a court date for our separation/divorce? The answer is very simple, "No weapon that is formed against thee shall prosper; and every tongue that shall arise against thee in judgment shall thou I condemn. This is the heritage of the servants of the LORD, and their righteousness is of me, saith the LORD" (Isaiah 54:17.)

This would have landed me in jail with her statement that I ran away from my marriage. As the court started, the judge asked me of my names and date of birth, I gave him all my data to confirm that it was really me. The charges were read aloud to my ear.

She and her lawyer heard me as I told the judge inside the court that, why coming to tell lies in the front of judge in the court of law? Why? To say I ran away from the marriage is a lie. We just ate Pizza yesterday night together, and you did not tell me that you filed for a divorce. The judge saw in my eyes that I loved my wife so much.

Here I was in the court, in love with my wife and wanting to save my marriage. Can somebody who loves his wife run away from marriage? Her lawyer saw that my speech was dominating the court and I am not an attorney, Her lawyer rebuked me instantly, that I should shut up my mouth. The lawyer died.

I am a prophet and he was a lawyer; our identities are very clear, I do not know how to read this in his ear that I am a prophet of the living God. Man as a lawyer has his boundaries. And if you go beyond the red line, you will face a divine execution. "M'r:10:9: What therefore God hath joined together, let not man put asunder". You are putting asunder what God has joint together, this lawyer was guilty. This lawyer insulted me that I should "stai zitto, chiudere la bocca" meaning in English language I should shut up and close my mouth. Such people will have eternal punishment.

We are in the days of grace and nothing the judge could not do anything other than his work. The judge removed himself from the case and another judge who is a woman took over the case. Yet, I won it. I was not guilty of this marriage. The truth was revealed.

The court clerk advised me to ignore her and let her run the paper work by herself since she is the one that needs separation, and not me. The new judge also told me that not to come to court again. The woman judge, she handled the whole process with her lawyer.

Italian women end up their marriages by first suing their husband for separation so that when the court grants them separation certificate by Italian law, they start to commit adultery.

My wife did not say anything, because she knew that she was lying. she kept silence, after her lawyer rebuked me as I was saying the truth, it was a humiliating to me, but I did not say anything.

In Italy, it carries punishment for a wife to lay charges before the judge that her husband ran away.

But God of heaven does not sleep. He will always protect, He is a Saviour.

The judge told my wife she should consider me and let us continue the marriage. The judge was persuading her. My wife responded that she would not come back to me and she wanted a separation.

This is how my marriage ended. I knew the pains I went through in life. As I woke from my bed in the morning, and she was not by my side, the response from me was, "where are you, sweetheart?" Tears would always gush from my eyes, I could not stop crying. I was only holding her photos, but I said, this is just a photo. I need you honey, not pictures. I would ask the photos, where are you? The tears could not stop. This is a pain that has remained me.

What really happened, in the second hearing of the court, the lawyer was sick and became thin as a broom, the sickness affected his movements; he could hardly walk. Seeing the lawyer, you would know that there was no way he could survive his illness, and you could see clearly that he had a short time to live. Before the third hearing of the court, that was when he died. The judge himself washed off his hands from the case and he resigned.

Rebuking a prophet of the living God who is saying the truth carries a death sentence. You were told as written in the bible. When you hurt a prophet, the war is not over, justice awaits you on this earth and in the world to come.

Italian women know that if the court does not grant them separation, there will be danger of committing adultery by law. So they rush the court for separation and when the separation is granted, they believe they are legally committing adultery, as they hold the separation order from the court. So that the husband cannot do anything because she will present the certificate of separation from the court if there will be any dispute.

A marriage separation approval from the court is a certificate of fornication and adultery for Italian women.

The paper you call marriage separation approval written with ink issued by the court, is a death panel.

Any law written with ink kills. Jesus did not write any law to anyone either with ink or written in stone, the name of Jesus was designed to save you from the shameful death of ink and of stone and even though you commit the most horrible sin on earth including fornication and adultery, when you love Him your sins do not count and you will be set free indeed.

But today, the world is living by His grace. The bible says work out your salvation with fear and trembling.

I know that some may say, "ah, Thomas Bayo is an African man; this is African culture", but you are making error. The power that has been given to me by God Himself, and He lives inside me. The same God who Created all human beings. This power that has been given to me is a physical fire that lives inside me, as revealed to you by apostle John in the book of Revelations 11:5: "And if any man will hurt them, fire proceedeth out of their mouth, and devoureth their enemies".

This power that is inside me lives forever. Let me try to describe this fire to you. This fire is like that of a gold smith that he uses to do his job. The capacity of this fire that lives inside me is blue and it is crude, like that tools of the gold smith that he brings forth to do his job. This power and fire has no mercy, yet this is the glory of God. And the power that lives inside me, He cannot forgive when you sin against Him.

The word devoureth here as written in the book of Revelations is, in the next world to come, the governmental power that has been given to me by God is of high capacity. Our government will be the sword of Christ to threaten evil.

By using soft hands to treat evil, evil will definitely be out of control. Grace and liberty will make enemies want to show their power, meaning they will wax strong and breed more enemies. Such things will not exist in the world to come; they will be devoured with fire. This is the reason the bible revealed to you that do not hurt these two witnesses, "And if any man will hurt them, fire proceedeth out of their mouth, and devoureth their enemies" (Revelation 11:5.)

In all areas of life, when you are a holy prophet of the living God and you are living with all kinds of people both young and old, including the wicked, see how they deposit their evil acts, which are their anger that they refused to control, untamed tongues; poisonous tongues, disgusting souls to the Holy Ghost.

But for now, God has made me harmless as the dove and He has made me wise as the serpent. When you live in a world that has no wisdom, this is when you use wisdom to live with them that are of the world, a peace maker as a child of God so that in the world to come you, will inherit eternal life.

Any man whosoever that carnally lies with the wife of a prophet, either married, separated or divorced, this carries a death penalty. Eternal death to him and his entire house. The bottom line here is power. Such a soul has trespassed a high power.

In the stone age, Pharaoh the king of Egypt was worshiped as god, was like the world's super power at that time. Egypt, at a time, was the highest world economic giant, Abraham was an immigrant in Egypt. Sarah, Abraham's wife was so beautiful, her beauty was so thrilling, that as she entered into the nation of Egypt, everyone recommended her to be taken into the house of the king of Egypt. Pharaoh, for romance, attempted to have Sarah as a wife because of her beauty, what happened? God plagued the house of this king because of His prophet.

The man Pharaoh, a king who was worshiped as god pleaded with all his heart and returned Sarah to her husband with a great possession, sheep, oxen, asses, she asses, camels, including human servants men and women were given to Abraham. You can see how much the wife of a prophet is worth. In the stone age, for Miss world to visit to any nation like Egypt, from the point entry, the army will take her straight to the house of Pharaoh for romance. This present world is different from the past. These kings were worshipped as gods on earth during the stone age. Abraham experienced this, at the entrance of Egypt, Sarah landed in the king's palace because of her beauty.

The new world tradition, " have your say", didn't exist in the time of the stone age. Christ gave you grace to live in freedom and in liberty in this present earth, but many do not know, although the grace has been abused. Human beings do not like liberty. God gave you liberty but man messed it up. Some even curse God, their own Creator. The Blood of Christ brought liberty, freedom to the entire world.

I strongly believe without any doubt in my heart, that every believer is beautiful. The wives of prophets are always beautiful, starting from Noah up to this hour.

It is only death that can separate married couples; twins do not separate from each other. Disagreement between two people does not mean separation.

Who will put asunder what God has joint together? Why do you want to destroy yourself?

I did everything with all my strength, telling my wife to come back to the marriage and let us have as many children as she wants, even a quiver full. She said no. I begged her with tears, she said no. I know how much I loved her.

We are in the days of grace. That is why you see many divorce cases even woman divorcing the men of God around the globe, which did not happen in the dark age.

That does not mean that these women will go to hell fire, but they will be punished in the last day. Since they believe in Jesus, they still have salvation. This is what the Spirit of God says. God will create a new heaven and a new earth, and God will establish them on this earth. These are not qualified to inherit the kingdom of heaven. This is same salvation.

Grace is as a system used to experiment the human behaviour. When grace is given, the wise will watch and see the impact and the reaction of it on human behaviour. When God laid the foundation of this world, grace was not in the sketch. The law was very simple: do not eat, if you eat, you will die, period. This has nothing to do with grace.

Disobedience produced immediate results in the past. Many do not know what grace is all about, some believe that grace is a birth right, but grace came into the spotlight many years back.

So, when the God of heaven sent His prophet to give you a message and you stone, humiliate and kill all of them and God is silent, it has a meaning. If you think that it is a routine to kill prophets, and hurt them, you are making an error. It is only people that have wisdom that know the definition of grace.

Grace will produce good results in people that have wisdom and understanding. This is a great advantage of a system of grace, they that have knowledge live with wisdom, breath with wisdom and wisdom is in their mind. This wisdom, is not a question of academics, this is what you have to work out yourself.

In anything, there are advantaged and disadvantaged, and the disadvantage of grace is not good for the ignorant. On the other hand, if table of stone can create an impact to make a away for the ignorant to escape destruction, this system will automatically be switched back to the stone age after the rapture. Because we all know the result of grace.

"It hath been said, Whosoever shall put away his wife, let

him give her a writing of divorcement: But I say unto you, That whosoever shall put away his wife, saving for the cause of fornication, causeth her to commit adultery: and whosoever shall marry her that is divorced committeth adultery" (Matthew 5:31-32.)

The Creator gave a commandment:

Thou shalt not commit adultery.

(Exodus 20:14.)

This commandment was written and carved in stone.

The Creator commanded forever, thou shall not commit adultery. Who is going to break this commandment? This is a commandment from the Creator Himself. They that broke this commandment during the stone age, they got the wages.

God did say, as written in the book of Revelations, that He will give a great tribulation to any of His servant that commits fornication.

Jesus commanded the world to drop the stone of death against any that commits adultery, because of His grace. In the stone age these things did not exist; there was no room for mercy. I know that some humans hate Christ, but I tell you that the grace you are enjoying today, He gave it to you.

In the world to come, all these things will not exist. God will create a new heaven and a new earth, and no sin shall be found in it. Divorce will not exist. Be assured. Everyone will have the best.

You cannot swear an oath of marriage with someone and later break that agreement. This is evil. It is good that you maintain any of your words, even your spoken words that are idle, maintain them to the end, this is what makes a man.

I have seen how people killed their wives and ended up in jail, they prefer to be on the leather injection than to live on this earth. Living on this earth without that particular woman is worthless to them. I have seen murderers because of this kind of passion when I was in jail in Austria. I did have personal experience. This is among the highest causes for suicide on earth. I have seen people whose partners left them and were depressed and depreciated in body, soul and spirit.

When my wife left me, I was no more a human being; I saw myself like as a dead- living being, I was totally empty. I could not even enjoy sleeping with another woman, all what I was thinking about was my wife. I told my wife I would not end this marriage. This is a pain from the soul and people that cannot control it end up doing what they are not supposed to do.

At a time, a voice pounded in my heart a heavy tune that I wanted her dead, but I love God I will not commit murder. I cannot even hit a woman. In the time of my marriage to her, I did not even insult her.

Even my own mother, I honour her. All the time I lived with my mother, I did not challenge her when she gave me instructions. The bible says, thou shall not kill. But God healed me of this passion and I forgot the past. I even prayed that God would bless her. I put all the blame on Calli Lilja and Ingrid; they symmetrically made me marry an unbeliever. I do not condemn the unbelievers; not all of them that are bad in this area of life. Some of unbelievers are nice people and I love them.

People like Calle Lilja and Ingrid, these are geniuses, they know human philosophy. These are people who spent many years studying how life is formed, how it's matured and how it try to win. They know all the methods of human behaviour. Most of them are professors. People and nations depend on these category of people to give to them suggestions or information. And many rely on them for guidance.

Calle Lilja and Ingrid know perfectly that I am a real human being, and I have a passion, they know what to do and how to destroy me, since I was already in their net (school.) These are the people who gave me admission to the bible school. It is their signature that made me have a resident permit in Sweden and travel to study. If you are not a genius, you cannot do such a thing. Some of them are not like us who did not study. God hid wisdom in us that a genius cannot see.

In this world, I am for peace and I will maintain it, this is what makes a child of God.

We true Christians have been humiliated, with lots of sufferings and with great tears, punished because of our faith and many have been killed by the wicked.

We who are children of God love peace on earth and as Christ lives forever and we shall hurt no one.

The earth is the basic place to make peace, our Father in heaven is good enough to have given you the chance to come and reason with Him even though your sin be as a scarlet, it shall be as white as snow; though they be red like crimson, they shall be as wool.

God gave man a great opportunity, but it was misused. Not one apostle was left behind by the people of this world; the world killed all of them. Many do not know the liberty they have now, and that was given to you by Christ. Christ will come and take the ones He loves, saved them from death, this is the end.

In the world to come, the holy mountain of God will not accommodate any type of evil in accordance to what has been written in the holy bible.

When the God of heaven wants to do His things, He performs a righteous judgment. For now, He is silent, giving man time to repent. But man has chosen to do evil than to do good. They that rule in this evil world, they govern this world and kill in the name of peace.

The Lord God of heaven has created a destroyer. Let me give you a detailed explanation and example of what physically happened in the past. "And the earth opened her mouth, and swallowed them up, and their houses, and all the men that appertained unto Korah, and all their goods. They, and all that appertained to them, went down alive into the pit, and the earth closed upon them: and they perished from among the congregation" (Numbers 16:32-33.)

This will give you a perfect understanding that in the world to come, evil will be destroyed. No negotiations with evil. By negotiating with evil, it gives them more chance and power to re enforce and the people are more in terror of the wicked. Evil does not know peace.

Another example we can see in our daily lives is, how many false prophets have came to cause confusion in this world, different kinds of false prophets in different religions. These have their portion in hell fire.

Children of evil are glorifying deaths and killings. Evil is in the world and the masses are in fear, many are not safe on the streets, even in their own houses, any strange noises make many feel unsafe.

The false prophets have created a false religion and they are leading people in the wrong direction of faith. The seed of evil normally starts with only one man. To initiate any evil idea, it always starts with one man.

The foundation of any confusion starts with one man; it is not good to give such a man a long rope, because when he has recruited other people to join him, this is as planting a seed. When the seed has grown, it will produce more and more. Meanwhile, when they have increased, they will wax strong. And it will be too late to destroy them.

There will be nothing like confusion in the world to come; such a thing will not exist in the new earth that God will create. Before any soul makes such a move to bring confusion, he will be consumed. If such a soul is not consumed immediately, the earth will be polluted again. There is no place for evil. The kingdom of Christ shall rule with a rod of iron. The greatest joy of all is that evil will not exist in the new earth that the God of heaven will create, Satan will be in prison, this is hell fire and the world will be at peace.

The wicked who refuse to repent, your days have been numbered. God is strong to execute His judgment.

However, it is only by the power of the Almighty God that the kingdom of Satan will be no more. And the world will rejoice and live in peace, but not by the power of man or any other power.

Jesus did not offend anyone, neither did He kill anyone and He never hurt any. He came healing people and doing good and giving everlasting life to as many that believe.

The God of heaven is kind, He gave you a last chance to repent, or get the wage of your sin.

It is appointed unto man once to die, then comes judgment. Since evil has become an ecstasy in lives of many people, the pit which is hell is waiting for them. It has already been prepared.

In the new earth that will be established, evil people shall not live on it, and they shall not see heavens, they shall be locked and sealed under the pit.

"And he shewed me Joshua the high
priest standing before the angel of
the LORD, and Satan standing at his
right hand to resist him" (Zechariah 3:1.)

Zechariah was a Jewish prophet, and in this revelation in the verse above he mentioned the name "Joshua". What is actually Joshua here in this verse? Biblical records shows that Joshua was a high profile prophet, meaning that this verse is not talking about a physical Joshua, this is spiritual Joshua.

The question is, what is a physical Joshua and a spiritual Joshua? A physical Joshua is a prophet that existed in the past in the time of Moses and lastly in the land of Israel. A spiritual Joshua is a prophetic mechanism use as a message to identify a specific person that will be born on this earth. Physical Joshua is dead long ago and the time of this prophecy physical Joshua was not even in existence.

The prophecy of Zechariah is an encrypted message. Pointing a sign that this is a private message and only the owner of message a gift from God that can be able to descript it and reveal it to the world—a trade mark. The dictionary define trade mark as a device (such as a word) pointing distinctly to the origin or ownership of merchandise to which it is applied and legally reserved to the exclusive use of the owner as maker or seller.

Another question is, why is Zechariah chapter three is heavily encrypted? Because false prophet are out there and they are spiritual thieves.

Because when the false prophets read the prophecy of "Zechariah chapter 3" they will get confused and they do not know where to start from and where to begin. By the time they carry their spiritual weapon to rob a prophecy and when they read in the bible that, "And he shewed me Joshua the high priest standing before the angel of the LORD, and Satan standing at his right hand to resist him", What will a false prophet interpret here? To say you are the dead Joshua? To rob these prophecy? When a false prophet try to crack this verse, God of heaven will laugh in His Throne; myself will laugh too and laugh and laugh.

This is the power of God, the prophecy of Zechariah is left intact and cannot be stolen or robbed. Many will say I am prophet, I am a prophet God sent me, bla bla bla.

God of heaven protected all potential prophesies against those false prophets. These are the evil people enemy of righteousness who in the outward appearance they look nice but the inside of them are full of chronic evil.

When the people came to meet Jesus and asked Him to show them the sign of the end, the Lord Jesus used a name "Jonas". The core of His message to the people was that, you don't expect Jonas, a prophet already laid to rest in the grave to give you a trending prophecy. The spoken word of Jesus regarding Jonas is an indication of message referring to a prophet that was not yet in the spotlight.

God chose two witnesses, which is me and another being whose residence is in heaven, which makes us the two witnesses of the living God. The second witness is an angel in heaven.

When it comes to a spiritual subject this is where faith is

involved, because without faith, it is impossible to please God and without faith it is impossible to become a good Christian. Unbelievers will go to hell because they refuse to believe.

The spiritual Joshua here is talking about another prophet that will implement prophetic duties similar to the duties the physical Joshua performed at his generation. I, Thomas Bayo, I am the spiritual Joshua, which apostle John also revealed that, this is given to the Gentiles, as you read ahead you will see. So the spiritual Joshua is a Gentile but not a Jew.

The Joshua of the past is of biblical historic record. But spiritual Joshua is referring to another prophet that is not yet in the spotlight. You don't expect the past Joshua that has been laid to the grave to execute a trending prophecy, it does not work that way. God is not the God of the dead, but the God of the living.

"For he is not a God of the dead, but of the living: for all live unto him." (Luke 20:38.)

This explanation is to give you the knowledge that I, Thomas Bayo, the author of this book is the living witness of the Almighty God and power has been given to me.

"and Satan standing at his

right hand to resist him"   (Zechariah 3:1.)

If you look at the verse taken from the book of Zechariah, what is the purpose of this prophecy? A prophecy that involve an angel of God, a prophet the spiritual Joshua—Thomas Bayo, the heavenly host, including Zechariah the prophet himself that brought this prophecy to an account, God of heaven heavily involved.

Another question you need to ask here is that, why Satan is resisting me the prophet — Thomas Bayo? Thirdly, why did the angel of God here in this verse protesting against spiritual Joshua—Thomas Bayo? The angel of God is indicating here which you can pinpoint, is against Thomas Bayo? Protesting? Look at it again, "And the angel of the Lord protested unto Joshua".

Fourthly, what do you understand by filthy garments that is on spiritual Joshua—Thomas Bayo? Because we know the truth that physical Joshua (a prophet) will not wear a filthy garment.

The answer to the above questions is this; what involves the Creator here, Satan, angel, Thomas Bayo, the heavenly hosts. The purpose of this verse, this is an inaugural ceremony of the day me and my angel were inducted into a new position as officially the two witnesses of God. And to announce the date of the end: The evidences are here, look at what the bible says here in verse 4, "And I said, Let them set a fair mitre upon his head. So they set a fair mitre upon his head, and clothed him with garments. And the angel of the Lord stood by"

So we do know that, mitre is a tall headdress worn by bishops and senior abbots as a symbol of office.

This shows clearly that this is inauguration and this is a crown that was given to me and my angel by the Creator Himself. The ceremony took place in prison, the evidences are here in verse 3, "Now Joshua was clothed with filthy garments, and stood before the angel" As a bad boy this was the time that I was in the prison. Take notice of the behaviour of the angel of God here as written in this verse enable you the reader give your true judgment.

There is filthy garment involved in this prophecy which means a sinful man. The identity of the sinful man here shows clearly that the angel of God did not stand by this sinful man (Thomas Bayo.) Angel of God is holy and cannot and will never stand by a sinful man. The sinful man stood before the angel of God. Hope you agreed?

There was a distance between the two beings here, the angel of God and the sinful man. Look at it here, "standing before the angel of the Lord" This is face-to-face. And 'standby' or 'stood-by' is only a close relation can do this, example of husband and wife.

So the filthy garment here means prison because I was a bad boy, a sinful man, heavily polluted with fornication, with all kinds of women both the posses and all kinds of unbelievers. So the angel of God cannot stand by me since I am a sinful man, angels of God are holy.

It was in the prison that I was heavy anointed by the Creator and power was given to me and I saw this power live. I am not saying that I read it on newspaper that power was given to me, this was live in the physical realm. Or I am not saying someone called me and told me that power has been given to me. I saw my angel.

You need to look at the behaviour and the movement-manner of the angel of God here, very important, for you to get the correct identity of who is this angel of God and what is up to. Prophecy requires a lot of intelligence to get the clear pictures of what is happening because this is a work of a genius.

It was when the filthy garment is removed from the sinful man—Thomas Bayo, this was when I was anointed by the Creator. It is impossible to anoint a sinful man except such person is given the garment of righteousness. And after I was anointed the angel of God changes position and stood by me, you have a look, "And I said, Let them set a fair mitre upon his head. So they set a fair mitre upon his head, and clothed him with garments. And the angel of the Lord stood by". Mitre here is a crown. I was heavily anointed in the prison and filled with the Holy Ghost and with fire, power was given to me, and the bible says, "And the angel of the Lord stood by." For example is only a strong relationship as husband and wife can be able to stand by each other, so in this prophecy it shows clearly here that this is my angel, my partner and the second witness of God Almighty.

There are lot of questions to be asked in this revelation of prophet Zechariah. If I begin to interpret the complete details of this prophecy this book will end up to 500 pages or more, I just want to be brief and try to minimise it and push more of it to the next book.

So with common sense, why do you think that an angel of the Almighty God who Created the haven and the earth, will have such powerful relationship with a filthy human being or a prophet that is filthy? The word filthy is disgustingly dirty. And the bible telling you here that the true identity of this person is bad guy! Look at the capacity of this relationship how close is the angel to a prophet of God.

The angel of God in this prophecy is woman who is second witnesses of the living God. I am not saying that there are marriages in heaven so don't prove me wrong.

If you read the verse, "and Satan standing at his right hand to resist him". The bible says here, Satan standing at his right hand? So this is impossible to stand at the "right hand" of somebody that involves resistance without a contact or a relationship has not been established within the two parties, no man can argue this. There must be an history in connection with these two parties, that requires to reveal a secret. Why Satan beside him, who are they, what are they up to and what is their relationship? Because this is Satan with a man that is filthy. For you to understand perfectly what it means of someone standing at the right hand of another, according to Notorious B.I.G, beside every bad boy there is a bad girl.

Prophecy of Zechariah here pin-pointing that Satan (the God of this earth) is standing by the right hand of the bad boy, and again to resist this bad boy. Is not this bad boy resting the right hand of Satan.

To stand by the right hand of someone either filthy or holy, it shows clearly—physical intimacy is characterized by romantic or passionate attachment or sexual activity because the bible made it clear that there are dirty things involved to identify of this prophet. A filthy garment meaning a sinful prophet. You see how the Creator hide a treasure on the chemistry of a bad guy to as many to keep eyes off, for safety measures, is only powerful being such as gods that are above humans that have the capacity to detect this chemistry. Satan saw this treasure, kept it and using it.

In the book of Zechariah here, this Satan is a woman. Satan is referred to as a being who is rebellious, they were once angel of God but they sinned. And Satan resisting this bad guy. Prophecy of Zechariah did reveal this Satan as a woman and titled her wickedness. Also in this revelation in the fourth chapter, Zechariah was on a deep sleep when the revelation came to him and his two eyes were full of sleep.

The prophecy of Zechariah is not saying that Satan is fighting with the angel of God or fighting with spiritual Joshua? The bible says, "and Satan standing at his right hand to resist him" Right hand, Satan is struggle to retain the relationship holding the right hand of this bad guy, don't ever leave me, don't ever go; the picture of this is like the songs of Brandy & Monica - The Boy Is Mine, Satan need to give it up. The angel of God successfully collected me from Satan. Any talented biblical prophecy genius will tell you that the Antichrist is a woman and she is called Satan. The full story that carried almost the half of my coming book, Deadly Secret The United States Government Is Hiding.

Another question is, what is so important that made Satan to resist? What is so important in the live of this bad guy that made Satan to say you know what, I won't let you go? The bible never pointed out here that Satan is trying to kill this bad guy, the bible says resisted. This is not an arrest and there were no combat involved, the issue is when the angel of God projected that the boy is mine, heaven knows and prophecy knows, that is when Satan said hell will let lose than to give it up, but at the end I saw Satan break down, a hard hit.

This secret relationship between me and the Antichrist is revealed in my next book. This revelation will give a perfect understanding to believers around the world that we have eternal life, the reason why we are on this earth is because the earth is our origin the beginning of the point of where we were created and we are heading to where we will begin our eternal life of joy without end, a place that there is no age. This is why salvation is very important to a wise person. God did not condemn us despite evil is in our mist and the devil drag us into sin. God cares for us and He will give out the kingdom to them that loves Him.

When you read a revelation or a prophecy the easy way to understand it, is what are the motive of this revelation? What is the benefit? Who are involved? As for me I do not what to be selfish in just focusing on by my prophctic biography or whatever. This revelation is of the end time, which is revealed here.

The Antichrist resisted that no way, over her dead body that she will not leave my hand this was when I saw the spirit of the Antichrist try to enter to me, came aggressively as a white cow. This was very, very terrible.

Let me describe the Sword of The Almighty God here. The Sword of the Creator is Sore, Great and Strong. The word Sore here is painful and sensitive, like a Buzz Saw, the word Great here is, possessing great and impressive power or strength—performance of Superior Power, and the word Strong here is Marked by a Great Physical Power. For Satan to resist me Thomas Bayo the spiritual Joshua, this is when Satan fell into a Buzz Saw.

The Lord God of heaven rebuked Satan and everything went successfully.

On this day that I was crowned on this ceremony, my angel used her inaugural address to present her vision and to set forth her goals to me and for the ending of the world which you can see here, "And the angel of the Lord protested unto Joshua, saying, Thus saith the Lord of hosts; If thou wilt walk in my ways, and if thou wilt keep my charge, then thou shalt also judge my house, and shalt also keep my courts, and I will give thee places to walk among these that stand by. Hear now, O Joshua the high priest, thou, and thy fellows that sit before thee: for they are men wondered at: for, behold, I will bring forth my servant the BRANCH." (Zechariah 3:6-10.)

For behold the stone that I have laid before Joshua; upon one stone shall be seven eyes: behold, I will engrave the graving thereof, saith the Lord of hosts, and I will remove the iniquity of that land in one day.

In that day, saith the Lord of hosts, shall ye call every man his neighbour under the vine and under the fig tree." .

You can see how powerful is her addresses in the above verses.

On her speech she presented perfectly the Government of God. If you look at her speech here is shows clearly that this is a government that requires me to follow the right process, follows all the commandment of God.

Toward the ending of her message she mentioned BRANCH, creating a forum for me to message address and announce the date of Christ return which is this prophetic book that I have written.

The word BRANCH is the elected law-making branch of government; power of authority. You can also see on her speech that in this ceremony there are heavenly hosts present in that day.

If you also look at the Revelation of apostle John is sates clearly in chapter 11 that this power will be given to a Gentile.

Heavenly host were there as the ceremony of my anointing was spiritually air around the world, in heaven, sea, and things under the earth all in the spiritual realm. The greatest moment of my angel, as she read the end time message in heaven and in the earth and in the sea and for those under the earth.

What do you know of Satan? All what you know of Satan is by what you have read but you did not see. When the word Satan is pronounced the answer is always evil which is correct.

There are differences and this subject is not taught widely in the church so the identity of this woman has been a mission impossible and the bible called her mystery. If there is no prophet to encrypt a decrypted prophecy this is impossible for the people to know.

This Satan is not booted from heaven because there is no biblical evidence of this, is Lucifer that has been cast out from heaven, this woman is still in heaven and nobody knows the identity of this woman and bible pointing to you in this prophecy of Zechariah that this spiritual Joshua will reveal this woman to you because Satan standing at his right hand.

So, which false prophet will say I know it more than Thomas Bayo who Satan stand at his right hand? This woman is God of this earth as you will read below in the revelation of apostle John in the book of revelation.

You can see how the prophecy of Zechariah projected the relationship between Thomas Bayo and Satan. So if you want to know anything about Satan, Thomas Bayo (spiritual Joshua) will give you the clue, but this is not an easy journey.

But mind your language the prophecy of Zechariah never projected that the spiritual Joshua—Thomas Bayo is a devil, the prophecy of Zechariah pointed to you that Thomas Bayo is a prophet, an elect, heavily anointed and a servant of the Almighty God called The BRANCH. Satan knows the position of Thomas Bayo as a big fish and romantically fell in love with him and do not want to allow him go and Satan was making trouble as you can see on the prophecy "resisted" that involves the Powerful Sword of the Almighty. Sore, Great and Strong.

All power is from God, the power of angel is given by God and the power of a prophet is given by God and the spiritual identity of my angel is also revealed on this encrypted prophecy of Zechariah.

In my next coming prophetic book on revealing revelations, what you will read is, it happened that Satan resisted and she was rebuked by my angel that pave way for the inauguration ceremony to be held and power was given to me. So the question is, did Satan gave up after the ceremony? Was there a death threat to the living prophet by Satan? Satan didn't give up but came back and what happened is what makes part of my next book.

The two witnesses of the living God is also revealed in the book of Revelation by apostle John, Apostle John says, "These are the two olive trees, and the two candlesticks standing before the God of the earth" (Re:11:4.) This is the same revelation that is in this verse above, Satan is resisting in the verse above. Face to face.

Revelations have strategies, and if it is not properly designed, it may not properly balance in all the generations. The bible properly balances all revelations, many revelations have keys and if you are not given the keys, there is no way you can know it.

If you are in power and you are revealing revelation to a present generation for the future generations, you use a reigning name in that present generation to seal the revelation for the people to have hope, hope is big and wide as the sea.

The first people that heard this revelation were the people at the time of Zechariah, and Joshua was the reigning name at that time. You have to use a reigning name to match the topic of the discussion, this is how it works. And when that generation has passed, the sharp eye will look at same revelation and understand its meaning and what the revelation is referring to.

In the time of the apostles, they believed that Jesus would come in their life time, based on how the revelation was designed to suit their hearts; they waited, generations and generations waited. If Christ had told them in His time that He would come back by 2035, if they calculated the years ahead, the churches may be empty, nobody may go to church and the printing press may not have printed the bible materials immediately. The apostles may have said it doesn't make sense to preach the gospel now, when the world ends in 2035. They may have said let that generation of 2035 take control of the gospel.

Jesus that says He will come like a thief in the night, and He also says He does not know the day and hour of His coming, are you wiser than Him? Jesus is wiser than you, my friend. The bible is a well done job. And I really thank Jesus for such a wonderful wisdom for saying He would come like a thief in the night. I also thank Him for saying He did not know the day and the hour of His coming. It is a foolish man that will say "I don't believe that the world will end in 2035", then he will go and sleep and slumber like the five foolish virgins and the rapture will come and they will be left behind, while the wise will act like the five wise virgins and watch the year 2035 month of May and...., they will not sleep but watch.

The angels in heaven rebelled against the Father, but not all did, some remained loyal to Him. Now, these loyal angels, God loves them dearly.

The angels love the saints of God and God gave them power to defend us anywhere and at any time, according to His will. The saints will not offend any man, because we are perfect people, faultless people, repented people.

The woman who will sit with God on His throne, such a

woman on earth there shouldn't be any dent on her. Not fairly used in any way or with a second hand heart or a heart that has been destroyed by any man. A woman that has not bowed down to any or face east position or west position to worship man. A pure heart. God gave this power to one of His angels in heaven to inherit this crown.

The crown was already going to Maria, but she was snared and taken.

Two chosen will sit with Christ in His kingdom. This two chosen are one flesh, a man and a woman. One on the left and one at the right.

We are created as pair, and so shall we live in God forever. Man and the woman and Maria eat her salvation and she became a fading flower.

Chapter Four

2035, the End of Age

"These are the two olive trees,
and the two candlesticks standing
before the God of the whole earth"
(Revelations 11:4.)

I, Thomas Bayo, was in the spirit and immediately I saw the Lord Jesus appear to me and coming toward me. I was going toward Him at a distance of about 12 meters and we were coming towards each other. I could not wait to meet Him, this is the Lord God of all the whole earth and heaven, the Emmanuel, God with us. In this crossroad of revelation, many things happened. This was a revelation that came to pass.

After many years had passed, I surveyed this revelation and I asked myself why did Jesus appear to me? What was His mission to me? I was still studying this revelation in a very critical way. How am I so sure of this revelation? Was I not standing in eternal judgment, already face to face with the Lord? I reasoned within my mind again, can the living face eternal judgment when he is still yet alive? A wise man must need to study what he has seen before making any decision.

Part of my survey resulted that, I am to fulfil a mission however, and another question is, my testimony will be based upon what truth? As you read on. you will get to understand that truth is written in all our hearts.

In this revelation, it resulted that, I burst into tears as I came alive. And I could not stop crying. These were tears of guilt mixed with Grace, grace. This was my immediate reaction. Meanwhile, in the beginning of the revelation, my understanding was not opened so I left it idle, and I focused my attention on the area of my sins, why Jesus appeared to me and I was grieved based on the situation I kept myself, I was lost. A revelation from God is treasure to the whole world.

The Creator gave me a mighty revelation and I kept it carelessly, not knowing it was a valuable treasure that was given to me and I misplaced this revelation. By the time I knew the usefulness, of the revelations it was too late. The reason why I lost the revelation was because I was so much involved in the pleasure and the cares of this world, all my attention was taken away due to pleasure of women, parties and money.

There are many reasons why the Lord Jesus appeared to me. They that are wise will reason with me here and accept the truth. One of the reasons why the Lord appeared to me is: biblical records show that Jesus does not appear to righteous men. Any righteous man that says Jesus appeared to him, such a person has lied. The heavenly Father will only appear to a holy man as He did to Jacob; any evil man that says the Creator appeared to him, he has lied.

The Lord Jesus will only pay divine visits to a sinner like me. And there must be an evidence of that sin you committed that will motivate the Lord Jesus to come to you as He did to the ancient prophets. The evidence must show an image, since image is available in our time, including any medical evidence or coupled with people that will stand as a testimony to say, yes, this is true. Technology was not available in the time of the prophets, so there were no images. Wise men will have to review it and if there is any lie, the wise will not accept it.

Jesus does not appear to people that are already in the ministries such as pastors, bishops, prophets, evangelist, deacons or anyone that partakes in activities in the church or any spiritually established man, because it is unbiblical for Jesus to appear to them. These are the just; they need not repentance. Jesus has nothing to work on their body. Any pastor that tells you Jesus appeared to him when he is in the ministries, avoid such a pastor.

It is only the heavenly Father that will appear to them that are just, to give a potential message that will reflect to all people that dwell on the earth, a powerful message that when you hear it, you will tremble. You need faith to stand such a message. Jesus loves sinners, He appears to them and saves them, this is what He does.

If any person tells you Jesus appeared to him or her, the question is, why did Jesus appear to you? What will you respond to Satan when he asks, who are you? Do you have a testimony to prove the reason why Jesus appeared to you? What message do you have from Jesus to the world? Is the message a head scratching, similar degree to that of apostle Paul's manner?

The underlining message is, the message Jesus will give to any man that He pays divine visit to, it is always astonishing when you hear it. It is a message that, when you hear it, a man will even question himself who am I? You need to be saved. Some will say Jesus came to me, I saw Him, and the question is, for what?

If Jesus appears to anyone, the message must be terrible because Jesus is dealing with a sinner directly and his or her testimony must prove it.

In my case, it never came to my mind that Jesus is coming; the level of my night parties with girls was on an industrial scale; at that time I never one day slept in the night; from Monday to Sunday, for me, it was parties, women and wine. I shifted from one club to the other, I only slept in the day time. On special occasions, I slept with women in their homes. You can imagine the level of my night partying was beyond control.

In the days of my partying, the police knew my car in the city, they knew my name. Many pull over me many times. I partied across Europe, airlines knew me as I flew frequently and I was given a special hand language tag. I had discount based on my air miles. I got my income through the business I established as CEO/MD, I employed workers, my life was holiday and parties.

There is one message I hate to hear from the club bouncer, "this is a private party, you cannot come in." I regarded this as "blacks are not welcome". I got a broken rib one day when I started a fight at one party. The fight was so intense that the owner of the night club came out; I wounded him on the chest with an iron. It was the police that came to separate us. I knew it was God that sent the police to rescue me that night; it was almost resulting to a gun fight. I will never forget what the Lord did for me that night to save me from death. I went home with a broken rib. Later I was healed by God.

There are many people in the world, and there are many characters in the world. A casanova will pick different girls at a night party, and at the end of the party, a fight will break out. In the days of my night partying, I moved with my weapon 24/7. I experienced women that are evil to the core; their passion is to set guys up to fight and the strong would take them home for a night stand.

These are not prostitutes, these are girls that work in cooperate companies as lawyers, bankers, students, medical doctors, young police women. They just want to have fun at night parties with models, TV stars, university students, air hostesses, tourists, stars and much more, these are the kinds of night clubs that were my choices. In this kind of life I was living, Jesus appeared to me.

At the end of my survey of this revelation, it was then that I knew exact the reason why Jesus appeared to me, and it was a wonderful thing, this was the time my understanding opened and I wept again. When you read this complete revelation, I will say I am very sorry for the readers of this book, the revelation that was left, you have to manage it, and some people will be angry with me to have been careless of a mighty revelation that was given to me by the God of heaven.

In this revelation, as I saw Him, this is Jesus Christ of yesterday today and forever. His form was like a person that doesn't talk much and he was a meek looking and straightforward Man. His hair was very short, like 7 millimetres long and very curly, the colour of His eyes were dark and the appearance of His age was within 27 to 30 years old, not above 30 years old, there was no beard on His face. His dressing was simple and the cloth He was wearing was like a normal garment. I believe that was reigning at His time. The appearance of His face was very gentle and did not look troublesome, he looked the type that minds his business, and is very, very watchful.

This revelation made me to remember the spoken word of one of His disciples.

Thomas said, "Except I shall see in his hands and the print of the nails, and put my fingers into the print of the nails, and thrust my hand into his side, I will not believe.

Ten people persuaded Thomas to believe that Jesus appeared to all of them and that He lives forever. Thomas did not believe but argued. God loved him. But he later repented and stop arguing after seeing the reality. That was the measurement of his faith.

Jesus appeared to His disciples and Thomas was there. Jesus said, "Thomas, Reach hither thy finger, and behold my hands, and reach hother thy hand, and thrust it unto my side: and be not faithless, but believing. And Thomas answered and said unto him. My Lord and my God. Jesus saith unto him, Thomas, because thou hast seen me, thou hast believed: blessed are they that have not seen, and yet have believed" (John 20: 27-29.)

This is the Lord Jesus who is more than a prophet, more than angels, the Lord God Almighty. This is the Man that I have heard of since my child hood. The Jesus that I have read about in the holy bible, who has been working miracles and raising people from the dead.

The Lord that rose from the dead after the third day, He ascended into heaven and went to His glory and joined Himself together with the heavenly Father.

He was called God the Son on earth, because He wonderfully separated Himself and one part was in heaven and one part was in the earth. Above human understanding, a spiritual matter that is hard-talk for the unbeliever. He made a great solution to save all human He has created from eternal death, eternal life.

God is a Spirit and not flesh, in heaven He was called God the Father and when He was on earth He was called the Son of Man, manifested through the womb of Mary. He used her as a transit to this earth, and He called her woman, not even mother. It was not the impregnating fluid of Joseph, the husband of Mary that formed Jesus, He was conceived by the Holy Ghost, It was grace in Mary and she was used as transportation and passage for Jesus.

He used His own power to form Himself. The truth remain forever that Jesus was conceived by the Holy Ghost. And the Holy Ghost is the Spirit of Jesus.

Christ did have the power; He took His own life when He was on the Cross of Calvary. His holy blood was the only remedy to save mankind and He did it with great love. If He did not die on the Cross, there would be no hope for anyone.

When I saw Him, this Jesus that walked on top of the water in the river in the presence of His disciples. This is the Almighty that I pray to always, that has the power to say, "your sins are forgiven" and immediately your sins will be forgiven. This is the Lord that has the power to cast into hell. This is the Saviour. This is the Man many wanted to just see His face.

The bible declared, "When Jesus therefore perceived that they would come and take him by force, to make him a king, he departed again into a mountain himself alone" (John 6:15.)

The Lord Jesus, His kingdom is not of this world, we that believe our kingdom is not of this world.

The Son of the living God, angels bow down and worship Him, the earth worships Him, the kingdom of Satan is troubled by His name, He that has the Almighty power, that has the key of life and of death. And only He that gives eternal life, He put His breath in the nostril of man and man became a living soul. Through breath He gave power to the apostles.

Apostle John in the bible was a witness to all the testimony of Jesus. And the witness of John is true and his testimony was published to the entire world which is known today as written in the Holy bible, in his testimony he wrote, "IN the beginning was the Word, and the Word was with God, and the Word was God... All things were made by him... In him was life; and the life was the light of men."

The most righteous prophet that has ever lived, John the Baptist, bears witness that Jesus is the light of all men, John was respected as one of the greatest prophets that has ever lived, and he testified to the people face to face that he was not worthy to untie the sandal of Jesus.

Kings on this earth, they bow down to Jesus and they pray to Him for deliverance, this is the Saviour; this is the Man the believers are waiting for to take them to heaven.

When I saw Jesus, in the beginning when this revelation was manifesting to me, I rejoiced because I was seeing the Lord coming toward me and I was going toward Him, but I did not know what was going to happen. I never knew what was in the mind of Jesus as He was coming toward me. But inside this revelation, to see Him to me was a great joy. I could not endure it, I could not wait to see Him. Although it was a nice and wonderful experience.

When I saw the Lord Jesus coming toward me, patience didn't exist in my life again, I could not wait to see Him, and my mission was running to embrace Him while He was walking toward me, words are not enough to express how I could not wait to hug and kiss the Lord.

When I saw Him coming toward me, it was like a Daddy had come back home, let me hug Daddy and touch His face and believe His presence. This was what prompted me running to hug Him and with a kiss.

This scenario was like a manifestation and revelation of love between two people. Jesus did reveal to me in this place that He is the heavenly Father. I should study the bible very well.

When I studied the bible very well, I saw the revelation of apostle John plainly written in the holy bible, after God appeared to John, and introduced Himself to Apostle John He said, "I am he that liveth, and was dead; and, behold, I am alive for evermore, Amen; and have the keys of hell and of death" (Revelation 1:18.) The question here is, who was dead and rose from the grave and is now living? If you say Jesus, then, you have rightly judged.

The wonder of Jesus originated from heaven and He lived on this earth and He was called the Son of God.

It was Matthew, one of the writers in the New Testament who wrote on his book that Jesus is the Son of God, while Mark wrote on his book that Jesus is the Son of Man.

There are no qualms if you believe that Jesus is the Son of God. You are saved. If you believe Jesus is God the Father, this is a real faith.

Some are confused about the actual figure of Jesus, if He is God. If you want to know the actual figure of Jesus by much questions, you are disturbing yourself, just believe Jesus is the Son of God.

Relax your mind and have faith. All these things works with faith, depending on what you believe. Your own faith can profit you and your faith can also destroy you. Our basic faith is the holy bible.

Categories of apostles as of John, these are men with powerful revelations. And the things of God are of wonders. Wisdom is needed from above to understand them, however, the bible is there for us to use, since it is what we have at hand to live our life through Christ. This is what we have in our hands, the testimony of Jesus, the word of God that saved us that believe.

In all this my 100 meter race running to meet the Lord: could you believe that were I was heading to meet Jesus was His judgment Throne?

If somebody had told me, "Thomas Bayo, take it easy and walk normally to meet the Lord and wait and hear what He is going to tell you first before you even plan to kiss or hug", I probably would still ignore any kind of advice from anyone that would have told me to take it easy.

In the position that Jesus was standing, at His front was the judgment Throne of God. Jesus was not there to laugh with me; He came to give me one simple message. And to show me something.

After I heard a short simple message of Jesus and the things He showed me, I burst into tears. My joy in that place was turned into sorrow and I was grieved. Jesus was gone, I was alone in my room crying and looking helpless.

And the place where this revelation manifested, there was nobody by my side to help me and say "Thomas, do not cry, things will be okay, God loves you". There was nobody with me. And no one by my side. I was alone.

The bible explained to you be ready to stand the Son of man in the judgment. It is a terrible thing to fall into the hands of Almighty God. "It is a fearful thing to fall into the hands of the living God" (Hebrew 10:31.)

The Father judgeth no man. Can you stand Jesus? Under the judgment Throne, is hell fire.

In the name of God, blessed are they that shall be able to stand Jesus in this specific position, a place where all will walk toward Him to give an account of their lives how you spent your life in this earth.

In my experience, in the judgment of God, you cannot know your faith until judgment has been pronounced on you. You may say that you are a Christian and you judge yourself that you are saved. But I know exactly that many of you do not know what you are talking about, because you have never heard the judgment of God on you. And you have never seen the judgment throne of Christ and of the saints, how it looks like.

Immediately the breath of man is gone out of him and falls dead on this earth, there is no chance of coming back to this again. Next, you will be working towards Jesus and he will be walking towards you.

When I saw the Lord, I was joyful in this revelation, but later the game changed.

Hell is under His feet. How many people know that hell is under the earth? That position where I was meeting Him was His Judgment Throne, the place where Christ will pass His verdict.

What was the actual skin colour of Jesus? When Jesus was on earth, He was singled out of the public because of His colour. This was exactly the interpretation of what prophet Isaiah wrote when he was describing the physical looks of Jesus, and the detail of His word is in the book, What Do You Want? Slim fit, tall and gorgeous. Very simple looking.

We speak what we know and testify what we have seen... (John 3:11.) Anyone who is trying to debate the colour of Jesus, he did not see anything.

Now, prophet Isaiah also revealed in his book and wrote, The crown of pride, the drunkards of Ephraim, shall be trodden under feet: (Isaiah 28:3.) The word under feet here is hell fire, hell is under the feet of Jesus Christ. The words "crown of pride" here are those that have been intoxicated with pride, the way alcohol moves some people, that is how pride moves them. They are always tipsy with dignity, self-esteem, arrogance, self-importance and much more, but they shall be trodden under feet. This explanation is to give you a perfect understanding of what the judgment of Christ looks like, and the end of the world.

Jesus asked a question in the bible by saying, "be ready to stand the Son of man in His judgment". Are you able to stand Him?

What I learnt and what I have seen in this revelation was that I was a child to Him, and I saw Him as a Father and God Almighty. When I survey this revelation more and more, the love between a truthful believer and God is perfect like that of child with the good mother, this is the picture to give detailed explanations the kind of love that is flowing between us and the Lord, the truthful ones that believe in Him as the Son of the living God.

They that believe in Jesus as the only Saviour of mankind have already been established in righteousness and are not crowned with pride or intoxicated with self-importance. In that day, when you as a believer shall see Him coming towards you in judgment, believe me, you cannot wait to see the Lord in the last day. You will run joyfully to Him.

In this revelation, I know the capacity of this divine love that bind us believers together with God. I saw this love in reality and in practice, because I touched the Lord and I felt Him and I know Him; He is a righteous God and at the end, tears upon tears came out of me for a specific reason after I came back to life. There are many reasons He appeared to me.

Perfect love takes away fear. The angels in heaven behold the face of God, the word 'behold' is to touch, feel a great love of the Father.

When this revelation manifested in my life as Jesus appeared to me face to face, at this time in my life I had a girlfriend by the name Bianca, but I was a Christian and I partook in Church activities, preaching repentance to people and I was attending Assemblies Church of God, and my pastor knew me as a God- loving person and always appoint me to lead prayers. But there was error in my life.

Me and Bianca, we were living together as boy friend and girlfriend however, I did not know anything about Bianca's faith. Neither did I ask her if she believed in Jesus, and even if she's a Christian at all, my relationship with her was only for sexual intercourse, but I was not marriage minded; marriage was far from my mind and in my life at this time. I never even thought about marriage.

But Bianca was nice. She's is a girl hoping for serious love and relationship but I told her a lie that I loved her. She fell in love and continued to give me story of her life. As the only daughter of her family, her dream in life was to be a lawyer. She was in the first year in her university, and her parents already bought a house for her, probably to commit me into relationship. Of a truth, she is nice.

She was living with her family in an apartment and she had her personal room, because I am black, she snucks me into her room, because she wanted me to sleep with her every day. At age 19, she was still under the authority of her parents, and she was not allowed to sleep outside. I was living with her in her house secretly, but her parent did not know. She was suggesting that we should live together in the house that was bought for her. She said that everything depended on me, she said she could convince her parents that she could live alone. You can see how wonderful she is?

I was with Bianca and I studied her life style; she's a person who is loyal and is not an arrogant type of human. Very easy to deal with, due to my experience with women, I know that there are some humans who are brought up very educated and they take things easy with people, but character is not based on salvation. I can assure you that Bianca has credit.

Even though my character was not good and people take me as a very bad guy, I had to cool down in life and behave gentle for the sake of Jesus and follow His commandment and treat people well.

Bianca, is the kind of person that, if I had told her that the foundation of our relationship and life should be the biblical, we should live as God fearing people, she would have yielded with joy. But I was after sexual intercourse and I was stupid.

God was grieved in me that I was having a relationship that was unbiblical, not only this but I was deceiving her that I loved her, and at the end I knew I would dump her and her life would be miserable, and she would be heartbroken.

When a woman is frustrated in the name of relationship, love and romance, looking for a genuine relationship, it affects the soul and the impact of this can make her get depressed.

Depression is very terrible and it can make a person totally lose control of oneself and it affects the daily activities. Sleeping in your bed alone, fed up with masturbation, when you see your own body, you start hissing, despite your beauty, moving alone and very lonely just like a bird that the feathers have been removed and under the rain and the cold.

Humans that heaven declared unsaved that I was sleeping with. I ignored the priority of a good chance to sing the song of the prophet, if she can be saved from eternal death. And heaven will rejoice.

One thing about unbelievers' relationship with Christians, no matter what, if you are a Christian and you are faithful, loving and loyal, there may be every possibilities that the unbelieving partner can give his or her life to God.

Anyway, since unbelievers are flesh and blood, the best way

is to depart from fornication and adultery, and there is more guarantee in the spiritual life of a man.

I have seen women who are dubious compared to Bianca. she's a reasonable woman.

Before I met Bianca, I had just broken up with a Jewish girl who was deeply in love with me. Before we started this relationship, she warned me that she would give me a prayer of evil if I dared leave her. Another Jewish girl warned me again if I leave her, she would report me to her father and make sure her father bullies me.

The Jewish girl that I was with before I met Bianca, I did not preach the gospel to her. Our relationship was broken by me without any reasonable reason, she made all efforts for our relationship to function, but it was difficult for her.

She got to understand that I am Christian and I love church, she traced my church, and started attending regularly. Because there was nowhere else she could see me. The only place where she knew she could see me was my church. She was attending church regularly. This is the girl I was with before I met Bianca; her heart was broken by me.

There are people in this world who have not heard a sound gospel, like this Jewish girl. God has committed us to preach the gospel to humans to have salvation and instead of me to preach to such souls like these girls, I started fornicating with them and destroying their minds. I became lukewarm in hands of God. These were people who were ready to accept Jesus as personal Lord and Saviour.

I kept my faith secret from Bianca because I knew that if I let her know that I am a Christian and latter disappointed her, this may affect her if at all she will one day become a believer. If a God-fearing man comes to her in the future for a serious relationship, what will come to her mind is: another. For this reason I was I keeping my faith secret.

It was immediately after this relationship with this Jewish girl I started with Bianca and our relationship was going on.

I knew that I would get married, but not at this time, commitment was not on my mind. My plans at this time in my life were to get married to a believer like me. I made up my mind that I would not receive any woman that is a Christian, and not fornicate with them, because I knew that by doing it, I would definitely break their hearts, and it is more evil to break the heart of a sister, to me this is something that I will not do.

This period that I was with Bianca as my girl friend, I planned to travel to Messina in Turkey to clear my consignment that I had shipped. And this journey was very long. I decided that I was going alone. And I told Bianca of my journey, that I would travel alone. I had never been to Turkey before, it was my first time, neither did I know where Messina city is, but in my thoughts, Messina as a city in Turkey should be very close to Istanbul.

Then I travelled to Turkey, when I got to Istanbul I asked of Messina city and I was told that Messina is very far away from Istanbul.

I had to travel through Ankara and many other cities, in fact, it was the beginning of my journey. From Istanbul I travelled through Ankara, and Tarsus. This was the city that was in the bible, the birth place of apostle Paul. The journey was so long.

When I got to Messina I walked through the city and visited their restaurants and some shops. Messina is city on the sea side, but not as big as Istanbul and Ankara. This is Turkey's largest sea port. Messina has always been a port city through history. Key prophets were there. There are recorded biblical events in history in this city. These region, Tarsus and Messina or Mersin.

The reason why I travelled to Turkey was to go to the sea port and clear my consignment.

In my thoughts before I travelled to Turkey, I was hoping that I would be able to clear the consignment in same day and same hour and start my journey back home. When I got to Messina, it was a different story. Not thought as in west Europe where I could clear my goods same day and same hour.

I had to spend some days in Messina, and I was going

to the sea port and visiting the customs and they were always asking me to come back. I ran out of patience and I yelled at one of the uniformed men; I was given a dirty slap. I looked at myself helplessly and it came to my memory that I am in Turkey this is not Italy, I told them okay, and I went to my hotel room. I decided that anytime my consignment was ready, I would wait. Since then, I started using the wisdom of Solomon to approach them. These officers were mean. For me coming back home in safety, I glorify God because the journey was too long. I had to drive long distances. And the roads were not so nice like the ones in Italy, accidents were smelling and on my side God was in control.

I stayed in Messina for about three to four days, because I cannot remember the accurate number of days, but it was not two days as I did lodge in a hotel.

In this paragraph, this how my revelation took place. Out of one of these three or four days as I was in Messina, I cannot even remember if it was morning, afternoon, evening or night in this hotel.

Suddenly, I was in the spirit and I saw the Lord Jesus and He appeared to me and I saw Him coming toward me, I could not wait to see Him coming toward me, I joyfully ran to Him and hugging Him and He cast me to the ground with His hand, what I heard from Him was that: none of my friends is a fornicator. Go and check the bible very well. I knew I was guilty and I had sinned against the Lord because I was committing fornication. I was convicted of my sins and I wept bitterly. I knew that I was committing fornication.

His messages have a lot of meaning. He gave me ahead revelation, step by step, how I would be snared.

I could not bear it, I knew that I was fornicating with Bianca, and I just disappointed another girl that has not recovered herself from broken love, these are the people that need salvation that I am supposed to preach to, but I was doing what the Lord does not like. Tears were running out of my eyes, the Lord Jesus said the truth that I was a fornicator, I was fornicating with women.

As I came back from Turkey, I called Bianca on the phone and I told her that I was back from my travelling, and we should see. We needed to talk. I told her not to come to my house, and I am not coming to meet her at home; we should meet somewhere else. As she came, we were facing each other and the bible was in my hand, and I continued my message, and telling her that Jesus said I should stop fornications and our relationship should stop. I saw in her face a sudden surprise and disappointment and sadness. Out of anger, what she responded was that, "you are a devil". I saw her walk away.

I stayed in little bit, seeing her as she was walking away in a letdown mood. I knew it was all over. When I was telling her about the end of the road, she saw in my face that there may be no sign of negotiation and she did not resist. I never forgot the four words that came out of her mouth.

Some girls, if you tell them that this is the end of the road, some tell you straightaway that I am not going anywhere. And anywhere you go, I follow you. To insist that the relationship must end, that is when they insist more. Bianca was not like this, she just left. Although she was sad, she did not insist.

I should have told Bianca my plans and hear her reactions before telling her good bye. Am I ready to accept the responsibility to become a daddy?

Bianca's case was different; my relationship with her was only for the bed and nothing more, not that she could not be a loving wife, at this time in my life the issue of marriage had not come. After this issue, I made up my mind to stop fornication and I deviated from it. Because of this revelation I made up my mind to finally get married, but to a sister.

At this time in my life, I only had Bianca as a girlfriend, and I was not controlling two girls at same time, just her. Some humans do meet daily challenges and temptations and faith is needed to overcome this.

I have the right to a partner (female) according to how God created it, but it has to be a truthful way and I did it a wrong way. My relationship with Bianca did not break the greatest commandment on earth; Jesus only let me to know that I was committing fornication and His judgment is true The relationship between me and Bianca might have been rectified with understanding and sacrifices.

To be unequally yoked is very wrong, if two partners are unbelievers and along the line one of them repents and accepts Christ, one has saved the other.

You will see many women greatly in love go to any length, and when the relationship is broken, they have great pains, but they do not know the love techniques. That's why some suffer greatly and cry for a broken up relationship. Some even face tough depression.

However, some of the women are very wise. And the wise ones know how to play the game. Some men know the right women who know how to love. The best and the greatest woman is the woman that will insist and say, "I am not going away, anywhere you go I will follow you, if you like kill me but I am not going away". This is a great woman.

Normally, in another way, a wise woman, if she's in love, and the love or marriage is out of control and the relationship is on its way to being over, the wise ones will say to her partner, "we should be open to communication, depending on if the other partner is willing to communicate." This is where they will see if they can rectify any negative force that is trying to hold their love to ransom, and with good communication they can stay together again.

This is the area where the woman will use her wisdom to persuade, insist and convince her partner, and miracles can happen, except there is no love. Situations change from bad to good. If Bianca would have use this method, up until this day I could have still been with her, because she would have won my heart; I have a pure heart. Pure hearts do not insist, and a pure heart is open to communication and very sympathetic. I know that I sinned against the Lord by fornicating.

God acted according to His word; the pure heart shall see

Him, which manifested in my life and the life of the prophets. Prophet Isaiah said, "Isa:6:5: Then said I, Woe is me! for I am undone; because I am a man of unclean lips, and I dwell in the midst of a people of unclean lips: for mine eyes have seen the King, the LORD of hosts."

Isaiah never said his heart was not pure, he said, his lip were unclean. This was the time the LORD appeared to Isaiah. These were strong boys. Isaiah said, I was in the midst of unbelievers. Isaiah was probably partying with the girls, he testified that he dwelt in the mist of people that have unclean lips, these were unbelievers. This was the time God delivered him and started using him to speak to nations in all the earth.

Searching the pure heart, this is a person that have the heart to forgive. Before you open your mouth to say 'sorry' to a pure heart, he has already fallen in love with you.

When the bible says "blessed are the pure in heart for they shall see God." this will give you a great understanding of the potency of how pure that heart is. The bible did not say "blessed are righteous, for they shall see God". It is only the pure in heart shall see God.

The angels of God in heaven always convince God to get what they want. The bible says they behold the face of God. Beholding somebody is to show a great love and such heart is pure.

Bianca did not mastermind me or sell me out on a racist level, and I did not mastermind Bianca. We were not officially married, and she cannot claim any rights; the relationship was illegal, although out of anger did she call me a devil. Both of us were enjoying the pleasure of sin. I later came to a conclusion that the best option was to give up this relationship. That doesn't mean Bianca will not get my blessings. She will have the reward of a prophet. This is her destiny to have met a prophet unknowingly. Bianca will not be destroyed in the last day.

Jesus speaking to me face to face is a potential proof that I did not create myself, so I cannot just do what I like. I was created by the Creator and it was out of love that He informed me that there is judgment over a sin that man has committed. This is the greatest love from the foundation of the world for the Father Himself to counsel a man face to face. The Lord was pointing me to studying the bible. So, the law has been written for man.

He gave me the bible, He still appeared to me and reminded me of what is written in the holy bible. He told me before hand, so that I would not face this judgment ahead to come. Even though I did not have the strength to repent, He did strengthen me to repent. This is exactly what He did to Peter His friend. "But I have prayed for thee, that thy faith fail not: and when thou art converted, strengthen thy brethren." (Luke 22: 32.)

They that refuse to repent of fornicating and adultery, it will not be good to face the judgment of God. It is a terrible thing to fall into the hands of Almighty God. After this earth, there are no more chances. Earth is the basic place to give up sins. You did not create yourself. God created you and He gave you a commandment to follow. It is up to you to be obedient or not or you get the wage of your sin in full scale.

In the time past, the earth was guilty of sin and they were destroyed by flood; God will do it again but this time He will create a new heaven and a new earth. Some of the angels in heaven sinned against God and He spared them not, and they were cast out from heaven and now in earth, chained to darkness, waiting to face eternal judgment.

If your telephone lines become like a public telephone line and the girls are calling you for pickups and for fun, then, you are at a big risk of getting HIV. Also, remember that HIV is in great circulation and hardly will you escape it.

HIV is hitting the world hard right now, and many have contacted it. Many are still contacting it and this is increasing.

When I was in the bible college, God gave me a vision about the warning of AIDS disease, including my chance of getting into jail. And God still uses sister Elizabeth to inform me to continue my school somewhere else, if I was kicked out of the bible school. I should not give up; I should continue my school somewhere.

Do not go to the extent of committing fornication as what Jesus has told me before, the warning of HIV was so strong that it was revealed that it had been planted on the way to affect me.

People, who are geniuses, have advised the people of the world theoretically that rubber can save them from contacting HIV through sexual intercourse. But practically, stop fornication and adultery, and there is every possibility that you are safe from being contacting this satanic disease. This disease is very dangerous.

AIDS has no cure. There is every possibility that condoms can burst, and can also pull off in the middle of sexual pleasure and at this stage, if HIV is involved, it will be too late.

How many people at the point of sexual intercourse think of using condoms? HIV activists may only tell you in theory the danger of unprotected sex. "Be not wise in thine own eyes: fear the LORD, and depart from evil. It shall be health to thy navel, and marrow to thy bones" (Proverb 3:7, 8.)

Do not follow what your thoughts say, obedience is better than sacrifice. This is what I have learnt in practical, and this is the wisdom I will give to all that I love.

Get the warning of fornication and adultery and stop it, God is silent for a reason but in days to come for those who refused to repent, the result of sin will be on a full-scale.

God commanded, "thou shall not commit adultery". And it is good that you should not do it. Take the counsel of a prophet and do not do it. Exactly the words of God toward prophet Isaiah, from the mist of sin and in the mist of sinners He did choose prophet Isaiah and established him into perfect righteousness and He used Isaiah to speak to the people.

Jesus gave me the warning of fornication, yet I did it. I received punishment for this, a great tribulation. I was kept in captivity and I forgot prosperity. This punishment was given to me because of love. So that He would take away His anger from me in the last day. Because He has chastened me like a father will chasten his son.

When it comes to HIV, Jesus told you already that some of us will not taste death until He comes back. Satan is using this disease to destroy the church of God against the rapture. You are expected to be without spot and blemish before you will be taken in the day and the hour of the rapture. This disease is a plague to the world. Do not let this plague affect you. Any avenue the disease is coming, try all means to avoid it; Christ will save you. The disease of HIV is what the devil is using it to shorten the lifespan of his victims, because of the rapture.

That is why, if God put you in prison do not regret it. His thoughts toward us are not of evil. This is how God saved me from contacting this devilish disease.

The call of God was boiling in my heart and I could not stand it. I repented of fornication, here came the issue of my admission to the bible college in Sweden. To proceed and get equipped to be a work man for God.

In Turkey, as the Lord appeared to me and gave me the warning about fornication, (I have tasted the fruits of the unbelieving life, and I know it will not work for me as a spiritual man, this is empty) I took a break and I was alone for some time. After some time, I made up my mind that now, I was hungry and thirsty for marriage just to avoid fornication as written in the holy bible, and I proceeded to chose a sister by name Maria. I found Maria stunning because she was a Christian. My spirit was stirred, I know with her I have a perfect love, as I was focussing it or as I did gauge it, and any relationship without Christ it will be vain.

It was in the bible college that I made the full decision that I would be a daddy, I was ready then, and that was the right time. My eternal wife is in the spiritual arena. This was my target. And I should have a perfect love for her in the name of the Lord, no matter her race or ethnic background or nationality, since she believes in Jesus as the only Son of God this is okay for me but nothing more. Maria whom I met in the bible college, my looking for Christian romance, love and marriage,   turned to horror.

The woman that I had chosen, she became wicked and she masterminded me, her and some of her country folks who are the teachers and the elders of the Church I was attending, they hurt me so hard. They refused to let me marry her and she did not marry me. Not getting married to me was not enough, she betrayed me and I was kicked out of the bible college, which is why today I am a school dropout. Sister Elisabeth was kind to me, she advised me to attend another school, there was no strength in me again, and today I am a college drop out.

I trusted Christians because my heart is so pure towards them, and they put tears on my face because I love them in God's name.

I consider that since one church can do this to me, others will do the same, in my mind, I told God that I would forget this road, even to be a preacher, I cannot even do it, is your love and fear that made me come to this school, these people that do not even like me how can I mix with them? Mixing with these people is like fooling myself. Let this be a forbidden thing to me.

What shall it profit to mix with these people? But I told Jesus that He is my Lord and my Saviour, "I will not deny you, you did not offend me, I did not see any single evil in you my Lord, the problem is not you but this is a problem of man.

God you are innocent in my case" and said within myself, I will go back to unbelievers, humans like Bianca and continue where I have stopped and let me enjoy myself with them and take any for marriage. I changed my mind and said, my life is based on discotheque, party, smoking, sword, violence, that is where I belong, my wife is waiting for me in the clubs and in the street corner but not in the church. Any road this unbeliever will follow I will follow it, to any length, in their games of romance, love and marriage I was ready to play it to any length.

God knows that I was going to destroy myself in the place I called discotheques and living the night life! What He did was that He did not abandon me nor did He forsake me but He was always with me even inside the nightclubs to save me, not let anyone hurt me. God of heaven has spoken that fury is not in Him.

But one thing I also said, I will never, ever pay evil with evil. If I run into any Christian on the way, I must give a helping hand and I will not see them falling and refuse to give them any helping hand, but I will not have any connection with them for my own personal reason because I may not like to see another Maria.

If I see any gospel preaching person, man or woman on the way and if they approach me, I give to them huge amounts of money, some when they see the money 1 give to them, some remain shocked and frozen. Some will not even know what to preach to me again. I felt their heart; they would wonder; what type of a kind man is this?

I carefully surveyed the whole thing and I concluded that these are bunch of wicked people; this is not a matter of racism. My own black brother was among them that saw me falling and refused to give me a little kindness, he connived with these teachers. Having joy to see me afflicted? This is wickedness.

God knows full well that is because of Him that I went to join the bible school to answer my callings and disengaged myself from the world, and if not for this, I would have spent my time in night clubs partying. This was not a matter of skin colour because I have dealt with unbelievers who are whites. I know the differences.

I did love them greatly because of our heavenly Father. This is a commandment which I must follow: to love my neighbour.

What the bible college teachers did to me made me backslide. I was swallowed into more fornication and adultery after Jesus spoke to me that "none of my friends is a fornicator", I gave up bible college, and I forgot that Christ is coming now. I went deeply into the world. I went and got married to an unbeliever, she divorced me. More details of what really happened in the bible college, my church, Maria all these are fully explained in my book, What Do You Want?

I went back to the world, mixed up with all kinds of women apart from believers. This was the counselling Jesus gave to me, I went back to Egypt. There was no strength in me again.

What next? God knows what to do. I was chastened and I saw red. God systematically put me in jail in the nation of Austria. The complete details how my captivity manifested is in the book, What Do You Want?

In the prison, I repented and the Lord strengthened me. The Lord is good. "For the LORD will not cast off for ever: But though he cause grief, yet will he have compassion according to the multitude of his mercies" (Lamentations 3:31, 32.)

Twelve judges, including the Austrian president were involved in my case. When it was too tough, God used the office of the Austrian president to release me from the prison on the grounds of official pardon. The first five judges gave me four and half years to stay in jail. I made an appeal.

Another five judges took over the case, on the day of court hearing, I was hoping to go home from the court, but these five judges requested me to maintain the four and half years. I requested that the judge to allow me go home on two third counts, the first judge refused. I appealed to another judge to allow me go home, he refused and he said I should maintain four and half years. All the reactions of the judges was that I should maintain the four and half years to the end. God reacted: the president released me on the ground of amnesty. It was in accordance with what Jesus said.

This is what the Lord God already said in the book of Revelations, that He would give tribulation to His servant that specifically refused to repent from fornication and adultery.

He, as God the Father will not reject any of His servants that commit fornication and adultery. They will be chastened. This is exactly what manifested in my life and I saw great tribulations. I wept and rebuked myself for the error.

The reason why I said Maria and her squad hurt me as written in my book title, What Do You Want? Is that, they yielded to Satan and through them, I was snared and I went to prison. Actually, I would have died in jail through the work of Maria and her squad, as revealed to me. However, God did not allow death to manifest through fornication. The Lord delivered me from death. Through captivity, He delivered me from the snare of the Devil.

When I was in jail, my brain cooled down. At this time, there was no woman and there were no parties. I remembered all my revelations, my callings, I remembered Turkey, Bianca, and Sister Elisabeth I accepted to fulfil my ministry in captivity like that of prophet Jonas. It was in the jail that I recovered myself, and the Lord was kind to me.

I sinned and went into more fornication and adultery as I left the bible college, I was motivated to live a wayward life like a pig. After I was established in righteousness, I began to wonder if really, it was I who did those things. Through captivity, I was established into perfect righteousness.

Heaven is designed for angels and only the believers on this earth that have accepted Jesus as Lord and Saviour also established in righteousness. Those will inherit the kingdom of God, these are the ones chosen by God the Father, that practise the biblical principles. Angels, they rejoice over any sinner that comes to God

To avoid being seduced by Satan, it is good for a believer to flee from marrying an unbeliever. If you were already married to an unbeliever before you came to the Lord, this is a different case and you are advised by the holy bible not to leave her or him. But if she wants to leave, let her go, and remember that a believer is not under bondage.

The angels in heaven sinned, He spared not the angels that sinned against Him and cast them down to hell and chained then under darkness, reserved to be punished with eternal fire and the smoke of their torment will rise up forever and ever.

If you are a believer and you are married to a believer, you are safe from that anger of God that will wax hot against the children of destruction.

After believers depart from this earth, when they get to heaven what will be relationship between a man and his wife?

The wife that you are married to here on earth will still be your eternal partner in heaven, this is only for the living when Christ will come and rapture the church. Since you have one already, you do not need any, there is no marriages in heaven. The ones that will be rapture by Christ will have a glorified body.

Those who have died without Christ, they have gone on their own way and now, they are in outer darkness.

In the rapture, angels will accompany Jesus as He comes to rapture the saints, and we shall meet Him in the air and so shall we ever be with Him. This is the power of God, not your own power. The bible also revealed to you, "Take heed that ye despise not one of these little ones; for I say unto you, That in heaven their angels do always behold the face of my Father which is in heaven" (Mathew 18:10.)

In captivity, I remembered all my revelations and I asked myself; is it not me that has seen the Lord God Almighty and He has spoken to me? What I am doing here? And I came to myself, and I regained my lost memory from the church called "Word of Life" in Uppsala, Sweden, caused by Calle Lilja, Ingrid and Maria.

In the prison, I began to remember all the Lord had told me, and I remembered that we are in the end of the world and Jesus is coming very soon. Fornication and pleasures of women made me forget that Christ is coming; this is what the Lord God of heaven has revealed to me face to face.

I tried to think and recollect all the revelations about when Christ is coming. God the Father has revealed the end of the world to me, the year, month, week, day, the hour and the minute, He revealed it to me as a secret, and I forgot. But God opened my understanding. I did not remember the year when this revelation was given to me. I forgot the year.

What I did was that, I started asking people that I knew, calling them and asking them about some events that happened in that period, if I could get that part of the revelation, even to get the actual period. It would be great. But the day and the hour, it will not be possible for me to recollect it.

When I had this revelation, the God of heaven gave me the year, month, week, day and hour, when Jesus will come and rapture the Saints.

God does not reveal what He has revealed a second time, just like the date of the end written in the bible and people asking Jesus "tell us when the end will be", Jesus will not tell anyone, except the world searches the bible very well.

When I came out of prison, after some years, I lost all what I had; I did not find any single paper. I lost all. God will not give the revelations He has given again. He will only provide the best means to help.

My backsliding was so strong that I was swallowed up, and I did not preach the gospel.

I was creating companies with offices and money was flowing and my job was only vacations and enjoyment, flying here and there. I was transacting all my business through phone calls and instructing my staff on what to do and I was satisfied. I thought I was rich and increased in goods and had need of nothing. I never knew that I was wretched, miserable, poor, blind and naked. I was going deeply into the world until God gave me the last chance to repent, but with a strong hand.

My understanding opened in captivity and I vowed that I would fulfil my ministry. The complete details of these revelations is called "the fat valley" that was revealed by prophet Isaiah and I have written it in the book titled, What Do You Want?

The Lord God spoke many generations ago, before we were born into this earth that He will personally rebuke and chasten the ones He loves; and this chastening of God is grief and sorrow, and is not good to see.

Many prophets experienced the hands of Almighty God and they wept in the time of their captivity. They were in hell and their lives in hardship, because they committed sin. Some wept bitterly and they rebuked themselves for their foolishness and confessed that only God is holy, and there is no One like Him,

He is the only Saviour, we are saved by His grace.

As written by the Hebrew writer" For whom the Lord loveth he chasteneth and scourgeth every sons who he receiveth" (Hebrew 12:16.)

In the bible, Jesus said, "But of that day and hour knoweth no man, no, not the angels of heaven, but my Father only". The people did not ask Jesus if His Father in heaven would reveal the year, month, week, day and the hour when He will come back to this earth a second time.

The mystery of the end is this: The Lord Jesus was perfect in His speech when He spoke about the end of the world and He was a man that had no power to make mistakes. He has no power to lie, the power to commit sin is not in Him, He remained perfect in His sermons and and He live forever. With His Almighty power, He established His name in heaven and in earth forever, and all knees shall bow on earth and in heaven.

Jesus' speech was so perfect that He did not say nobody knows the year, month and the week when the world will come to an end. He used two words: day and hour. "But of that day and hour knoweth no man, no, not the angels of heaven, but my Father only. Why Jesus did use these words - hour and day? Because the heavenly Father will reveal the year, month and the week to them that dwell in the face of the earth through one prophet, but no one knows that day and that hour but the heavenly Father only" (Matthew 24:36.)

This is not a new song, that Christ is coming very soon. This song has been going on before me and you were born into this earth. Even your ancestors sang this song until they fell asleep.

For the Christians, the rapture may leave you behind when you refuse to keep your eyes open to see what shall happen. As the lightning is coming out from the east and shining to the west so shall the coming of Christ be, "For as the lightning cometh out of the east, and shineth even unto the west; so also the coming of the Son of man be" (Matthew 24:27.)

If you do not watch, it will be your own fault. In the bible, the Lord gave you examples of the ten virgins, you already know the scriptures. "Then shall the kingdom of heaven be likened unto ten virgins, which took their lamps, and went forth to meet the bridegroom. And five of them were wise, and five were foolish" (Matthew 25:1,2.)

These ten virgins were Christians, they all believed, five were wise and five were foolish. The wise Christians will follow the revelations of God from the bible about the two witnesses and keep watch on the year, month, the week and the interval of days when Christ will come and take you home to heaven.

Within the interval of days as we expect Christ, sleeping is forbidden because Christ will come suddenly, in a twinkle of an eye, He will take His people home, they that keep their eyes open and do not sleep are like the five wise virgins. Nobody knows that day and the hour but the year, month and the week will be revealed. Do not slumber and sleep, meanwhile, pray so that you will be able to escape the terrible thing that is coming ahead of time to the people that dwell in the face of this earth.

When Jesus says do not sleep, He is not telling you not to sleep throughout all your life time, this interval of days is the period that you will not sleep since He will come like a thief in the night.

"Watch ye therefore: for ye know not when the master of the house cometh, at even, or at midnight, or at the cockcrowing, or in the morning: Lest coming suddenly he find you sleeping" (Mark 13:35, 36.) They that have wisdom can understand clearly what Jesus said here. He did not mention year here or month. The interval of these days will be revealed so that you do not sleep but watch.

In the revelation, when I saw the Lord as He was walking toward me and me running to Him, in the city of Messina in Turkey after I was present in the body, I said to myself that God has brought me to this side of the earth to give me this mighty revelation and show me in the bible the date of the end. This is the last day that He has revealed to me face to face.

In this revelation, after I saw Jesus, my understanding began to open slowly, slowly to get the full details of the revelation. Recently, I began to understand His spoken word and as He opened my understanding to get what He is saying, the pleasure took me out of this world, the Lord instructed me in His word to go and check the bible very well. None of Jesus' friend was a fornicator. Jesus used the word "friend" with me; He made me His friend, so I am the friend of Jesus, confirmed. I will hold a potential secret that no one on earth has any access to. For me having, the date of the end is a secret that was given to me.

The Lord also commanded me to go and check the bible very well. This was exactly what Jesus said in the holy bible, "Henceforth I call you not servants; for the servant knoweth not what his lord doeth: but I have called you friends: for all things that I have heard of my Father I have made them known unto you" (John 15:15.) Who is a friend of Jesus? He chose me and made me His friend, I did not choose myself.

All of Jesus' friends, their biography is written in the bible, which made me understand that my life history is written in the bible as the end time prophet, including what the Lord told me and all the revelations that I saw face to face. I checked the bible very well in my captivity, and I saw myself right in the bible and I was astonished and I praised the Lord God. Nothing will be added to the scriptures and nothing will be removed, the Lord only instructed me to go and check the bible very well, revelations has ended, what is written in the scriptures are fulfilling.

It was like, Thomas you do not know yourself? If you know whom you are, you will not do all these things, you will not commit fornication. I am a man whom God the Father the King of heaven paid a divine visit to on earth. After I checked the bible very well, this was when I knew myself. The Creator has made me His friend and His Spirit lives inside me.

Here, I will now give the complete revelation that manifested in Turkey when I saw the date of Christ return: I was in my hotel room in this revelation, after Jesus told me that none of

His friends is a fornicator and I should check the bible very well, the spirit took me to see two trees. These were olive trees.

These olive trees were standing by each other and the trees are in the north positions, about tree meters from each other.

As I was gazing at the trees, the Spirit was telling me that I was one of those trees, and I am planted here, the one on the right side was me. For a long time, I stood looking at this tree, in this tree, there was a date written in figures attached to one of the trees, that was mine, and the number written on it was forty.

Since when I was a kid, I get astonished when people surrounding me sing a song to me that there is something hidden me, some tried to tap into it and see what is hidden inside of me, but God covered it with a veil, and the more the third eyes want to see it, the more they were troubled. This is the date of the end that has been hidden in me which I did not even know myself, and the God of heaven revealed it to me in Turkey that I am one of the olive trees. That He hid the date of the end in my body and now it has been unveiled. It was written in my tree, I am the olive tree. The date of the end is on the olive tree.

Generally, tree means controversial wisdom while the olive tree in particular means blessed wisdom. The man, which is me, revealing the end of the world, even though I am not academically intelligent, to pronounce such revelations, my wisdom has been blessed by God of heaven.

This number was not written in words, the number was written in figures. This is a total calculation of years, this is the second coming of Jesus Christ to the earth to take the saints away, and this is the end that was revealed to me by the heavenly Father.

When heaven opened, and I saw Him, He looks like precious stone in His throne in heaven; this is a secret that was given to me by Him. Numbers in figure means information. In the bible, God would always use forty years to accomplish a mission. Do not be surprised that God has revealed secret to the ones He loved. "The secret of the LORD is with them that fear him; and he will shew them his covenant" (Psalm 25:14.)

God will always reveal secrets to the one he loves, the year, month, week, day and hour, the minute and the second Christ is coming to this earth; it was revealed by the good God of heaven to me but unfortunately, I lost this information.

For my partner, who is the end time witness, my angel, there was no number written on her tree. So, no angel in heaven knows that day and that hour when Christ will come to take the Saints, if a number that is a figure was written on her tree, it means the angel will definitely know the year, month, week, day and the hour and minute when Jesus Christ will return to this earth.

On her tree, there was no number on it, only mine; It is only I that was given this revelations. I was careless and women took my heart away. I remembered that Christ is coming when I was in captivity, when my brain cooled down. I remember the messages of prison warders; they would always say, you have time to stay here.

I would say, I am so sorry for those who would have loved to know the exact day and hour when Christ will come back in His second time. The world is so hungry and thirsty to know the exact minute, hour, day, month and the year that Christ will come back to the earth.

People should not be offended if they did not get the date that was given to me that I lost. This was exactly what happened to King Solomon, the bible says, "For it came to pass, when Solomon was old, that his wives turned away his heart after other gods: and his heart was not perfect with the LORD his God..." (1 Kings 11:4.)

This was exactly what happened to me as a prophet of the living God, women turned my heart away from the works of the living God that I was supposed to do, preaching and crying Grace, grace, be ready to meet your Lord God that you have been waiting for ages.

The feast of the bride and the bridegroom is ready. King Solomon did not see Jesus; the prophets of old wanted to see

Him and hear His sermons, but it was not their time, they wanted to be baptized with the Holy Ghost and with fire, but it was not their time. This was exactly what Jesus said as recorded in the bible. "For verily I say unto you, that many prophets and righteous men have desired to see those things which ye see, and have not seen them; and to hear those things which ye hear, and have not heard them" (Mathew 13:17.)

The number 40 that was found on my olive trees, God will always use the number forty to accomplish a mission on earth; this is the number that the Lord God has chosen to do His work. In calculations this is where we can get the date of the end.

Israel stayed in the wilderness for 40 years, and this is the symbol of the last years the gospel will still be preached from the mouth of only one prophet, as the last gospel to everyone in all the earth. Salvation is still available from the mouth of the Holy Ghost, and also the world will face a terrible judgment and God will punish and destroy them for their sins. Also, as written in the scriptures, 40 is a target number of the Lord God of heaven.

"And thou shalt remember all the way which the LORD thy God led thee these forty years in the wilderness, to humble thee, and to prove thee, to know what was in thine heart, whether thou wouldest keep his commandments, or no" (Deuteronomy 8:2.)

"Thus I fell down before the LORD forty days and forty nights, as I fell down at the first; because the LORD had said he would destroy you" (Deuteronomy 9:25.)

"Forty years long was I grieved with this generation, and said, It is a people that do err in their heart, and they have not known my ways:" (Psalm 95:10.)

"And afterward they desired a king: and God gave unto them Saul the son of Cis, a man of the tribe of Benjamin, by the space of forty years" (Act 13:21.)

"And when forty years were expired, there appeared to him in the wilderness of mount Sina an angel of the Lord in a flame of fire in a bush" (Act 7:30.)

"No foot of man shall pass through it, nor foot of beast shall pass through it, neither shall it be inhabited forty years" (Ezekiel 29:11.)

"And Jonah began to enter into the city a day's journey, and he cried, and said, Yet forty days, and Nineveh shall be overthrown" (Jonah 3:4.)

"And when he had fasted forty days and forty nights, he was afterward an hungred" (Matthew 4:2.)

"And the children of Israel did evil again in the sight of the LORD; and the LORD delivered them into the hand of the Philistines forty years" (Judges 13:1.)

"So let all thine enemies perish, O LORD: but let them that love him be as the sun when he goeth forth in his might. And the land had rest forty years" (Judges 5:31.)

"And the rain was upon the earth forty days and forty nights" (Ge:7:12.)

"And it came to pass at the end of forty days, that Noah opened the window of the ark which he had made:" (Ge:8:6.)

"And Moses went into the midst of the cloud, and gat him up into the mount: and Moses was in the mount forty days and forty nights" (Ex:24:18.)

"And he was there with the LORD forty days and forty nights; he did neither eat bread, nor drink water. And he wrote upon the tables the words of the covenant, the ten commandments" (Ex:34:28.)

"After the number of the days in which ye searched the land, even forty days, each day for a year, shall ye bear your iniquities, even forty years, and ye shall know my breach of promise" (Nu:14:34.)

"And the LORD's anger was kindled against Israel, and he made them wander in the wilderness forty years, until all the generation, that had done evil in the sight of the LORD, was consumed" (Nu:32:13.)

"And it came to pass at the end of forty days and forty nights, that the LORD gave me the two tables of stone, even the tables of the covenant" (De:9:11.)

"Thus I fell down before the LORD forty days and forty nights, as I fell down at the first; because the LORD had said he would destroy you" (De:9:25.)

"Forty stripes he may give him, and not exceed: lest, if he should exceed, and beat him above these with many stripes, then thy brother should seem vile unto thee" (De:25:3.)

"Forty years old was I when Moses the servant of the LORD sent me from Kadesh-barnea to spy out the land; and I brought him word again as it was in mine heart" (Jos:14:7.)

"And the land had rest forty years. And Othniel the son of Kenaz died (J'g:3:11.)

"And the children of Israel did evil again in the sight of the LORD; and the LORD delivered them into the hand of the Philistines forty years" (J'g:13:1.)

"And it came to pass, when he made mention of the ark

of God, that he fell from off the seat backward by the side of the gate, and his neck brake, and he died: for he was an old man, and heavy. And he had judged Israel forty years" (1Sa:4:18.)

"David was thirty years old when he began to reign, and he reigned forty years (2Sa:5:4.)

"And the time that Solomon reigned in Jerusalem over all Israel was forty years" (1Ki:11:42.)

"And he arose, and did eat and drink, and went in the strength of that meat forty days and forty nights unto Horeb the mount of God" (1Ki:19:8.)

"And Jonah began to enter into the city a day's journey, and he cried, and said, Yet forty days, and Nineveh shall be overthrown" (Jon:3:4.)

"To whom also he shewed himself alive after his passion by many infallible proofs, being seen of them forty days, and speaking of the things pertaining to the kingdom of God" (Ac:1:3.)

"When your fathers tempted me, proved me, and saw my works forty years" (Heb:3:9.)

In the bible, the olive tree is the core message of the end that God of heaven gave to the prophets, the two olive trees. This is the position the world can get the date of the end. The number 40 is where God made major changes and trans-formations.

The olive tree is linked to the time of Noah during the destruction of the earth with flood, and number 40 is also linked to the destruction of this earth in the time of Noah. He was a wise man when he survey the number 40; this is the number that the Creator uses to act.

The tree is wisdom, the same tree in the garden that gave

man knowledge and man began to create; if not for the tree, there is no way man would have the knowledge of arts. Man ate the fruit of the tree and became wise as God. He knew science, business, technology, entrainment, tourism, travelling, politics, sports, health and much more.

What you do not know is: the tree gives you the answer, because there lays all wisdom. The date of the end is hidden inside the olive tree, not just any tree. The reason why the Creator is giving you the date of the end as written boldly by prophet Zechariah here is, Grace, grace.

Forty is an important number in the mind of God. History has shown that forty is a mighty revelation. Number 40 cannot be accused, because this is a biblical number, God's own number; nothing false can survive the number 40.

Number 40 is the foundation of this book; the same number that made my revelation. The manuscript of this chapter, 2035 The End of Age in Microsoft word is exactly 40 pages long, and I marvelled as I saw it.

There is a fellowship that is called 40 days, this number is special in the heart and soul of some believers with a spiritual force behind it that some may not even know of, a number that is spiritually potent that will even draw the attention of the Father. If you see a revelation and see the number 40 in figures, this number will only come from God. These numbers belong to God.

In the prison in Austria, when I got to understand how important this revelation is, I trembled in body, soul and spirit. I prayed to God not to consider my foolishness, or I would perish.

My tree, and Maria in this revelation as she stood between the judgments seats of the Saints.

The time I saw Maria in Sweden, I even told her that before I met her I had already seen her in a revelation that was given to me by God but she rebuked me and said God did not showed her to me. This is always the case for the unbeliever; they never believe.

I perfectly remember the two olive trees, I remember the seal of hell, I remember a fading flower in front of the fat valley.

People mistake the kingdom of heaven for the earth; God will create a new heaven, and He will also create a new earth paradise.

Humans will continue to dwell on this earth, since God did not create this earth in vain, this earth was created for man to live in and enjoy paradise like in the days of the garden, a symbol of beauty.

Many people have different views old heaven. God, the King of heaven will give the kingdom to the unexpected. The kingdom of God suffers, violence and the violent take it by force. These are believers who are strong.

The saints are in the mist of multitudes. It is those who flatter with words who are mostly known and influential.

I always remember the word of Jesus: "None of my friends is a fornicator. Go and check the bible very well". I took my time in the prison and I started reading the holy bible.

The number 40 is a very powerful one; there is a saying that life begins at forty. "And the rain was upon the earth forty days and forty nights" (Genesis 7:12.)

There are many important events that happened with the Almighty power of God in the scriptures, it was recorded in "Deuteronomy 8:4 - Thy raiment waxed not old upon thee, neither did thy foot swell, these forty years."

One thing I remember perfectly was, I went with a travelling visa issued inside my passport by the Turkish Embassy, I put-up in a hotel, and there are records with the customs and they should have my name in their system. The shipment left Italy from the city of Laspezia to Messina in Turkey.

I planned to check these records that I may get the year, month, week and the interval of days that I checked in into a hotel; this is the period that Christ will come to this earth in His second time.

It may be possible that through records, I may get the year, month, week and the interval of days, but the actual hour and day, it will not be possible, because there are no records for this; I did not take care to write it down.

When the revelation was given to me, I did not know the meaning, I thought that Jesus had been appearing to all of people in this generation, that such a revelation is very common to Christians, that everyone who said he is born again must have seen God the Father and Jesus Himself face to face themselves, because I heard from many people that God spoke to them.

I came to find out when I was inside the prison by listening to many preaching's that their testimony is based on what they had read, but they did not see anything. They have never seen God, never seen Jesus, never seen heaven, never seen the Holy Ghost. For three good years, I was listening to the radio in jail and my stations are mainly religious stations around the globe.

God began to reveal things to me and I was surprised that I was holding a mighty revelation that I did not even know of. Then, I re-examined my life and my spiritual status.

That particular passport I used to travel to Turkey is no more in existence; I don't know where it is. I started planning to go to Turkey to ask of these places, if they still had the records.

When I came out of jail, I did not have a passport, getting a new passport in my country embassy in Rome is not a day's job. This is on the grounds that your passport is stolen. Even though I had a new passport, I needed my Italian stay permit to apply for a Turkish visa in Rome, but my permit expired while I was in jail.

As I came back to Italy, I told the immigration police the truth, that I was in jail in Austria, and I did not make up any story for them enable me to get the permit quickly. Since I became a completely repented soul from the prison, I became a child that would not lie as spoken by prophet Isaiah, " For he said, Surely they are my people, children that will not lie: so he was their Saviour" (Isaiah 63:8.) Since the righteousness of God started flowing in my life, I became a child that maintains the truth in my lips. And this will be forever. The fire of God lives in me.

The process of renewing the stay permit was not easy. For

ages, I had been expecting the residence permit in the police station, but they had not given it to me, so I could not even travel to Turkey. In the year 2005, a thought came to me, should I call the Turkish embassy? What would I tell them?

I came out of prison, and I needed money to process many papers and to get a new passport. But even this was not easy; my resident permit had a question mark in the police station, due to this prison record that I told them about. How can I get to Turkey? The city I shipped this consignment from was Laspezia, I could not remember the name or the address of the shipping company, but I knew it was a storey-building, probably two or three floors; I had to try some shipping companies addresses in Laspezia.

I travelled from Pisa to Laspezia, for many hours I asked different shipping companies many questions, most answered that their ships did not go to Turkey, and one even directed me to Genova, another city that was not on my itinerary. I could not remember the building and the street number; I knew that all the shipping companies were located on one long street facing the sea port in Laspezia.

I latter found one shipping company that told me ship to Messina, Turkey, and I told them the whole story. They were so kind to me and treated me fine, they even gave me a sit in the visitors' room. I gave them my name, they searched their systems and they came back telling me that they could not find anything, not even my name. They said according to the law, any documents ten years old were destroyed. I went back home.

I remembered one thing, when I came from Messina in Turkey, after I told Bianca about the end of the road, this period the word of Jesus was still burning in my heart.

Jesus revealed hell to me and I knew how terrible how it was, under His feet was the hell. It has been constructed with a strong seal, the mouth of this place was open for me to see, what I saw, the mouth of hell was like the funnel where the heat and smoke came out; it was a like sulphur.

It has only been constructed and no one is there right now.

This is serious. In that period, I behaved well to all women, because the revelation was not so easy to bear.

Then, another greater one given to me again to see; I saw where people are kept in detention, waiting to be cast into hell on the great judgment day. This place was outer darkness, it was so terrible that I could not look at it, I covered my face with my hands, but I heard noises of torment, suffering and pains from them that are inside.

Any time I remember this noise, I always tell God to have pity on me, and the response from Him is that I am already saved in Christ Jesus. This was the place where I wept and covered my face, I came alive trembling.

Within an interval of this days when I got this revelation, I said I would not commit fornication again, and I really repented. It was in this period that I met one girl called Claudia; she's beautiful, but because of the fear of that revelation in my life, I did not touch Claudia, fear could not let me kiss her. She was in my home, and she was nice and helped me put things in order.

If I had not repented, Claudia and I would have ended up in bed. But I did not touch her, and sex did not even cross my mind. She was clever and she studied the situation. Her response was, "Bayo, you love God so much". I liked Claudia, but when I remembered my revelation, how I was cast down to the earth with His hands, I gave up touching Claudia. One of the most beautiful girls that I came across. Claudia was telling people that I love God so much, but she did not know what I had seen. She never knew that God saved her from my hand.

Claudia was not born again at this time, but she is an open girl, the type who is ready to blend with a man to any angle, she is a type of person that is open to the gospel, and I know definitely that God loves this girl so much. God brought her to me for a purpose. If you see Claudia, her face is full of love and peace, she is very gentle and not arrogant. She has beautiful blue eyes, she's blonde. When I say Claudia is nice, I mean she is really nice.

This is just the beginning of this revelation, as this time, my understanding had not opened yet. To me, since Claudia was not born again, she was not qualified. This was where my knowledge ended. When your knowledge ends in a certain position, I wonder if it remains in that position; who can even change it? This is a good human being that came into my life, yet, I refused to open up to her.

But I did not understand what God was trying to do in the relationship between me and Claudia. I knew that she had a part to play in my life. I did not proceed into anything; I made up my mind to just relate with her as friends. Another thing she did was that she gave me her passport photograph to put in my wallet, I collected the photo and I kept it in my wallet. Claudia's photo was in my wallet, and sometimes people would ask me if I had a girl friend. When I didn't have anything to say, I showed them the picture of Claudia, and they would always complement her.

I did not see Claudia for many years as I went on my own way and lived my life. I went to the bible college, and many things happened in these years, I went to prison, came out and lived my life in a different fashion.

Since I could not travel to Turkey, because I had no resident permit to obtain the visa, I started calling old friends, and carefully asking them if they had any idea of events that I remember happening in that period to bring the date back to remembrance. Of all the people that I called, nothing came of it.

I was fortunate to get in touch with Claudia after ten years. I asked her about her welfare and she said she was fine and happy in life and I was happy with her.

I asked Claudia on the phone if she remembered the day I first met her. I knew Claudia as a secretary that worked for a friend of mine; it was in his office I met Claudia as I came from Turkey.

When I asked Claudia of the date we first met, she said she could not remember the day, but she quoted the year and month perfectly. She's the type that keeps records. This was the month that I came from Messina Turkey. It was 1995 in the month of May.

The date of coming of Jesus that the Spirit of God showed me on the olive tree which I thrown away because I did not know the important, Claudia the blond girl that was a rejected stone became the cornerstone; Claudia remember the date and gave it to me but she did not remember the day and the hour. This was how I recover some part of the date.

I was in Messina in Turkey when Claudia was employed. As I came back, I went directly to my friend's office and I saw a new girl in the office, newly employed. This was the beginning of my friendship with Claudia. Because immediately I left Messina I came directly to Claudia office. Before I departed to Messina Claudia was not employed, it was the interval of this time that the date was given to me by the Creator. After 10 years Claudia remember the date of her employment but she did not remember the day and the hour. Thank God that we still remember some part of the date of the coming of the Lord Jesus.

When I was in Messina, many guys went to my friend's office and they saw the new secretary and all the guys wanted her, but immediately I entered my friend's office, when Claudia saw me she was in love already, and I knew. She was no more comfortable speaking to any other guy and everyone knew.

I have one strong policy regarding women, it is against my principle to sleep with any of my workers. My workers were mostly young girls. The old workers would always advice new employees that are girls not to make any move regarding romance with this guy (Thomas Bayo.) He will not even look at you despite your beauty.

This is his policy. If you have a friend that comes to visit you and she's a girl, director may be interested in her, but not you. All my workers love me to this day, no matter the offence they committed in my company; it is against my policy to fire any of my workers. I always give them same chance and the best advice.

I remember the last day I spoke with Bianca; that was when she started to wear summer clothes and it was in spring, summer was just about to begin.

People do not understand the spoken word of Jesus, because great wisdom is needed to understand His words. Flesh and blood have no power to believe. Jesus used a story in the bible, to describe the end. "For the Son of Man is as a man taking a far journey, who left his house, and gave authority to his servants, and to every man his work, and commanded the porter to watch." (Mark 13:34.)

In the teachings of Jesus, you are expected to know His sermons with the wisdom of God that is in you, but you cannot understand the sermon of Jesus with the wisdom of this world that is of vanity. To know the exact time of His coming in connection to me, the end time prophet like Jonas, it is from 1995 to 2035. The calculation is complete—40 years. Also written, "and he shall bring forth the headstone thereof with shoutings, crying, Grace, grace unto it" (Zechariah 4:7b.) Headstone carries date. Headstone here is the date of the end.

This is a terrible time. A year of doom, but the doomsday and the hour is not known, not even my angel in heaven knows it. Because in her tree, there was no number. This is when God will filter His wrath to the wicked in the entire world. The prophet already told you that the last day is terrible. This is the wrath of God that is coming to this earth in the year 2035 both the dead and the living.

Some think that when they die, that is the end, but they are ignorant. No flesh and blood will escape this day, because the day of the Lord is terrible. "For behold, the day cometh, that shall burn as an oven; and all the proud, yea, and that do wickedly, shall be stubble: and the day that cometh shall burn them up, saith the LORD of hosts, that it shall leave them neither root nor branch" (Malachi 4:1.)

Who spoke here as written by prophet Malachi? Here is written, saith the LORD of hosts.

If you hear the word of the Almighty God of heaven and you do not tremble, then, be ready in the year 2035. This is your year, the year of the wicked, not only the living, but also the dead, including angels. The devil himself trembles when he hears of the end, how much more the living. For the powers of heaven shall be shaken.

Revealing the date of the end is not a matter of a promised land in Israel, and Palestine issue, this is something that concerns the entire world. Israel has its own biblical history, just as the Gentile nation has its own biblical history. The Creator is not only for the Jews, He is also for the Gentiles.

He Created all the creatures on the planet, so when it comes in knowing when the world will end, the Jews are out of this issue. For this reason the Creator chose a Gentile to execute this powerful revelation, to give the date of the end.

You cannot be a witness without seeing or knowing who you are witnessing for. This is the reason why the Creator personally paid a divine visit to me, so that my testimony will be based on truth, not what I have read, this is a great revelation. My book title, What Do You Want, tells more of this.

For the Creator to choose a Gentile and give me power to implement this revelation, it tallies with the end of the world message from heaven. This is something that affects the entire world, and affects heaven, so an angel is involved as my second witness. By focusing on the olive tree, the year 2035 month of May, is the date when the world will end. The purpose of the headstone is the date of the doomsday.

When you survey this revelation, how Jesus appeared to me and the condition I was in, it shows clearly that all my tears are cryings of Grace, grace from the Lord God. Believers do have this date based on His marvellous Grace, grace. To have this date believers should rejoice.

The Lord Jesus Christ said to those fools who asked Him, "tell us the end", He simply answered them that He did not know the day and hour of the end, because they were asking a question that had already been answered. You cannot fool Christ. When you ask an ignorance question, what do you expect?

Martin Luther, the German theologian and religious reformer who was the catalyst of the 16th-century Protestant Reformation, tried to crack the date of the end, but he cracked the wrong tree; he started cracking the apple tree and it was a mission impossible, however, he knew that tree is wisdom and date of the end is on the tree and he even told the world to look at the tree that is where they will see the date of the end and me and my angel are the trees. The bible says the two olive trees, the two candle sticks.

Jesus pointed plainly that the end time date decoder has a violent behaviour, the same capacity of prophet Jonas, yet the Creator gave to him power, and made him His own witness by His loving Grace.

❧❧❧❧

I was still fighting the flesh as I was in captivity in Austria, and flesh persuaded me to go back to live with the Egyptians immediately, as I was released from the prison. And I asked myself, what is special about Egypt?

Who am I to announce to humankind, the word of God concerning when the world will come to end? It was the Holy Ghost that was given to me, which is the source of my strength to accomplish my mission to announce to you the coming of the Lord. This is the headstone that carries the date.

After the death of Jesus, there was no strength for the disciples to witness Christ. It was that power that was given to them that was their strength to accomplish their mission and proclaim Jesus as Lord. The Holy Ghost made them fulfil their mission on earth.

"Now learn a parable of the fig tree; When his branch is yet tender, and putteh forth leaves, ye know that summer is nigh:" (Matthew 24: 32.)

Now, look at what the bible says here. You should learn the parable of the fig tree. When you learn the parable of the fig tree, as spoken by the Lord, you will get the information about the season when Jesus will come back to this earth. The word "learn" here is to study and understand what this fig tree is all about. Jesus knew that some people had never seen a fig tree in their life, but learning about it will give you a good idea of the parable of the fig tree.

When I was in captivity in Austria, in the second year, we fellowshipped together in the prison; this was a church in the prison, which was organised by one of the protestant German churches. The pastor brought a picture of a fig tree and displayed it, in teaching us the parable of the end. So, showing the picture of the fig tree is another way of learning the parable of the fig tree.

The Lord used the parable of the fig tree to tell you when He is coming back to this earth a second time. The fig tree is not in the country of my birth, and many do not know what a fig tree is. Thank God that I have seen the fig tree and I have already eaten it's fruit, touched it physically with my hands and my testimony is not based on what I have not seen.

A fig tree is a plant that has multiple fruits, this fruit is soft and pulpy, sweet and pear shaped, having numerous tiny seeds, and the colour of the fruit is green.

Through the grace of God, I was opportune to be in Europe to see this tree, with my two eyes.

One day, as I was hungry and tired of walking, the bar was not even near the environment where I was, and this was in the city of Lucca in Italy the area where I live. An idea came into my mind, to go and pluck fruits to eat along the way, so, I walked past one tree, I did not even know the name of this tree. I turned back and walked to this tree, I plucked some fruits, near the tap and washed it, and started eating. This fruit was yummy and I was satisfied. I gathered much strength to continue my journey. I ate about six to seven of it in this hour; this was the month of July the year 2004 in Monte San Quirico, Via Della Chiesa, Lucca. Italy. I only ate this fruit because I was hungry, but I did not know actually what this fruit was.

As I was studying the parable of the fig tree, I decided to learn what the parable of the fig tree is, Jesus has already commanded me to go and search the bible very well.

At first, when I did not know what the fig tree was, I wondered where on earth this fig tree was located, where would I see this tree and feel it and learn of it and understand what Jesus said of it.

I asked one Italian woman if she knew what a fig tree is, and I called it 'fico' since I already knew the name in Italian. The tree that I was asking about was just behind us, and she pointed the tree to me and she said, "questo" meaning, this one. In this time, it was already November, the leaves were wearing out and the fruits were gone. After I saw the tree, I knew it was the fruit of this tree that I ate just months before.

This woman and me, we started discussing this tree and I ask her many questions about the tree, since she knew it from her childhood. I got to understand that all its leaves will fall out in the winter and the tree will become naked.

The season of the year occurring between winter and summer, during which the weather becomes warmer and plants revive, extending in the Northern Hemisphere from the vernal equinox to the summer solstice and popularly considered to comprise March, April, and May, is a time of growth and renewal.

The coming of Jesus is not in summer or in the winter, you will know by studying the fig tree and understanding His parable, that Jesus is coming in the spring. "And when these things begin to come to pass, then look up, and lift up your heads; for your redemption draweth nigh" (Luke 21:28.)

The Lord Jesus used the word behold, the fig tree. The English define the word "behold" as to perceive through use of the mental faculty. Or gaze at. So, use your mental faculty to know when Jesus will come to take you. This subject is very serious.

I will always repeat, Jesus told you already that you should learn the parable of the fig tree, the word learn is to gain knowledge of, or become skilled at.

The most tragic thing that has ever happened on this earth was in the times of Noah, Lot, and Jonah.

There is nowhere in the bible that God has not revealed secrets to His servant concerning the things He will do, He reveals secrets to His servants at the appointed time, when He will take His action in accordance to number 40 either days or years. All what has happened to the world, the Father sent His prophets to let them know what He would do. Flood in the time of Noah was 40, Nineveh was 40, and wilderness was 40 and much more. 40 is a target number, terrible time.

In the period of 40 years in the wilderness it was the harvest period so shall be the end. These period of forty years the seal of God will still be going on to them that will still believe, 40 years is the time of the harvest separating the good from the bad, in manner like that of the wilderness in the time of prophet Moses, God of heaven gave the promise land to the chosen ones that were selected directly by Him.

My lifestyle notwithstanding, the God of heaven continues to show me His favour with His grace above my imaginations, always revealing His love to me.

The mightiest blessing He gave to me was His own Spirit, the Holy Ghost. He has filled me, another mighty blessing that He gave me is my angel; I saw my angel face to face; she's a queen, I will continue to testify it, her garment was rolling on the ground that looked endless and the Lord has joined us. She remains my angel as God lives forever.

The scientist has already revealed to the world that the asteroids are coming from another planet, they are fasting approaching and will hit the earth in the year 2015. Christ already told you that you will hear many rumours, but do not be afraid.

The year 2035 is not long from now.

When I tell some people that the world end 2035, they are afraid, you do not need to be afraid when you are established in righteousness and trusting Jesus as your only Saviour. Blessed are they that will be patient and avoid sins.

For many generation, humans have been predicting the year, month and sometimes day when this world will come to end, some have said the world will end 1998, 2005, 1990, 1998, 1999, 2000, 2001, 2002, 2003, 2004, 2005, 2011, 2012. The prophets have almost always predicted that the end would happen in their own immediate future. All of these predictions share one factor: none have ever come true. These people predicting these dates, they are like foxes in the deserts, they did not see anything.

And some have prophesies, false revelations, the heavenly Father will always use the number 40 to accomplish a mission, and the Lord God of heaven has spoken, "Behold, I am against them that prophesy false dreams, saith the LORD, and do tell them, and cause my people to err by their lies, and by their lightness; yet I sent them not, nor commanded them: therefore they shall not profit this people at all, saith the LORD" (Jeremiah 23:32.) The fire of God will authenticate all revelations to try them, whether they are true or false.

Some scientists say that asteroids are coming and will crash the earth in the year 2028, the earth will go beyond this and the end will not exceed 2035 in the month of May. This is what the world has been asking since when Christ was in this earth, when shall the end be? The year has now been given to you.

The bible did not say, pray hard so that you will be rapture, regarding the rapture, the bible said do not sleep. The point is, do not sleep. If you pray and go to sleep, you are still like the five foolish virgins. The five foolish virgins knew how to pray, but they slept and slumbered. And the door was shut against them.

In the rapture, do not sleep, but watch for the coming of the Lord Jesus in the year 2035, the month of May. The week and the interval of days may be revealed

if I have it, but I do not know the day and the hour. What I have is the year, month, week and interval of days when Christ will come.

If I had committed fornication with Claudia, there is no way I would have gotten the date of the end; it was that revelation I saw when Jesus appeared to me face to face and also spoke to me that made me tremble, and when I remembered that revelation, I refused to kiss Claudia. I just hugged her while still trembling within myself. I knew what I saw in that revelation.

If I had any sexual intercourse with Claudia, I definitely would have broken her heart and try to get any information from her would remind her of the past the pains she went through.

I did nothing with Claudia and we are not in debt of each other. Anytime we see, we will always smile and show the human love and wish others good luck and blessings, and if it is the will of God, we will even be together in heaven, what a great fun.

"Except the LORD build the house, they labour in vain that build it: except the LORD keep the city, the watchman waketh but in vain" (Psalm 127:1.)

Prophets are people who have experienced life. They know what the difference is between the inside world and the outside world. There is no prophet who has never experienced captivity.

These prophets that have experienced life, they will tell you the consequence of evil.

I give you an instance of the people of this world, a judge in a court is an expert at dealing with crime. When the police bring anyone to the court, if the judge sees an evidence, exhibit A, of a quantity of cocaine presented by the police against anyone, the judge can draw punishment with that quantity that is the evidence brought before him.

As an expert, he will give the prison sentence of the drug quantity. So are prophets; if you commit any sin against God, a prophet is an expert, the divine wisdom has been built in him, and he will be able to tell you the consequences of sin that you have committed and the punishment that you will receive. Prophets are able to describe the fire of God because they know it. Any preacher who tells you that the wages of sin is not death, such a preacher has deceived you and you are deceived indeed.

Jonah was an expert. He told Nineveh the consequence and the gravity of sins they had committed, and he told the people that in forty days, they would be gone. But repent and you all shall live. They got the message.

Prophets with the wisdom of God will always give good counsel to believers to keep away from the wicked, so that they touch you not. If a wicked man gives you water to drink, do not drink it.

One thing the God of heaven will not do is, He will never, ever allow anyone to go to jail that has no ability to take it. Instead, He will use another means to chasten such a child. Because not all have the ability to take captivity, some commit suicide inside the jail. Jail is a suicide home. Most people that commit suicide do it when they come out of prison, under pressure, lacking the ability to start afresh. When they saw how rough the road is, they do not have the power, so they kill themselves.

God will not allow temptation that is above us to overtake us. Satan will bring the temptation that will manifest in prison, this is for sure. But God will make a way, knowing full well that by the measure of faith He has given to a man, such a man will identify his error and become wise when he is out of captivity. Everything in life is faith. Satan will think it will be end of such a man, but through it comes a great victory to the man of God.

Prison is a place where you learn and see the truth, and get very close to your Creator.

For spiritual men, getting out of jail is a great wisdom. Captivity is among the strongest places where you can be assured that God is with you. The greatest men of God, key prophets all were in captivity. Kind David said, "If I ascend up into heaven, thou art there: if I make my bed in hell, behold, thou art there".

For example, the greatest blessing in my life, God gave it to me when I was in captivity. He comforted me with this great and mighty blessing which I have already written in my book, What Do You Want?

They that are of the world will define being out of prison in their own understanding, but we that believe have our own definition and interpretation, which is different from they that of the flesh. When you study the bible, you will have a clear picture and interpretation how the prophet defines captivity. No soul on earth has not trespassed the law.

But God sent His loved ones to captivity for a specific reason, to fulfil the scriptures. As the bible defines it; "For whom the Lord loveth he chasteneth, and scourgeth every son whom he receiveth. If ye endure chastening, God dealeth with you as with sons; for what son is he whom the father chasteneth not? But if ye be without chastisement, whereof all are partakers, then are ye bastards, and not sons. Furthermore we have had fathers of our flesh which corrected us, and we gave them reverence: shall we not much rather be in subjection unto the Father of spirits, and live? For they verily for a few days chastened us after their own pleasure; but he for our profit, that we might be partakers of his holiness." (Hebrews 12:6-10.)

That is why the prophets could not bear the joy when they found themselves in captivity and when they came out, because they knew that God would reveal His wrath to them that dwell in the face of the earth, and on their sides they are saved. Job said, "Behold, happy is the man whom God correcteth:" (Job 5:17.)

Captivity is a complete identity or proof of a believer's repentance in accordance to the bible. You have only one chance to repent on this earth. If you cannot repent in the world, God will give you a chance, if you repent when you are in captivity, this is fine. It does not matter the place when you get to repent, even if it is in the hospital or forest, battle field, God accepts all.

The prophets, many of them repented in captivity, and God sent some of them into captivity to repent. And we are established into perfect righteousness. We are perfect like our Father in heaven. Those who do not believe they need repentance, God is looking toward them.

It is not a good thing to experience the wrath of God. The Father does not have pleasure in death of the wicked. The tears of all the key prophets that have gone and come out of captivity, their message is: repent.

Those brothers who were once in jail and the world looked up to their moral standards, speaking of being rejected by the world due to their prison records, these brothers and sisters need to have one knowledge that even though you do not go to the jail, you're commanded by heaven not to unequally yoke with the children of flesh. Pray for them, even though they condemn you. God has already taken His anger away from you and you are saved in Jesus name.

Before Christ will take you as He comes the His second time, there shall be no single fault be found in your life. Not even one. You are expected to be without fault in body, soul and in the spirit. If Christ comes and takes you when there is one single fault found in your life, do not ever call me a prophet.

What I mean is that, no fault should be found in you before Christ takes you, this is to say as written in the bible: "but we know that, when he shall appear, we shall be like him: for we shall see him as he is. And every man that hath this hope in him purifieth himself, even as he is pure" (John 3:2a, 3.) This is what I mean, and I do hope you understand me.

As we are approaching the end of the world, climate change, world economic crisis, immigration, religion crisis, humankind is troubled with marriage definition, outshoot of terror is that people are in fear, outgrowth of crime, political chaos, social and environmental, prisons, disease and much more. These will be tough times as we approaches 2035, and things will get tougher. But for the elect's sake, the Creator will soften things.

Trouble, conflict and great affliction; believers need pray hard. We have our salvation in this tough time in accordance to what Isaiah has spoken, "O Lord, be gracious unto us; we have waited for thee: be thou their arm every morning, our salvation also in the time of trouble." (Isaiah 33:2.)

Look at what the bible says here, "But LORD…Be our strength every morning". There are going to be every day challenges and different shapes of trouble will manifest. We do know how it will come and how it will stop, but the human race cannot survive more than the year 2035. Prayer is needed in every nation before the end. The world is in peril.

The fool says there is no God. The Lord Almighty created the heavens and the earth, and all creatures that dwell in the face of the earth. I have seen Him face to face with my two eyes and He spoke to me, and I heard His voice like a roaring waterfall, a mighty voice, not once did speak to me, and His eyes like fire.

The world should understand and know the truth: that Lazarus was never a major security threat to the rich fool, which the rich fool also knew, so beware how you fight terror; do not afflict any believer that loves Jesus as the Son of God in all the earth, these are people of peace.

When you begin to afflict the poor, then, are you not a hypocrite? You will be allocated the same portion with the terrorist in the last day. Or if the master delays his coming and the senior servant begins to afflict the junior servant, where shall the senior servant end? So, Christians should love each other and not afflict the disadvantage ones.

The judgment day is very close. People should adjust their belts and stand in this coming judgment. All will give account of his life, the good and evil you have done. Be ready to face Christ and His Saints in the judgment throne.

$$\mathcal{S} \diamond \mathcal{S} \diamond \mathcal{S} \diamond \mathcal{S} \diamond$$

When you study the fig tree, focus on the month of May. Jesus coming to this earth on His second and the last time, to save us once and for all, when you carefully study the month of May, this is a month of Grace, grace. This month of May is a nice month in all the earth, this is neither summer nor winter.

In Europe, the month of May is neither cold nor hot, this is spring time, here in Italy we wear T-shirts in the month of May. We do not wear jackets like onions because of the cold. Also, in Sweden, folks wearing T-shirts and in the rest of Europe.

I am in contact with my people in Sweden and I will ask what the weather is over there? The reply from Sweden is warm. The sun is shining. This is the month of May.

The first time Jesus came to this earth from heaven, it was in winter. But this month of May is a target. God is excellent in Judgment and He is holy.

This is a good month when Jesus is coming to the earth, we have prayed hard for this.

In the rest of the world, I understand that in the continent of America, in the month of May, people still wear T-shirts.

In Australia, their winter is June, July and August, while summer is December and February. So, in the month of May in Australia, the weather is fine, they also wear t-shirts. In Asia, by month of May, they wear t-shirts.

In Africa, winter does not exist. Only in the south. In the month of July, they have winter, but compared to winter in Europe, it is still a perfect and balmy month. The target is the month of May. May whether in Africa, Europe, America, Asia, Caribbean, in the month of May, the weather is perfect.

In any part of the world, by 2035, in the month of May, if there are places that are still experiencing winter, they should get out of that city because it is not good that the end meets you at winter time. Because, when the seventh angel shall sound, there is no time. The game is over.

The trumpets of the seventh angel, I have heard the sound in revelation, and I know how it is. I know the tune. This is dread. That sound is sound of judgment. When this sound goes off, your strength is gone. No man can stand that day; the powers of heaven shall shake.

In the month of May, in the year 2035, make sure you watch and always be dressed, even when you take your shower in the bath room or you are using the rest room, make sure you pray hard, so that in that day, you will not be taken unawares. Because you will not even have the time to wear your pants or your knickers.

May is the month of grace, with common sense you will know that the second coming of Christ is this month of grace. In the whole world, the only month that is generally honoured is the month of May, this is the month the Creator has chosen and the whole world honours it.

The month of May is unique, no other month ends on the same day of the week as May. The month of May is a free day and May Day, which usually occurs in many countries, with the celebration of spring. It is also a national holiday for workers worldwide, but keep your eyes open on this day, month of May.

All that is written in the holy bible, shall come to pass. In the month of May, year 2035, keep watch. I do not even know the day and hour but the week and interval of days shall be revealed soon and be published, when I go to Turkey and investigate, but it is not guaranteed. Not by my power or by my strength, but by His Spirit.

"Then let them which be in Judaea flee
into the mountains:" (Matthew 24:16.)

The word "Mountains" here is the Church. In this period of days, I hope we shall have it. I hope to travel to Turkey to collect the remaining revelations, if the Italian police agree to renew my stay permit. Edward who is my friend has same problem as mine in Germany, but the police in Prato gave him his stay permit but the Pisa police station has refused to renew mine.

However, my residence permit in Italy was seized by the immigration police in Pisa and they said they would not renew it again, so I cannot even travel because I came back from Austria and told the immigration police here in Italy the truth that I was in the prison in Austria.

For years now, it has been seized, this made life harder for me; pray so that they give me the permit to travel and to get it. If they refuse to give me the permit, there is no way I can travel to Turkey and the week and interval of days will not be known. Then, you have to maintain the month of May and stay in the church.

So, when the week and interval of days are revealed, make sure you stay in the church and do not go home from the church. Take food with you that you shall eat, take water, if you have the power to fast, this is not bad.

"Let him which is on the housetop not come down to take

anything out of his house" (Matthew 24:17.)

If you love to stay at home, remain in your house and do not move. Save food in your house when the seventh angels will sound.

"Neither let him which is in the field return back to take his clothes" (Matthew 24:28.)

If you are working shifts, make sure you remain in your work place, take food with you within these intervals of days and remain where you are. Do not enter the flight or in the ship. In the interval of days, watch, if you refuse to watch, this revelation will click and go off. In the judgment, the saints will tell you face to face that God has no pleasure in the death of the wicked and obedience is better than sacrifice.

That day is a terrible day; this day is the beginning of sadness. That day is a day of lamenting and screaming, for fire is coming ahead of time, a fire that has not been treated, this is crude. Pray hard, so that you can escape that terrible day. That day is not child's play. This fire that I am talking about, I have seen it. God showed it to me, I touched it. When I saw this fire, I repented. That is why I am using all my strength and ability to write what will happen to you ahead of time, because I have seen it in the physical, I touched it, felt it and I know the capacity.

The source of my revelation is not what I read or what a man told me.

It is that fire that I saw and touched that made me vow to God that I would live a faultless life and I will be pure for Christ. With the relationship I have with the Lord God, I still pray to Him to have pity on me. The Lord God made me know that He has favour on me already.

The prophets already told you as written in the holy bible, "The earth shall reel to and fro like a drunkard, and shall be removed like a cottage; and the transgression thereof shall be heavy upon it; and it shall fall, and not rise again". (Isaiah 24:20.)

This is also what prophet Isaiah told you as written in the holy bible, "The earth also is defiled under the inhabitants thereof; because they have transgressed the laws, changed the ordinance, broken the everlasting covenant. Therefore hath the curse devoured the earth, and they that dwell therein are desolate: therefore the inhabitants of the earth are burned, and few men left". The word burn here is fire.

People may think that the bible is child's play. Every single word written in the holy bible must be fulfilled. It took Noah to warn the earth for forty years the last warning and they regard not Noah. This world fears not the Lord God.

"And woe unto them that are with child,
and to them that give suck in those days!"
(Matthew 24:19.)

"But pray ye that your flight be not in
the winter, neither on the sabbath day:"
(Matthew 24:20.)

Sabbath day here is your rest period. They that, with sleeping garments, there is no time, take care and watch, so that your flight not is in the winter or the rest time.

This earth shall melt away with fervent heat. Nothing shall be left. This is a terrible day. God shall reveal His wrath to all children of disobedient.

"And take heed to yourselves, lest at any time your hearts be overcharged with surfeiting,
and drunkenness, and cares of this life, and so that day come upon you unawares" (Lu:21:34.)

In the Month of May, stay clear of any kind of television programmes that do not give glory to God, keep clear of forni-cation and adultery, keep clear of anything alcohol in this month of May, and do not attend night parties, because I am not so sure of the week. And I am not so sure of the day and the hour of Christ's arrival in the year 2035.

In this specific month of May, make sure you do not involve yourself in the things of this world, re-read the verse above. You will be left behind if any trace of alcohol is found in your body system in this specific month of May when Jesus arrives. Do not fight in this month of May, and do not us curse words against any, do not cheat anyone on this month of May.

The bible says, "Abstain from all appearance of evil. And the very God of peace sanctify you wholly; and I pray God your whole spirit and soul and body be preserved blameless unto the coming of our Lord Jesus Christ" (1 Thessalonians 5:22, 23.)

You have to be faultless when Jesus arrives, watching of movies and cinema, fictions, thriller, comedy, science fictions, romance, detectives, Television shows, horror, musical, dramatic, historic, TV and computer games, imaginations, actions, night clubs dancing, theatre, festivals and all kinds of shows that do not give glory to God, books and films that relate to affairs, they that do these things shall not be taken when Christ comes.

Do not let this day take you unaware. Make sure in this month of May the remnant Christian sisters apply the biblical dress code, do not wear trouser (pants), cover your hairs in such of those catholic sisters, watch and do not sleep. Nobody knows the day and the hour in this month of May 2035, not even the angels in heaven, not even me, Jesus Himself does not know it, it is only God of heaven that knows it.

In this month of May, biblical prophecy is fulfilled, the year the forefathers waited for. Any who wants to go back to their land should do it before the month of May. Because at the end, there will be no flight to go back, or car or ship. It will be terrible.

In the month of May, stay where you are and do not travel.

In the year 2035, in the month of May, the rapture will take place suddenly and in just a twinkle of an eye, the believers will be caught up in the clouds to meet the Lord in the air, so shall we ever be with the Lord.

Exactly what the prophets told you, nobody knows this day when this unexpected moment of rapture will take place.

Christ will not rapture you if you are dancing at nightclubs at that exact hour of the last trumpet. When you are playing a computer game, you will not be taken or watching a movie such as thriller, action, romance, science fictions, reading a novel or magazines that does not give glory to God and much more as I have mentioned before.

If Christ will rapture you when you are doing the things that I have mentioned above, it means I am not a prophet of God, and God the Father did not speak to me and I did not see any revelation.

On this earth, one of the worst things that can happen to a man is when the rapture leaves him behind.

On the last day, when Jesus will return to this world to take His people, a mighty sound will articulate and the earth will be mightily shaken. Those who are not taken, they will run to and fro, they will jam and jump into each other, they will seek death, but they will not find it.

The worms in their body will run to and fro and seek to die, but they will not die, they will look for place to hide, but they will not see a place to hide. This is a terrible day in the history of humankind which has never happened before.

Everybody will dive like the spear, looking for rocks caves to hide their faces when they shall see the power and glory of Jesus Christ and the wrath of the living God. Those that have little babies, they will be highly sorrowful. The beauty of this world will be in vanity in that terrible day.

Those that will be in the bath, swimming pool, those taking a rest, either on the bed or anywhere, they do not have time, it will be dreadful for them, they will all run away naked, they will be in great torment.

God is strong to execute His word. All mankind that falls to the ground to worship the god that cannot deliver their soul, they will all be cast away in that day when they see the face of Jesus and the wrath of the Almighty God. The Lord God Almighty will cry out with pain like that of a travailing woman at birth, to devour at once for what the earth has caused.

Not accepting Jesus as their Lord and Saviour, killing and suffering the prophets in all the earth that were sent to them. Prophet Isaiah saw the revelation of the last day and he cried out from his inner heart and wrote in his book, "Fear, and the pit, and the snare, are upon thee, O inhabitant of the earth."

"The earth shall reel to and fro like a drunkard, and shall be removed like a cottage; and the transgression thereof shall be heavy upon it; and it shall fall, and not rise again" (ISAIAH 24:20.)

I feel sorrowful every day in my life when my mind flashes back to that revelation and the mighty power of God that I saw. If I did not see these things, it would be a different thing, but I saw it and I was shaken. God spoke to me with a strong hand to deliver this message to the earth.

The fools that say there is no God, they shall see the wrath of God in that day.

If you study the bible very well, in the book of Revelations as it is written of the two witnesses of God, the two olive trees and the two candles standing the God of the whole earth. The god of the whole earth is the devil that rules the world right now.. Which prophet Zechariah, says here, "Who art thou, O great mountain? before Zerubbabel thou shalt become a plain" (Zechariah 4:7a.)

The heavely Father made this very clear here that Satan will be revealed very clearly to the two witnesses of the Creator. You cannot stand someone that you have not seen. What are you standing? God of heaven opened my eyes and I saw Satan face to face in the physical realm and the details of this have been written in e my book titled, What Do You Want?

I know Satan, I know his shape whom have I seen him physically. The bible stating this clearly.

Chapter Five

My Testimony

All the remnant Christians have a testimony, if you do not have a testimony, it means that your life is not parallel to the Book of Life. It is the book of life that counts, and if you are ashamed of your testimony, Jesus will be ashamed of you.

We know the story of a Samaritan woman with Jesus at well of water. Jesus told her that any person that drinks water will still be thirst again, but the water He will give, if anyone drinks it such a person will not be thirsty of water again, spring of water of eternal life. The Samaritan woman told Jesus she has interest for such a water and she need it.

Jesus told her to call her husband, the woman said she has no husband, Jesus replied that she's correct. However, you have five husbands but the man you are currently with is not your husband. This woman was astonished.

Look at what the Samaritan woman said, "The woman saith unto him, Sir, I perceive that thou art a prophet" (John 4:18.)

The story of this Samaritan woman is to give an idea of my experience and explanation of when Jesus appeared to me and told me, none of My friend is a fornicator I should check the bible very well. As Jesus spoke to me I was astonished exactly like that woman at the well of water.

The photo you are about to see in this chapter: is an evidence that Jesus cannot be proved wrong. Jesus is a true Prophet of all prophets, King of kings and Lord of lords, the true Son of God and my Lord my God. He told me exactly what I was doing. Because I parties all over Europe..

I fled from the presence of the Lord after He spoke to me, went to camp myself with girls. The Lord dumped me in maximum security prison, in the prison I wept.

The last party I attended before I went to prison. In the maximum security prison I remembered my calling. The pleasures of this world made me forget that Jesus is coming.

To stand the god of the whole earth, there are many forces behind me, a great military. Nothing seems to be moving forward, my academics was a failure, work a failure, marriage a failure and much more, yet, I am a prophet of the living God.

I wake up in the morning every day and I walk by faith. If not for the Holy Ghost and fire that is with me physically, I would have still told God to please make another person His prophet, because I cannot follow this road. I was grieved in heart and I did weep.

It is prison that gave me wisdom to be wise in life, if not for this prison, there is no way. One of the greatest things I gained from God in the prison was patience. I will quietly wait for my salvation from the Lord.

It is not easy to become a prophet, this is not mirth. The challenges I see every day, I have to hold my faith and continue to thank God because of His love.

What happened to the ancient Christian brethren is exactly what we the remnant are still going to experience, it was not actually mirth. Paul said, "We are troubled on every side, yet not distressed; we are perplexed, but not in despair; Persecuted, but not forsaken; cast down, but not destroyed; (2 Corinthians 4:8, 9.)

Jesus did not say, God will not reveal the end. God does not keep secret from His prophets. Check the bible very well.

"The secret of the LORD is with
them that fear him; and he will
shew them his covenant"
(Psalm 25:14.)

If God made a man His prophet and calls him His friend, a revelation will go to that generation and the entire world. God did reveal the end to me, and I am revealing it to the entire world.

Captivity is hell. Jonah came from hell to give a warning to Nineveh. Jonah's message was: repent or perish. You were created by God, and He has given you a message. Repent and live.

The greatest prophets in the bible were captivity prophets; they suffered captivity, but in love, God allowed them to experience grievous sufferings in captivity, that through it they were all established into perfect righteousness, and this is the reason they preached the message of righteousness.

Jonah did not come in mirth to give a warning to the people. He came from hell (captivity.)

So, my message is same as that of prophet Jonah. My revelation came from a holy captivity. The source of my revelation is not what I read or what I was told; this is 20/20 vision. This is the work of God. Even though you do not believe, watch for the coming of the Lord Jesus in the year 2035 and do not sleep or slumber like the five foolish virgins and be left behind.

I am a man who has experienced jail sentence; I have seen where humans are emotionally traumatized over a jail sentence. What is greater than that is coming to this world. In the last day, I do not have the words to describe it. It is terrible for the world.

People think that prophets must wear white garments. There is a difference between a prophet and a priest. When Jonah was fleeing to Tarshish, he was not wearing a white garment, otherwise, he would have been identified as a prophet on the ship. Jesus did not wear white garments when He was on earth. He dressed like the ordinary man. He was even mistaken as a gardener. Gardeners don't wear white garments, they are like the normal people and they wear normal attires, which Jesus did.

The prophets in the bible they did not know the meaning of the revelations they were having, they only wrote down what they had seen and what they were told to do by God or by the holy angels.

Except a revelation specifically belongs to you, it is written of you in the bible by the prophets, and you see your DNA (body chemistry) in the holy bible.

God the Father Himself appeared to such a prophet, with all these evidence or astonishing disclosure with confidence and faith, you will tell the people in a very simple language that your message is true.

They that do not believe, this is up them, the most important aspect of it is that I have fulfilled my ministry, we all have a choice; either you believe, or you don't and reap the works of your hands. We, the prophets of God know that God has no pleasure on the death of the wicked.

Moreover, with this evidence in my life, the Holy Ghost told me that, if they do not believe, I should ignore them. I should stop arguing with anyone.

There is no time the people of the world have ever believed any prophet of the living God. The words of the prophet always itch the ear of the people. These are heavy words, and because man show he knows too much the world refuses to believe.

The word of a prophet is as sharp as a razor, because these words are from the Creator, and the word of God the Creator is like a hammer that breaks rocks into pieces.

If you check biblical history, when a prophet prophecies, the people of the world will not believe. When the prophecy comes to pass, that is when man believes, but at that point, it is too late. It is good to believe the prophet of God. Many look to experts to advice them, but experts will keep failing them.

God knows the number of hairs on your head and knows your future, before you were born He knew the life you would live, the Lord God knew well that Jonah would not go and preach the gospel, but yet He chose him, so that He would manifest His power before him; this is the work of God.

When Jonah saw the power of God and felt Him, with the experiences, it created a perfect get-up-and-go for him to speak firmly with all faith and confidence. God was out to do His wonders by using Jonah to accomplish a mission, and Jonah successfully accomplished his ministry.

Jonah did not just go to Nineveh and start shouting,

Nineverians heard the wonder God performed in the sea, because of Jonah.

Jonah told them his testimonies; there were witnesses who were in the ship who also testified to the entire world: this is Jonah the wonder man. God performed a miracle in that nation and in the next day, it was nationwide news that all marvelled at. This is the work of God.

The presence of a prophet in any nation, city, street, in such places there is presence of God, even the presence of the Holy Ghost is the presence of God in the world.

The decision of God to use Jonah was a perfect move. He knows the nation that has faith, a nation that will bring forth fruit to the kingdom. The Creator knows that the only person that has the ability to execute or fulfil his ministry for Nineveh to repent was Jonah, a radical. God did choose Jonah. When nations, people and kindred have hearts as hard as stone, God will chose a radical to blow the horn to the mean man.

And the question is, why did the God of heaven chose Jonah, knowing that Jonah would not be willing to perform his ministry? The answer is, the God of heaven is not looking for people who will say, Lord send me: God knows that if you say yes, you cannot fulfil your ministry.

You may not believe, but this is true. When Jonah said he would not go to Nineveh, God was happy to hear this message from Jonah, because that meant He would reveal His power to Jonah and that would create a wonderful energy for Jonah to fulfil his ministry. When Jonah saw the power of God, he trembled; with this energy, his mission was fulfilled and Nineveh became a saved land. No soul was perished. This is the wonder of God.

I was listening on that day, when Pastor Ayo Oritsejafor was preaching that Jonah was a rebellious man. Ayo Oritsejafor has a case to answer on the judgment day for speaking such negative words against the prophet of the living God. Jonah was a man that fulfilled his mission, a man that repented and was beloved. The meaning of this message is for you to repent.

God performed a miracle in my name in the nation of Sweden, that when people saw what happened, they believed. This is the plummet spoken of by the prophet as written in the bible. The news went round the entire nation of Sweden, it was published by the Expressen and copies of it are still available in any Library in Sweden up to this hour; what happened was a sign of the prophet.

The Holy bible was inside the boot but fell off to the ground, which you can see on the background of the car accident. The shopping bag you see on the background it is written The End. It is a message sign, the end of the world. That was a shopping bag where I went to buy clothes in a popular shopping, a company called THE END in Italy, because I drove from Italy to Sweden.

The wonders of God that manifested in my life in Sweden were same as Jonas.

The people saw the raging (Jonah 1:15.) fish as he swallowed Jonah. They marvelled and the people vowed to worship the God of Jonah. The fish deposited Jonah on dry land and the people were terribly afraid of the Lord God of heaven, same as written by Zechariah of me, that the world will see the Plummet in my hand. When the Swedish saw this Plummet as written in the holy bible, they rejoiced and their faith boosted in my school, when I was in the bible college.

The world is very wicked, the people saw the miracle of Jonah, and they heard the preach of Jonah and repented, but in this present generation, even the dead will come back to life and persuade them to believe, but they will still not believe. Exactly what happened to me at the school I attended in Sweden; they believed not the prophet of the living God. So, the God of heaven will not give to them the kingdom, the kingdom shall be given to another people.

Do not be surprised that false prophets will lead people astray by teaching the weak hearted that Jonah was a rebellious man. Jonah was not a rebellious man. Jonah's heart was pure. The point is that, Jonah saw the challenges he was going to face ahead of time. Do you know what it means to become a prophet?

Which of the key prophets is the holy bible said "God, send me"? The Lord God gives certain lectures to all His prophets regarding their calling to accomplish their mission.

These teachings are full of errors; they do not know the power of God, saying that Johan had a rebellious spirit. Saying that Jonah was a rebellious man is an act of Satan, an accuser. And such statements, condemning the Lord's chosen carry punishment on the last day.

The bible declared Nineveh as an unsafe nation, their destruction was about to begin, they had only forty days left, time was up. God was kind enough to save them through Jonah, His prophet. No prophet of God is rebellious. God loves His prophets. When God loves a man, such a man, any sin he commits does not count. The love of God is unlimited. God has the power to re-mould a man to be perfect like Him. Many lack wisdom and they do not know the power of God.

This is the time of grace, and time is running out. Only God is good. So do not boast of your salvation, but work out your salvation with fear and trembling.

Prophets of God are nice people; we are not wicked. Prophets are not happy in this world because of what they see. When they see the world without Jesus as their personal Lord and Saviour, we know that you are not saved; this will not bring us joy.

A man who does not believe in God is like a man who is taking the last local train home in winter and refuses to watch his train time in the wating room. So is a man who does not believe in Jesus as the Son of God.

Had I known! Is always the message of the fool. Believe in the two witnesses of God and you shall be established based on (Rev 11: 6.) The God of heaven gave me the keys of heaven, and I can shut it at anyone at my own will. He gave me the keys of hell, and He gave me the keys of death.

"When the morning stars sang together, and all the sons of God shouted for joy" (Job 38:7.) The word shouted here is, a sudden loud outburst; to overwhelm; enjoyment. And the word "joy" here is, the emotion of great delight or happiness caused by something exceptionally good or satisfying; keen pleasure; elation. In this paragraph is the picture of the rapture.

Lucifer and his angels now miss this action in heaven, and now they are angry and do not want you to be there. Avoid anything that will take away your mind from the gospel. Anything that will cause you not to be in heaven, try to cut it off.

God has given the believers the kingdom, not because of our righteousness, just because of His unconditional love. Rahab, was saved, but not by her works. People may ask, is there wine in heaven? The answer is yes, spiritual wine, not the physical wine that makes people dubious.

In the month of May 2035, since I do not know the day and the hour when heaven is set to come to the earth and Jesus will arrive with the heavenly angels to rapture the elect, this is when the seventh trumpet shall sound.

The sound of the seventh trumpets is more dreaded than the trumpets that the people blew in Jericho that fell down the walls of Jericho and the inhabitants fainted for fear. The city was captured, and all the strong men were killed in the days of the biblical prophet Joshua. No one on this earth should compare the trumpet of Jericho to the sound of the seventh angel that will sound.

Another explanation of the seventh angel, for you to have an idea how the dreaded sound will be, it is like what you watch in this real world television, when a deadly rocket is lunched toward a specific location. Some countries, for example, Israel has what is called a warning siren, the sound of the siren does not sound like party music, it is a sound of deadly warning to run for your dear life and hide in a place called the bunker.

The sound of the seventh angel is not a sound of warning to run for your dear life, this is a sound of "game over" for the world, judgment and hell. The sound of the seventh angel I heard in my revelation was, GGOOOOoooooo. Deadly sound, I saw the Antichrist fall down.

Since I was a child, I have walked past the valley of shadow of death, but I was not shaken; when I heard the seventh sound, I was shaken. It happened in the night as I was sleeping in a friend's house in Stockholm, Sweden. And it was in winter. The dread was so strong that all the worms in my belly were shaken, I ran out of the room naked in winter, because I thought it was the real rapture. Theo and his wife, who housed me as a guest, came out after me and ask, Thomas, are you okay? Theo had his first child not up to a week, I went to say greetings and I decided to pass the night in their house.

In Theo's house in Stockholm, I strongly believed it was a real rapture, for me to be convinced that it was not a real rapture and it was a revelation, I left that house immediately that night and drove back to my home in Uppsala where I was living and where I was in school, for me to be sure it was not the rapture,

I saw that all my school students were all in the lecture hall, I counted all of them, including the teachers all the numbers were correct, and I believed it was not the rapture, it was a revelation. The truth is that, I cannot explain this. It was terrible.

A new earth will be created, and the meek shall inherit the earth. Peace will be on earth and there will be no more wars, no crime, illness, no more human hate, terror shall not exist, no rape, violence shall not exist, only true worship shall exist, and no more religion. No more robbery and anything relating to crime will not exist, world powers, disparities between the rich and the poor will not exist.

A new structure of how every man will live his daily life in peace and in love throughout the world will be established in the new world that God will create. Among the things that cause crime in this world, is jealousy. "I want to be like that man, he a has Porsche, he has big house and he has money" This leads to stealing, kidnappings, hunger, prostitution, and the love of material things.

Another thing that makes this world a terror is religion; there will be no more religion. All religious books you see around will be destroyed by fire, even the phones you hold, computers, internet, vehicles and everything made by man. All will be destroyed. God will restructure this world.

God will create a new earth meaning that this present earth will be no more exactly as spoken by the prophets in the bible.

"Now I saw a new heaven
and a new earth, for the
first heaven and the first
earth had passed away
Also there was no more sea"
(Revelation 21:2)

I Appeared Unto You

Chapter Six

Small Thing

In Christianity, the basic principle of our faith is being spiritual-minded. This is what makes our faith solid. The question is what is a spiritual mind? When you talk of spiritual things, then you are talking about spirits. God Himself is a Spiritual Being or He is a Spirit.

You cannot see spiritual beings with your physical eyes. So, we walk by what we do not see exactly as spoken by apostle Paul that we walk not by sight. When a man or a woman has a revelation, he or she is already in the spiritual realm.

God is saying that to be spiritually minded is life, and anyone who is not spiritually minded is dead. Since God Himself is a Spirit, we worship Him in truth and in spirit. Spirituality is the foundation of our Christian faith, because through spirituality the church will have a vision.

Spiritual beings can see us, these spirit beings have powers, they can bless, they can also kill. Spirits beings can have a meeting on our absence, the meeting can be in our favour and some of the meetings can also be evil.

There are spirits that are out to war against Christians because of our faith, which apostle Paul revealed in the bible.

> "For we wrestle not against flesh
> and blood, but against principalities,
> against powers, against the rulers
> of the darkness of this world, against
> spiritual wickedness in high places"

207

Christianity is a battle, and only few survive it. Our only weapon to fight the enemies is the word of God and faith.

A meeting took place in the spiritual realm, among some evil people within us. One day, I was in my home and a woman visited me. This was a woman that I had never seen before. As she came to my home, she entered our compound as we saw her she said she had a message for us. This woman was a stranger, so we gave her a chair to sit down, we offered her a drink.

As we sat down, ready to listen to her message, she said, "this message is from our kingdom to you (Thomas Bayo)." In my mind I asked, kingdom? Her expression was very furious. She continued the message and said, "We know you by your name, but you do not know us. You are trouble to our kingdom; as you pray, bombs continue to rock in our kingdom. The explosions are so much that our world head quarter is totally destroyed. In the history of our kingdom, such has never happened, and we are all afraid our headquarters has traced your house, where the bomb is originally lunching from as you decree in your prayers. I am in the charge of our unit in this territory, and they have located your house to me, this is why I have come to tell you that, you (Thomas Bayo) will be killed by a car accident or we will have to make you a mad man, we have to fight for the survival of our kingdom."

She continued, "for you not to die by car accident or not to be insane, stop praying immediately, stop reading the bible and do not go to the church; you have to totally give up your faith, with this, you are safe".

If I was not a Christian, and such woman gave me this kind of message, I would faint for fear. When this woman came to meet me my faith was solid already. After I listened to her message, I calmly told her, "I am very sorry, I cannot give up my faith. Because of the love of Christ that I am experiencing, I cannot stop worshipping God". I left her in the sitting room, went to my room, I locked my door and I prayed. After I prayed, I read "For we wrestle not against flesh and blood, but against principalities, against powers, against the rulers of the darkness of this world, against spiritual wickedness in high places"(Ephesians 6:12.)

Can you imagine this? Somebody sitting in front of you face to face, telling you to give up your faith with a death threat. I know that in some parts of the world, in the days of the communist, Christians were physically beaten and tortured, and some were killed, but mine is different. A death threat from another world?

I had just repented not more than one month, the outcome of my faith had become a threat to the kingdom of the enemies.

There are mysterious things happening in our world, but with biblical knowledge, you will have the understanding of how people are killed either by illness, gun fire, car accident, physical killings by Islam and many other methods.

Lucifer performed what he said to me, but he did not succeed in killing me, because God told him plainly, "I that speak in righteousness mighty to save." (Isaiah 63:1.)

When I saw Lucifer in the physical realm, his garment was totally red, stained with the blood of people he had killed, and used the blood to dye his garment. The Lord God questioned Lucifer, asked why his attire is red. Devil is a killer. Devil performed what he said, but Jesus is my Saviour.

Devil knows where to weaken a child of God. It happened that when I was young boy, I believed in school so much and fell in love with it, and I concluded that my future lies in academics. Every day, I looked forward to being in college.

Meanwhile, my earthly father had the money to train me to any length, depending on my readiness. Devil knew this. He found the loopholes to make me frustrated in life.

I was about 10 years old when a revelation came to me that I should be a vegetarian and not eat any meat, With this, I could escape Satan, because my education was being targeted. My cducation would bc ruincd. I did not forget this. My response was that, it would not work, and I would not forbid myself to eat meat. Before anything happens to me, I get the information before hand, both in Africa and in Europe. Anything that Satan has in mind to do to me, he informs me first and he will carry it out, but God shows him that He is my Saviour.

Even in my love relationships, I got the same information in Europe, I got a prophecy about everything that would happen to me from people all over the world. A woman just came from an unknown direction, even as I was attending a church in Sweden, she told me what would happen to me ahead of time. Everything I was told came to pass.

Jesus Himself appeared to me and asked me to repent of sin and commanded me to go and study the bible. You will see the complete details as you read on. All these prophecies came to pass.

In my past, out of ignorance when I did not know the Lord God of heaven, I patronised soothsayers. I remember when I met a soothsayer, this man said to me that he would tell me the truth, he began to minister the gospel to me. He said that even if I met any other soothsayer, they would only defraud me, so I should stop patronising soothsayers, I should go to church, that is where I belong. If I lay my hand on anything, the power that is in that thing is destroyed, that even himself who is a soothsayer, my presence in his environment makes him troubled. He said I should leave, go and worship my God. Out of ignorance, I went away sorrowful, believing that this soothsayer did not want to help me. But out of His mercy and love, God called me.

Regarding my love for school, it happened that I am not academically intelligent, but at my age, I knew that school is a thing worth not giving up on.

In my first year of secondary school, I failed in one subject and repeated it three times. I remained in one class, while the students I started with had only two years to finish, I was still behind in one position.

Normally, if a student fails once in my college, this school will not ask the student to quit. The school only gives you another chance. And if you fail in the last chance given to you, then, you will be withdrawn from the school and no other school will give you admission, since they will see your academic records that is too poor.

At this time, I knew that if I was withdrawn from the college, it would have been my end, because I would have be depressed.

At that early age, I made up my mind that I would not learn handwork, I would be a professional. I had already started college, and I made sure that what I have started, I had to end it. My goal was education, it would not be good for me to end up as a labourer. I was desperate.

I was troubled and thinking of how I could pass my school exams and move to the second year. I failed and remained in one class for three years.

If I failed again in same class, I would be sent packing. At this time, I was just a boy of about 14 years old, I did not know about Christianity.

I was given a second chance in my school, and yet I failed again. However, there was a church in my school called the "Scripture Union", one of my co students was very friendly with me and he never failed any school exam, he was a strong and dedicated Christian, and always told me, "come to the Christian meeting". My best friend and me made fun of him, that God answered only his prayers, because he never failed his exams. We said that God would not listen to people like us.

I was reluctant to follow this boy to the meeting, but I wanted to see if attending church could make me pass my examinations, so that I would not be withdrawn.

I pressured my mother to visit a magician, so that he would give me magic to pass my exam. My mother went, but nothing worked out. I failed again.

So, I visited the church in my school and attended meetings regularly. The pastor would always ask, "does anybody here need prayers for something that's bothered him? You need God to help you?" I was among the people who would always raise their hands. The pastor would ask me, "what do you want God to do for you?" Obviously, I told him I want to pass my school exams and go to the next class.

The pastor prayed all the time, but at the end, I still failed woefully. God the Father is a miracle worker, He was watching the whole situation, and what He would do was on His mind. That prayer was answered. I prayed to Him, yet I failed many times, but He knew what He would do. He knows the best answer to your prayer. He is a God of wonder.

We humans, our thoughts are different from the thoughts of God, and our ways are not His ways. He knows the best way to rescue you. Why was I failing in my school? Why? There are two things, here. A boy may not have interest in academics or a boy may not like schooling.

Lack of interest will cause a boy to be serious in school. Secondly, a boy may have great interest in education, but he may not be book smart

I discovered that I was poor in spirit. Being poor in spirit, is the reason why a boy or a girl may not be the school's brightest.

Here is the miracle, what God did was that He changed the head of the college, and brought a man that is from my home town that knows my family very well.

The year I was given the last chance by the former head of the school, if I did not pass my school exam, I would have been withdrawn.

So, as I went in to write the examination again, I failed.

The head of the school is not somebody that you just go to his office to see. Your reason must be important, or you will be directed to see his assistant, even to see his assistant is not easy, you will end up talking to an ordinary class teacher or a senior student to solve your problem.

My class teacher was responsible for preparing the withdrawal procedure.

He prepared my withdrawal documentation and forwarded it to the head of my school to put his signature on.

The head of the school was checking my records and he found out that I am from his own home town and he knows my family. He did not sign it. He refused to withdraw me. The head of my college knew that my father had money to pay my school fees, so he concluded that I should remain.

The head of the school was so nice that he wrote a letter of encouragement to my dad that his son did not have any bad record in the school, and he would continue to be a student of his college.

The letter he wrote to my family encouraged my father to pay the fees. My father was encouraged to be give me money for school, although it was expensive but he had the money.

However, all the days of this man in my school, I did not fail again, not even once. I passed my examination. Even if you reported me to the teacher that I cheated in school examination, as far this man remained in the school as the head, I was protected. He was the one who signed the promotions. Anytime I saw my results, I saw promoted. I did not see anything like failure again.

Happy is the man whom God loves. The English define love as partiality. And partiality is showing favour. God favoured Noah, Mary and many more of the great people of God. Jesus already bought us with His blood and He is our righteousness.

In my college, all the students have one strong policy and they never broke or abused this policy: any student who is a failure is exempted from bullying.

In my college in Nigeria, there was a high degree of bullying that was well known in the nation. I saw students in panic. Being a failure in the class really made me live with a peaceful and loyal in character. This was exactly what my late father told me, that the head of my school gave the reason in a letter written to him why I was allowed to remain in the college; because I was a peaceful person.

The head of my school was transferred to another school. This was where trouble began again. But God knows what to do.

I was in the final year. I concluded that when I got my certificate, I would work for a year to save money, and I would move to the UK to continue my education.

A harsh man was brought to be the head of my college and it was my final year. I just needed a certificate, I was not interested in position, just to show that I got a certificate that would make me get employment. I got admission into my secondary school when I was ten years old. I was supposed to spend 5 years in secondary school, but instead I spent 8 years. The luck I had was that I went to school at an early age.

In the final year, this is when we write the (WAEC) west African examination council, which means all the final year students, our names need to be sent to the ministry of education to be in the nation's record of people who successfully finished their secondary education.

I had just one exam to write for me to be qualified and my name sent to the state ministry. A week before the school exam, I was accused by the assistant head of my college that I raped her daughter, not only this, this man also accused me of burglary.

Breaking and entry into his own house and stealing things. What did this man have that my father could not give me? At this time, my father was still alive and a wealthy man. This time, I was 18 years of age, I had not even had sex with a woman in my life; I was still a virgin. I did not even know this girl that I was accused of raping. The girl they said I raped did not even know me.

This assistant head of my college vowed that I would not write my final exam, meanwhile, he did not even know me in person. I knew all what is going on; somebody committed this crime and he used my name, and I knew the boy that did it. I knew that if this girl saw me, she would say this is not the boy. The problem was that, it was the hour of my examination, if I missed one exam, for sure I would repeat again. Meaning that if I repeated and did not get to the final class, I may spend between 9 years to 11 years in the secondary school. This is on the grounds that I was not withdrawn.

The assistant head of the school was hunting for me so seriously in this time of my examination, targeting me in that particular examination to foil me and even get me arrested, and before I would prove innocent and be cleared, it would be too late. At the end, I would be requested to repeat again. How would I have born the shame?

If I succeeded in writing the school examination and submitted my examination answer papers to the teacher who invigilated, if the even if the president of Nigeria comes to take the examination paper from him, the examination invigilator will not hand it to him, this is the rule. A student who summits his papers is safe.

I was bold and I did not run away, because I saw this as my life. As we were writing the exam in the room, every student knew what was going on, and they knew the truth. Every student knew that I could never do such a thing as rape a woman and to steal. We all knew the boy that did it.

The assistant head of the school entered our class room to get me arrested. As he entered into examination room, he asked everybody to look at him and he called my name. One of the students told him immediately that the person he was looking for was not in that room, he should go to the second to the last room. He left us and went to the second to the last room. The ones in that room told him to go to the last room; he went to the last room, and that was how the students dribbled him until he went to back to his office.

My fellow students knew me, they were a very understanding people, they also knew my problem, that if I did not write that exam I would be totally frustrated in life.

I finished my exam and I submitted. The teacher who was coordinating our group, he was responsible for the examination supervision, he was a type of teacher who didn't want a student to fail, he was a kind of teacher that was liberal he would not fail any student.

At the end of everything, I was innocent.

To ask a student to leave school without failure required approval from the state ministry of education. And this was a long process. An external committee would need to investigate it, and if they were convinced of bad character, it may have ended up in suspension for a term or half, but I would not have been asked to leave school. What the vice was doing was illegal.

He was supposed to go the ministry and lay a complaint, and it would be the duty of the ministry to order an investigation before any action. Even when a student cheats in the examinations, the school would not kick you out. The worst thing that would happen was, the paper would be cancelled, and the student would be asked to write the exams again in presence of a single teacher; there would be no chance for cheating. I was able to escape that storm from the deputy and I was registered as a final year student.

This is now my final year.

A month before we wrote the final exam, which was exit and my victory, another teacher threatened that I would not write the final exam. I hid until the examination day, and this man would be in the exam hall to drag me out of the hall. Because he vowed to do it.

God will always know what to do. He is a wise God. We are talking about the Supreme, the Creator of man, who can give you knowledge or the academic knowledge that the world cannot withstand.

The Creator has the power to make me be the best student in the school, but He left my academic brain to be as it is, why? A man that God will use to reveal the end of age must have a virgin brain, a brain that has not been contaminated with the works of men, nothing has entered into it and no man has ever penetrated into it.

This is not talking about an illiterate who did not have the opportunity to be in school, people that are in school but the works of men could not go inside the brain.

To be an illiterate does not mean that your brain is pure. God left my brain to be as it is untouched. So that any of my works will not be based on academic works given by another man, or built up by another man. In my case, this is just the work of nature. I am not academically intelligent and no man can force it.

The final year is the most important of all. As another teacher threatened me and vowed that I would not write my examination, this teacher accused me of stealing. It was a smear. It was in this that season my own biological older sister, by name Lucky, graduated with a good degree and her certificate was fine. She was transferred by the federal ministry of education to my college immediately as a teacher, this was the work of God, and her rank was superior to that of the teacher that was a threat to me. Today, my older sister is the vice of my former college.

When the teacher who threatened to kick me out of exam hall saw my older sister, he gave up. I succeeded in writing my final exam, my sister was in the examination hall appointed to supervise by the ministry and this teacher was there and probably he was there illegally, because I think his rank was not enough to supervise a senior student like me.

In my teenage years, I had a best friend named Frank Oris, a school dropout due to poor academic performance. His father was not rich enough to follow the withdrawal up and fix him in another school. Frank had determination, but he had a poor family. After he became a dropout, I distanced myself from him, because I knew where he would end up. A school drop out? What was he going to do? What were we going to discuss?

If I had been withdrawn from my college, what I did to

Frank was exactly what I would have experienced from all my friends. All would distance themselves from me.

However, withdrawing me from the school that I loved and having to make new friends that were not of the same circle would had impacted another ideology into me, entirely different from the moral standard in my college.

The last time I saw Frank, as I went to his house, I remember what he told me, he saw me and he smiled. From a long distance, he started to hail me and shout my nick name, after much hailing, Frank said to me, "your face is dreadful and fearful", I did not know the reason why he said such words to me. I so much loved Frank and our companionship was all fun, we played together and did many interesting thing as one. During the holidays, we were always at the beach partying, but there was nothing I could do than to cut him off entirely.

After Frank left the school, his life changed, his ideology changed, his name became a horror and he kept tears on the faces of multitudes. He gave pains to people that they will not forget in their life time, crime became a glory to him and he worshiped it, believing he had nothing to lose. To him, killing others was like a game of cards he loved to play.

Frank, at the age of 17, committed one of the greatest robberies in my state, Delta, south of Nigeria, to the level that my state was shaken. And history will not forget him; as a teenager, he robbed and killed a mayor with a gun and fled with the mayor's car. This mayor was a tough politician and his bodyguards were known high profile thugs. History has never produced a politician like this mayor, Amos Emanowve. On the federal level, this mayor was called the young political lion. The death of this mayor was something that people could not believe. He was such a tough man.

Immediately we heard the news that this mayor was killed, I saw the thugs face to face as they put their two hands on their heads, speechless. Their boss was murdered. The mayor was shot in a strategic position that he couldn't survive. I refused to eat in that period, because of this case.

After Frank killed this mayor, he escaped and he was captured and jailed, awaiting execution by firing squad. Frank escaped from the prison. I give you this story for me to thank God for saving me. I know what I am talking about, I who insisted that I must go to school, this wasn't foolish.

I knew that my enemies were seriously waiting for the day that I would be withdrawn from the college, but there was no drama in my life, God protected me and my hands are clean.

Travelling abroad without a college certificate in my hands, such idea was not in me, what am I going to do there? But with a certificate in my hand, this was not a bad idea. Meanwhile, as a teenager, for me to start afresh again to learn a trade after gaining admission into college would have been an impossible project. So, my college was a must. Study or die.

A strong man in the government that held the key to power, Frank, killed him. And I remember what king David said in the bible, "no king is safe with the multitude of an host" (Psalm 33:16.) His son Solomon wrote in the bible, that man has no power in the day of his death, that day of your death, your power will be taken from you. "There is no man that hath power over the spirit to retain the spirit; neither hath he power in the day of death." (Ecclesiastes 8:8a)

People may say all manners of things against me, but as I live I will continue to love Jesus, bless Him, hold Him as my anchor. God saved me from pestilence and death. School does not save, only Jesus saves and He performed a miracle at the dying minute in my school.

Meanwhile, if my older sister had not come to that school, for sure, that wicked teacher would have made me miss my final exams. And if I had missed that final exam, it would have been the end of me.

I collected the money my daddy gave to my sister, since my sister was a teacher in my school, my father already knew that my name appeared on the board from the federal ministry of education among the students writing the final exam.

My sister was nice; she gave me the money and asked me

to go to the bank and pay it myself, she trusted me and I went to pay the tuition fees in the bank.

After I wrote my last examination, I was setting off to Europe to live. I did not have money on my own to buy air ticket, but I knew what to do.

After I finished my exams, I went directly to Kano city, north of my country. A friend introduced me to a Swedish man by name Lennart Olsson. This man worked as a manager in a company at the airport in Kano.

I went to Lennart and gave him the leaving school certificate from my college, I was employed. I worked as a radio operator. I learnt how to use radio language codes and the work was fine, I was also working closely with the accountant and this man really loved and enjoyed working with me. He would always say, "You are a smart guy, when I have a child, I will give him your name".

Lennart Olsson was nice to me and a really kind man. When Lennart Olsson got the message that I was leaving, the message he gave to me was, "do not use drugs when you get to Europe". There are people who are nice in this world.

After some months of working in the airport, I bought my ticket and I went to London, but everything went wrong, once you are a prophet destined for a mission on this earth, you are leaving your country. Satan will try to block it.

When the God of heaven calls a man, you may not go back to the position that you were, because going back to that position is like you did not answer that call.

Prophets are messengers of the living God, and this world is not our home. They that are of this world will remain in their world, but they that are not of this world will do the works of the Father in heaven until they finally go to their home in heaven. This was what happened all the key prophets. Because you are going to accomplish a mission that involves the entire world. A messenger.

Anywhere God calls you from, you cannot go back to that place again. I give you brief example of Jonah. He heard the call of God to go and warn Nineveh that either they repent or they get the wage of their sin in full scale, for God does not have pleasure in the death of the wicked.

Although he is not willing to go for the message, that position where God called him from, he cannot permanently stay that position again. Jonah was born and destined in his journey and God called him from his country to accomplish a mission in another country. The word of God is like an active force with fire. His word will not return to Him void. With methodical captivity, Jonah answered the call and the mission was accomplished with the power of God. After he has preached to the people of Nineveh, they repented and turned from their wicked ways. What next? "Therefore now, O LORD, take, I beseech thee, my life from me; for it is better for me to die than to live" (Jonah 4:3.) Why did Jonah prefer to die than to live after he has finished his mission?

Jonah ruled out the idea of returning home. Do you know the daily challenges a prophet is undergoing every day in his life? As you remain a believer on this earth, you are under war of the enemies. This is war as the holy bible revealed to you.

If God is telling you to go and warn a specific people, either they repent or they get the wage of their sin. As you are going for that call, you are totally evacuating from your home indefinitely, and there is no coming back because you are like Israel who is married to God. For example, if you are married to a woman that woman is not going back to live with the parents again. She will live with her husband, so is the call of God.

Jesus said, "And whosoever shall give to drink unto one of these little ones a cup of cold water only in the name of a disciple, verily I say unto you, he shall in no wise lose his reward". Jesus knew what He is talking about. These prophets and apostles will face what is called heat on this earth. Some prophets prefer to die than to live. Look at what king Solomon said in the bible, "Wherefore I praised the dead which are already dead more than the living which are yet alive" (Ec:4:2:.)

It has been ordained that power would be given to me, and

this power shall be given to me in Europe. The Creator chose me. This is a mighty treasure.

To get hold of this treasure is not bread and meat. The road to get hold of this treasure is very, very narrow. This treasure is hidden inside a lion's den, with no weapon in my hand, I have to collect this treasure from the lion's den.

"For where your treasure is,
there will your heart be also"
(Mathew 6:21.)

People may define treasure as monetary wealth. It can be physical gold, any kind of natural resources, precious object, creations, taking these as wealth means they are treasure. We that believe, any precious thing that originates from heaven is our treasure, and this goes with faith.

Whatever comes out of heaven is perfect treasure, because is eternal.

We who believe, the definition of our treasure is different from the definition of treasure of the world. This world, their treasure is something that is relating to wealth or anything that can fetch money. This kind of treasure is temporary; it doesn't last forever. The English define temporary as, effective for a time only; not permanent. The things you see in this world and their fame is not everlasting.

Moreover, in everything on earth, in heaven and things under the earth, whether they are beings or creatures, the biggest treasure is the Holy Ghost. The Holy Ghost is power. This is everlasting power.

He that has the Holy Ghost (treasure) is already in heaven, meaning that such a man is just staying on earth briefly to accomplish a mission, and will later go home. The Holy Ghost did not design Himself for earthly inheritance; the bible says, except you are born of the Spirit and of water, you cannot enter into the kingdom of God.

The bible says, "silver and gold have I none to give, but I

give you Jesus". So, Jesus Himself is a treasure. And He is greater than silver and gold. Having Jesus in your heart is a treasure. If you love Jesus, look around at your neighbours, look at the street if they have Jesus. Many do not know the way to Jesus, because they cannot find Him.

If you lay your hand on any kind of treasure of this world, whether money or gold, you will have a testimony to tell the world of how you got your riches. When it comes to finding Jesus, it is compulsory that you have a testimony to give how, when, where, what time of the day, and how it happened that you found Jesus as your Lord and Saviour. What resulted in you finding Him, you must have a reason. Jesus will always ask, what can I do for you?

Finding Jesus is like the actor and the bad guy going and experience to accomplish a mission and the bad guy the enemy putting hindrance on the way.

Some have experienced heat and hits from the enemy, and they stood strong and they were not shaken with their faith and the journey became smooth and successful. Even when Jesus was on this earth, many wanted to see Him. It is not easy to find Jesus. This is the truth. You can see how many in this world are like sheep without a shepherd. Some do not even know what to believe. You who have Jesus as Lord and Saviour, you have a treasure already. You must see the reflection of how you were saved by Jesus. Some may not know what they hold. Having Jesus as your treasure makes you a star already.

When you bring the issue of Jesus to some people, you need to stand strong because some will rebuke you and tell you this is religion, but when one of their family passes away, this is when you see them in the church making sign of the Cross. And it will come to their mind that life is not as you see it. This is when some begin to think of their faith. Man is like vapour; it comes and vanishes. But when they step out of that funeral, they remain unbelievers. Such people put their treasure in this world and the evil one comes and takes it away.

When the treasure of a man is hidden somewhere, in the

physical, you do not know where this treasure is located, but your spirit knows exactly where your treasure is located.

Your treasure can be hidden anywhere. If it requires the use of violence to collect your treasure, you have to do it.

My great treasure, I started smelling it since when I was about 14 years old, and I told all my friends that immediately I finished my secondary school, I would go abroad. Because I was always failing in my school, it made me develop the idea of going abroad, that it may be easier for me to study abroad. You must use a device to locate where your treasure lies. You cannot just go like that. It does not work that way. It can take a man many years to plan how to get his treasure.

All treasures are hidden. And where my treasure was hidden was inside the lion's den. This is called Landesgericht in Vienna in the country of Austria. This place called Landesgericht, is a prison in Austria. This is where my treasure was hidden, if I would had not gotten to this place, there is no way I would have located my treasure in life. Can you imagine this?

I planned to travel to Europe after I finished my school. Before I was allowed entry into Europe, it was my eighth time. I face seven deportations. All my deportations were only at the entry point. Complete details of this are written in my book, What Do You Want?

Flesh has no ability to understand this, because they look to the things that are visible. The power is not in them to believe because they walk after things that visible. But we who are believers, although we are human, yet we look up to the things that are invisible and we walk not by sight.

The greatest treasure is hidden. The devil himself does not know where this treasure lies, but in your movement, he will smell something fishy and try to block it. If Satan knows where that treasures is, humans have no hope. It was Jesus who encouraged Himself all the way from heaven and made sure He helped us find our treasure. He found our treasures for us. This treasure was hidden in the Cross. Can you imagine? Our treasure was hidden in the cross! If Satan knew that the Cross would bring victory to us, Jesus might have not died on the Cross.

Jesus was not stoned to death, rather He remained in the grave. Through the Cross, He made it for us. The Cross is the enemy of evil.

The reason why your treasures are hidden is so that Satan cannot find it and take it. If Satan knows that our treasure is laid in the Cross, he will definitely spoil it but he was taken unaware and we are saved through the Cross. The Cross is a symbol of victory in heaven and in earth.

As heaven was open for me to see, I saw the Cross in The Throne of God in heaven. Immediately you enter heaven, at the gate, you will see the Cross. That Cross is victory and power and this is what gave us eternal life.

From all of God's creatures, He will always chose one. When it comes to trees, He chose the olive tree to accomplish the end of the world, same as He did with Noah. The anointing of the old prophets was extracted from the olive tree. When we talk about birds, God chose the dove. When talk about nations, He chooses Israel. When you talk about Gentile nation, He chose Rome. When you talk about animals, He chooses the sheep. God is holy.

> "And the dove came in to him in the
> evening; and, lo, in her mouth was
> an olive leaf pluckt off: so Noah knew
> that the waters were abated from off
> the earth" (Genesis 8:11.)

When you want to talk about the end of the world, then, focus on the olive trees. Who is the olive tree as revealed in the bible? The candlestick is a ministry that is active until the last minute when Jesus will come, which is the ministry of the two witnesses.

The things of God are of wonders; you cannot find what is in that tree which the bible used to reveal the end. God hid the exact date of the end in that tree. Do you know where I found this treasure? I found it in Turkey. In the east position of the earth. The pillar of this book is the date, revelation of the end. God has made me an olive tree, the wisdom of the end was hidden in me, which has been revealed.

Even if you search me spiritually, you will not find anything in me. Even though you have spiritual eyes, the more you want to hurt me the more you are troubled. Satan tried it. What happened? Satan only heard a voice, a mighty voice sounding to him as many trumpets and he was rebuked. This is God Almighty rebuking him. This is what I saw face to face.

Why do you think the bible says do not hurt my two witnesses or you will be killed?

A friend of mine told me one day like a joke that he is a prophet, and that there is something hidden in me that has not been revealed, but one day it will be revealed. I do respect people for the wisdom God has given to them.

I have mixed with all kinds of people. If what you are doing is evil even though I do not know and I join you, that organisation is going to be destroyed. This is what the bible says; every counsel formed against you shall not stand.

The presence of a prophet in any place is the presence of God in that place, because the Holy Ghost is there. Any evil of men in that environment will be destroyed, because the Holy Ghost is a fire. The Holy Ghost is God and the presence of God on earth.

I have travelled Africa looking for my treasure, Europe and I was exploring America until I found it.

To find your treasure is not something that you give up, you may have to go to many places to search, but one day it will be found. Your treasure may lie in the back of your house, but you still need to look for it. Treasures are hidden in various places, but mine was hidden in a tough zone. And I needed to be tough to make sure I found it. I located my own personal treasure in Vienna.

"Again, the kingdom of heaven is like unto treasure hid in

a field; the which when a man hath found, he hideth, and for joy thereof goeth and selleth all that he hath, and buyeth that field" (Mathew 13:44.)

The word "hide" here as written in the bible, the English define "hide" as to conceal from sight; prevent from being seen or discovered. The English also define it as, not to tell.

When I was a young boy, I used to play with other kids. One of us would put a mask on their face, and the other kids would put something like a ball, or even a coin somewhere and they would hide it in at a very short distance and say this is your treasure please find it. While the eyes are closed.

These objects are usually placed after your eyes have been closed, not when your eyes are wide open.

The kids see you as you are blindfolded, trying to find your treasure. Finding your treasure is great fun, and we would laugh and wait to clap for you when you find your treasure.

Sometimes, your treasure is kept in a cupboard, depending on where the kids hide it, if it is in a room, we may keep it under the bed, if it is a parlour, we may keep it on top of a cupboard, if it is an open ground, we may decide to put it in your immediate front, or behind you.

As kids, some of us knew how to target and get it, because we think immediately when our eyes were closed, and guessing it would be under the bed or under the table, next on top of the bed, we give ourselves enough time to search and enough time to laugh.

You may not have to travel, your treasure may be under your feet. Our treasure is spiritual and not physical; we are inspired to look for it with all our might and strength.

What will you do when you know that your treasure is some-where? Jesus answered the question already, "and for joy thereof goeth and selleth all that he hath, and buyeth that field" (Mat-thew 13:44.) With wisdom, you know the meaning of this word.

When I was in Landesgericht in the first three months, this was when I made up my mind that I had to move immediately to United Sates, and looking for this treasure. But the Lord told me to cool down, he said the treasure you are looking for, you have found it. Immediately I saw this revelation that my treasure is not in the United States the revelation was so scary, this is here in Austria.

What happened? In the tenth month of my prison sentence in Austria, this was the time I found my treasure. I was given power when I was in prison, and the anointing was flooding like spring water all over my body, the anointing refused to stop and continue flooding all over me. I refused to laugh, but when I wanted to smile that was when the anointing increased on a very strong level. Only what I was hearing was,

Blessed!

Anointed from the top length of my hair and the anointing ran down to my feet, even under the skin. Another thing that thrilled me again was that.

I persuaded the world to rejoice and believe that God your Creator who loves you will now establish you, and you will experience peace like the way of the garden in time of Adam. Peace, peace, peace, earth, shout for your joy for your days are the days of the garden.

If the Lord had told me, your treasure is in maximum security prison in Austria, that is the place it was hidden. What do you think my response would have been? I might have said to God that He should not be angry with me, that I am alright in Africa in the place I am now and the life I live here I am contented with. I may have preferred to die of hunger if possible than to put myself in slavery, He should please send another person and I would not go. Did Joseph know that he would accomplish his mission through prison? God turns failure to a victory. And man will say "O' Lord, I am foolish, forgive me". Through the prophets, God revealed His power.

Some of the prophets were not willing to answer their callings, after they experienced the power of God.

They all trembled. And they knew that there is nothing the Lord cannot do and He is the God of grace.

To say yes to God's calling means you have the power to do it.

Even before you reach the middle of accomplishing a mission, some will give up. The road to heaven is narrow. Exactly what Jesus said, some will use all their strength to make it, but they will not.

Somebody asked me one day why God made the road so hard and very narrow? It is not God that made it hard and narrow, it is Satan that is a stumbling block to the life of everyone that follows the road of Jesus.

Satan had the power to destroy people's properties; he can destroy cars, kill children, destroy marriages, rob people, cause many women to be raped, destroy families, give a terrible disease, kill people's loved ones, gave heat to many, abuse, embarrass people, and he has made many to fall into temptation and sinned.

Satan has given many people hindrances, and their lives look like that there is no more hope, make people commit suicide and many other evil things. Satan will afflict the innocents, put tears in the eyes of people. But people that really know their God, shall be strong, and when evil comes to you, you remain strong and hold your faith.

If you know that your treasure is hidden in the prison, the question is how can you get there and collect it?

For to collect treasure in the prison is not the point, to get there is another point, on the way, there must be briers and thorns, set back and fight because you are going to get what is called a treasure.

Maybe people may not know who Lucifer is. Lucifer is the man who made war in heaven to the extent that the angels in heaven were fighting for their survival and fighting for their salvation.

Heaven says that the day Lucifer, who is also called the great Dragon was cast down to the earth, the angels in heaven rejoiced for their salvation and commented that "woe to the inhabiters of the earth and of the sea! For the devil is come down unto you, having great wrath, because he knoweth that he hath but a short time" (Revelation 12:12.)

The bible is able to describe devil to you, that he travels with the greatness of his strength. If you see Lucifer face to face, if you are not careful and if you do not have wisdom, you may think that he is God.

He still has his crown on him. That is why the bible warns you, to work out your salvation with fear and trembling, if you do not hold your salvation strongly, he can knock it out of your hands like the way he knocked down Maria's salvation including her house.

When you study the biography of all the high profile prophets in the holy bible, when God commanded them to accomplish a mission, they were not willing, because they knew that man, among the creatures of God, man is a very dangerous creature. If you tell man the pure truth, he will hit you. Some prophets know that when they are going to deliver a true message, they would be stoned by the wicked. Some even knew that they would be killed for telling the truth.

> "Jerusalem, Jerusalem, thou that
> killest the prophets, and stonest them
> which are sent unto thee, how often would
> I have gathered thy children together,
> even as a hen gathereth her chickens under
> her wings, and ye would not!"
> (Mathew 23:37.)

Lies give joy to man, and it entices them, but prophets are not for this, they are people who will tell you the truth, who will encourage you, who will always tell you not to faint, but stand strong. Man has been looking for material life and it has increased in this present world. How many really want to hear the truth?

Joseph was not told that his treasure was in prison. If the

Creator had told Joseph that he was going to jail in Egypt and later be crowned, what do you think Joseph would have responded?

Yet, he has been destined for this before he was born. It has been spoken before he was born that he and his generation would live in Egypt for four hundred years. This was what that has been seen ahead. A man needed to be chosen and used as an entrance for others to come into Egypt.

He was sold as a slave into Egypt. Selling him as a slave was not the main mission. This was just to activate the mission. Do you know what it means that you are sold out to be a slave? But Joseph was on a mission, at the beginning he did not know. His slavery was just a road with briers and thorns. He has to pass this process first before the action. But him as a prophet later knew everything. Joseph said, "And God sent me before you to preserve you a posterity in the earth, and to save your lives by a great deliverance." Joseph knew his mission on earth. All the prophets know their mission on earth and in heaven.

What actually triggered the imprisonment of Joseph? This is something that has been settled on his behalf in the spiritual realm. There are spirits who will volunteer to do the job. They will come to earth and execute it. The physical minded man does not know what is going on. This why it is good to have a spiritual understanding of life and it gives encouragement and unspeakable joy.

It resulted that Joseph was accused of rape, so, sexuality was involved in this case, on three charges: rape, adultery and rebellion; and regarded as a high profile case because a cabinet minister was involved. His wife, Potiphar said she was abused. Joseph said that he did not rape this woman and never pleaded guilty. It is wrong to plead guilty of the crime you did not commit for the sake of integrity.

Some women have evil foresight; they have some phoney eyes with the ability to know which man will be great tomorrow. Potiphar's wife had seen that Joseph had a great future, and she wanted to destroy him.

It happened that Joseph went to jail. His treasure was hidden in jail and he collected his treasure in the prison. If Joseph did not have this experience, how would he have gotten his treasure? Treasures are hidden. And they are hidden in strategic positions. Where the evil people cannot go and collect it. Devil is afraid to go to jail, he likes the posh and superior life. It is not a place where all can survive for anyone who does not know the mysteries behind it. Prison is a unique place designed for divine children.

Ultimate power is the biggest treasure that was given to me as a gift this is keys of heaven and keys of hell. Power that will continue to exist for eternity. A treasure that came with a sealed, Do Your Own Will. This treasure is God Himself that has no power to forgive, designed Himself to live with man forever and He does not depart. The God of heaven says I will give power to my two witnesses. This power has been given to me.

No man can say the world will end 2035 if power is not given him. This is the work of power.

God may give you a gift and seal it, and ask you to have it. When the appointed time has come, He will ask you to open what you hold and see what is inside. God may give you a revelation and you are seeing this revelation every day, but you do not know what it means.

If a man finds a treasure, there must be history linked to it. It does not come like that without history. The rape case was designed as the avenue for Joseph to be in jail for the treasure to be inherited.

What inspired me to travel abroad since I was a child was that I was a failure in school and I was hoping that it may be more easier for me to study in abroad.

I refused any kind of support from my family, because I decided in my mind to do all things alone by myself, so that if I experienced any calamity abroad, I would not blame anyone for it.

My brother graduated from a university in England and came back home in my country to work. He experienced life abroad, and when he came back home, he refused to travel again. As a professional, he was offered a great job abroad, but he decided not to travel again and the language he used was that he was satisfied with the life he now lives in my country.

Prophets, they curse the day they were born into this earth, cursed them that brought gifts to their mother, saying a male child is born on this day.

"After this opened Job his mouth, and cursed his day. And Job spake, and said, Let the day perish wherein I was born, and the night in which it was said, There is a man child conceived" (Job 3:1-3.)

"Cursed be the day wherein I was born: let not the day wherein my mother bare me be blessed" (Jeremiah 20:14.) The life of prophets were filled with stories of sufferings; when they told the truth, some were given dirty slaps. Persecuted and killed for testifying what they had seen and saying what they knew. Prophets are messengers and their kingdom is not of this world.

How did apostle Paul journey? Paul was placed under arrest within his country with hand cuffs, surrounded with deputies, suspected of felony charges, under appeal and was transported to Rome, yet he was on a mission for God. The chained were later loosed. This was how his journey was destined.

Actually, the warning came to apostle Paul in a physical realm that he would be chained both hands and legs. Paul could not see how it had been settled in the spiritual realm. When a man is destined for a mission, nothing can stop it. Some may wonder, a man going on a mission to Rome, he has to pass this process of being placed under arrest?

Paul would had been killed if he was not under arrest, and God used this captivity to safeguard for his mission to be accomplished. However, Satan wanted to make it unaccomplished mission with many obstacles on the away after he tried to kill him. It is easy for Satan to use unbelievers as tools to bring obstacles and hindrance against the children of God. But up to this hour, the Lord is our Saviour.

Prophets and apostles went through huddles.

That's why in the bible, God says, whom shall I send? Will

it be easy to say, "send me, God".

How many people will get the knowledge and understanding that Satan will always manifest his works, that the man the God of heaven is sending should be deported at the entry point.

So that when I am deported, I will give up the journey. God will always make Satan to clearly know that He knows whom He has chosen.

It was revealed to me that the road has been heavily blocked by the enemies, that Satan vowed that I would not cross any European airport. I began to examine this revelation. My question is why was the road blocked? What came to my mind was the revelation of Daniel the prophet, when Satan withstood an angel of God for 21 days and the holy bible concluded that this angel must fight with Satan when going back. This angel was bringing revelations regarding the end time to the world through prophet Daniel.

This was when I began to evaluate my life. I wondered that what was so important in my life that Satan was interested in me, to even not let me pass the immigration, I had visas, but I was refused entry. I had enough basic traveling allowance.

Satan knew that the revelation would be given to me abroad about the end time, and power will also be given to me abroad. Then, I did not give up, I had to fight, I knew that spiritual elements had already been involved in my journey, I did not give up. God is with me. As I was refused entry and sent back to my country, I knew I must be proceeding to west Europe again.

Me and my partner the two witnesses of God who will reveal the end of the world. The bible revealed we are the ones that is standing Satan the Lord of the whole earth. Have patience and long suffering, and do not complain. This is among the basic things in the life of a believer. Long-suffering.

This is what I tell people, if you like anything at first and you really need it, do not leave it and go. Do all your best and see the results. If you know the power of God, you will never be afraid of anything. God has the power to change all situations.

Small Thing

As I lived in Europe, I needed to continue my studies and probably study what I know, but the call of God was boiling in my heart, the details of my calling already been published in the book titled, What Do You Want?

I needed to go the bible college, since I heard my callings directly from God the Father face to face and from His mouth, I agreed to my callings. Man did not ordain me, I saw Him that ordained me face to face and I know Him. To further my education, I ruled it out of my mind studying to be a lawyer or a dentist. But to follow the line of the ministry, this is the truth. I enrolled in the bible school in Livets ord Uppsala, Sweden. This school is well-known university with all kinds of education you need even up to PhD level.

I went to this school in Sweden and they kicked me out of the school as I have said before; the excuse they gave to me was that I did not fit the standard of their school.

The head of the bible college told me face to face to leave the school. I did not believe this. This was the beginning of my failure, then, how can I be a preacher? My plans were completely ruined and destroyed. This was the time I told God I am ready to live by the sword and ready to die by the sword. I got one sword and I was happy. After some time, a friend called me from America and persuaded me that people are making millions of dollars and what were we doing? I was being drawn to be a criminal, and this time I was idle, no bible college and no more zeal to pursue the ministry.

All the money I saved for studies I had already invested in this bible college, but all was lost.

I knew that I was going to the street, I could not stop it, but I had not started anything wrong. Although I was doing genuine personal business in Austria, this had nothing in connection with what was I planning to do. I was in the process of drawing plans and launching a global fraud network with friends that were persuading me, this was exactly the time my captivity manifested. I never did anything wrong before I was arrested.

I was in the process of engaging in a fraud mission and we

were targeting world trade centre, what Nigeria called the 419, this was early 1999. My friend told me that I should think about it, that the job is easy, it was just writing letters to people and telling them that we belonged to the Nigeria government, if they can help us take 11 million dollars out of Nigeria that they have their percentage.

Anyone that responds, he is called Mugu. If the Mugu responds, we will invite him, and during discussion this is where the job begins. At the end of the day, we will collect money from the Mugu, some will even sell their houses and give us the money, some even borrow from banks, hoping that we will bring money to them. the Mugu can expect the 11 million dollar for up to a year, but still be paying to expect money. As my friend told me to think about this work, I replied him to let me think about it for a month, whether I like it or not.

In the process of my consideration of being a member of the fraud gang, I was arrested in Austria. This was not why I was arrested though; I did not defraud any one.

The Lord is a wise God and very patient. He knows how to handle situations that look difficult to man. He allowed me to be kept in captivity, and He used that captivity to strengthen me.

God knew that I would be going to the streets after I dropped out of bible college, the prison blocked any evil communication that would have corrupted my good manners. Can you believe I came out of prison wise?

Thank God for prison. The knowledge I have today, I acquired it from the prison. God gave me knowledge from the prison and I learned how to write a book in the prison. Practice makes perfect. Although, in any first work, you must see the signs of an amateur. There is no professional on earth that did not pass through the beginner stage. People will complain as is their tradition, but in finding your faults by yourself, you can build yourself up.

I was having a talent in me that I never knew. Secondly I forgot that Jesus is coming and thirdly the date of the end given to me which I thrown away. But if not for Claudia? Even me there is no way I would had be prepared to watch on the Month of May...2035.

You can see that these teachers are obstacles to people who genuinely want to repent and give their lives to God and worship Him in spirit and in truth. This is the problem. From their hair to their toes is anger and evil, and there is no wisdom in these teachers. They may be professors, but the knowledge they have is of the world.

If Calle Lilja and Ingrid had not kick me out of the bible school in Sweden, it might have prevented me from going to jail in Austria and carrying sword and involving myself in fornication with many girls.

I would have not been unequally yoked in marriage, and my wife to would not have had separate from me. But God is good. He changes situations from bad to good. See how my captivity manifested in Austria as you read on.

I overcame severe depression from been rejected by teachers in Livets ord and kicked out of the bible school.

I truthfully went to the bible college because of God, and was there to study and show myself approved as a work man, to divide the word of truth. But I was rejected.

The key to my heart is in God's name. Calle Lilja and Ingrid took advantage of this and broke my heart with it. No creature is capable of breaking my heart so much that it will cause so much tears. All my tears in life, the root of it all is linked to God's name. Because I love God with all my heart, soul and spirit. Jesus said, this is the law that hangs all the prophets.

When Calle Lilja and Ingrid rejected me, then, God decided to make me a living stone and now, He is using me to reveal the end of the world, meaning the stone the builders rejected has become the cornerstone of the house. The Lord's doing.

Calli Lilja and Ingrid are lairs, of a truth they are teachers and they are intellectuals, these are people that others depend on to obtain knowledge to live their lives, so you can understand that Calle Lilja and Ingrid are intellectual, so, they have records of students who are drop out and they know the lives and how they live, including the Swedish citizens who were also axed. Just for nothing.

Calle Lilja and Ingrid knew perfectly that it's a nightmare to anyone that has been axed from a spiritual ground. If Calle Lilja and Ingrid say they did not know that it causes pains, they have lied. School dropouts, the bible calls them waste, as spoken by prophet Isaiah, God of heaven has vowed as written in the bible that is this bible college dropout He will chose as His army and His judges. According to what God of heaven asked His prophet to write down,

> "In that day shall the LORD of hosts
> be for a crown of glory,
> and for a diadem of beauty,
> unto the residue of his people,
> And for a spirit of judgment
> to him that sitteth in judgment,
> and for strength to them that
> turn the battle to the gate".
> (Isaiah 28:5,6.)

This "crown of glory" here, is specifically going to exact people, not to anyone. And the question is who are these people? These are The Residue. The Residue here is a bible college drop out. People kicked from the church, for nothing. This are the people God has chosen to judge the entire world, judge the Christian and our judgment is holy and perfect. I am a residue.

The word Residue is a technical terms used in law to address a specific matter, is also used in chemistry and in mathematics and also spiritual, is also used even in physics. Politically a person who does not agree with conservatives he or she is called a residue, a terms used in politics. In the political live a residue is a person on a rational quantity under a radical form to make changes in a government of a country.

Residue is also a topic discussed in Britannica. Under modular arithmetic (with mod N), the only numbers are 0, 1, 2, …, N − 1, and they are known as residues modulo N. Residues are added by taking the usual arithmetic sum, then subtracting the modulus from the sum as many times as is necessary to reduce the sum to a number M between 0 and N − 1

Flesh and blood will say a "bible college dropout", but heaven calls them Residue.

The crown of God is not going to conservative Christians, it will go to the liberal Christians. When you study the bible, you have to focus on the key words, the key words are the foundation of you studying the bible and understanding the meaning.

If you have the knowledge, in some parts of Africa where hunting of animals in the bush is not controlled, and hunters do what they like, these animals are chased and they scatter in different directions, migrating to other parts of the world. This is how true Christians have been chased and they are scattered in the wrong direction within the society. But God will gather the residue of His people in that day. His anger is not on His Residue because He has removed His anger from them, and when the anger of God is not on, it means you have no fault, you are perfect. Just as God Himself, we know that He created the devil, but there is no fault found in Him.

When you are excommunicated, you have already fallen and there is no more strength in you again. But the Creator has spoken that He will give strength to the residue "…and for strength to them that turn the battle to the gate" (Isaiah 28:6.) The word strength here is power.

The word residue in English language is the leavings, and the word leaving is send-off, today, I am a remnant of Livers Ord Bible College, and I am not included on the main part, so heaven knows me as a residue, they that are successfully graduated are the main part of Livers Ord while I am the remains.

Let me use the fashion industry to explain the meaning of residue. In the fashion industry, residue is named as outlet or the remains. Every year, their fashion goods are placed on the stores for consumers needs, the ones that are not sold at the end of the year are kept aside, and the new ones for the new year are placed in the stores. Those ones kept aside are residue or the remains.

This is how residue works; the fashion industry does not sell their products to consumers directly, it is only the residue that is kept in the factory store, sold to the consumers directly. Their current designs cannot be found in the factory store, it is only the residue is kept in the factory store for consumers need.

Now, the fashion industry designed a public store for the consumers based on that residue, because they are the remains of the previous year. A residue is not a defective product. As a consumer, the product you buy directly from the factory store is residue.

For example, the Italian Cavalli current designed products are on sale in retail shops under the trademark name of Cavalli, normally in the retail stores, the residue are not kept there. A fashion designer wizard believes that no fashion is out of fashion, he can still make what you call "out of fashion" into new fashion. How much more the Creator who can create something out of nothing. The remains are not kept aside because they are defected, they are just simply residue.

Another example is, you want to make a telephone call to your friend or your family and you top up your phone with 10 Euros. After making the telephone call, there is still money remaining on the phone, probably 2 Euros. These 2 Euros are the residue or the remains. And you don't throw it away. You still use it to make another call the next time.

There are humans that are also residue, example is a school dropout, a school failure, people that are axed from competitions or any kind of contest, political residue and much more, these are residue. God loves the residue.

Now, the Creator will only select the residue, which prophet Isaiah wrote about in the bible. He uses the residue as His army, and uses the residue as His judges in the last day and

He gives to them spirit of judgment and wisdom. The residue are the ones that will sit in the throne to execute judgment, all who live on this earth will stand the judgment of God. The residue are very rugged people.

For example, God wrote my biography in the bible, that He has created the waster to destroy. A waster is school dropout; I am a residue, a bible college dropout. Prophets are the battle axe of God, the word of God is like a hammer that destroy the rocks into pieces.

My life in Austria? What I was doing, establishing a company is not what I was destined to do, although it proves that I established a GesmbH in Austria, a genuine business with thousands of Euro investment, I am the director, yet, I was a psychological child, based on how I was dealt with in Sweden.

I was always out; from January to December was holiday to me. The company was in existence, but I was never there in my own office, all my transactions were via telephones, and for this I was destined to fail, because this was not what I was called to do.

After I repented and accepted my callings, my dream work was missions with other missionaries, but my dream work was destroyed in the bible college by Cali Lilja and Ingrid. I was not interested in the income of how I will work for God, but I knew I would not die of hunger if I am serving the Lord and my thoughts and goal was just to look at the mission field.

They spoiled everything, even my marriage plans, all were spoiled. Which prophet Zechariah said because of a small thing. The question heaven is asking these bible college teachers, Calle Lilja and Ingrid, is that, who hath despised the day of a small thing? Because of a little thing that did not require me to be kicked out of bible college I was kicked out.

The bible says, "who hath despised the day of a small things?" (Zechariah 4:10.) Meaning who has spoilt the day (for me)? The man who will be a destroyer in the next world to come? Who has hurt that man whom God has created to be a destroyer in the next world to come? To be a destroyer is a message to my enemies.

A man who will accomplish a mission for God. The word despised here as written in the holy bible is, hate. I do not know why Calle Lilja and Ingrid hate me? These folks are not supposed to have been born. They looked down on me. I am a residue, and power has been given to me. The keys of heaven and the keys of hell have been given to me. I have seen the Creator face to face and He made me His friend.

Woe to anyone who says the holy bible is fiction. Jokes do not exist in the judgment of God. To hurt the two witnesses of God is a capital offence

The salvation that was given to some people through Christ it was out of pity, this is not your birth right and if you want to show too know (many masters), "My brethren, be not many masters, knowing that we shall receive the greater condemnation" (James 3:1.) This is why we should respect each other's. As I respected everyone including Calle Lilja and Ingrid.

You will be reminded as written in the bible that salvation only belongs to the Jews. This is their birthright. You will face eternal judgment. There is nowhere in the bible that the Gentiles have everlasting salvation. Do not lie. God says in the book of Isaiah that, His children are people that will not lie and He is our Saviour. If you are a child of God and you call yourself a Gentile, you have to always tell the truth and maintain it. Do not depart from it.

Moreover, If you want to show that you know more than yourself as many masters, you will also be reminded that you are a sinner and God is holy. All the sins that you have committed will be shown to you face to face, because the records are kept waiting for you. For is a terrible thing to fall into the hand of Almighty God. As you remain in love with Christ and obedient, God will keep your eternal life waiting for you and He will give it to you for free and not because of your works.

Not that Calle Lilja and Ingrid were not warned. My biography was written in the bible very boldly and they even hold my testimony. God has made me a signet. This is a very high profile position in the cabinet of God.

Calle Lilja and Ingrid underestimated me: and may say in their mind, Thomas Bayo what can he offer? Unknowing to them, the keys of hell has been given to me: I hold these keys, also I have been given the key of heaven: "These have power to shut heaven, that it rain not in the days of their prophecy: and have power over waters to turn them to blood, and to smite the earth with all plagues, as often as they will" (Re:11:6.) The rain is salvation, power was given to me stop salvation in all the earth which I have written the date salvation end in my book titled, What Do You Want?

"And to smite the earth with all plagues, as often as they will". The power that has been given to me and my partner, ability to plague the earth both land, sea and things under the earth.

❧❧❧❧

If I had married a woman I love at this point in my life, there is every tendency and readiness that I would be devoted to my wife, and there will be no room for any rubbish and she will act as a helper. There are women who have been destined to encourage their husbands. They will always say, "just find something doing, anything, even if it is one Euro that is your wage, let us eat in peace and be happy with it than to go to prison and leave me alone to suffer without you" Such words will touch a human being, the only precious thing you can give to a human being is not money but counselling, words that have life.

Even if your heart is iron, she has already sown a seed of encouragement into the heart, and it will be a fruit that manifests, love, and prosperity, and is also a challenge to be gentle and responsible. But when there is no wife and no child, this is among the reasons why some guys take unnecessary risks in life.

A virtuous woman who can find? A woman can give you tremendous help in life. But most women around us today are always full of anger. In these latter days, man needs wisdom to deal with them. Any woman or man who wants to live the way she or he likes, leave them and let them do their will. Their day is very near. The world shall go back to the ink age.

You have read as written that God will spring forth righteousness in all the earth, how will this be done? Do you think that God is going to beg you and pet you? This is the work of the rod of iron that will be used to spread righteousness in all the earth. After the rapture, we are going back to the dark age again. This is the work of the residue who are the army of God (Joe:2:11.) "And the Lord shall utter his voice before his army: for his camp is very great: for he is strong that executeth his word: for the day of the LORD is great and very terrible; and who can abide it?"

Do you know how many people in this world that do not know what to do? Because they are confused, and some of these confused ones are being cursed by other people, their hearts broken.

Biblically, If we, the true children of God have been scattered and destroyed by these present preachers in the entire world, and they cut us off from the church, this is not our fault. We are perfect. This is the judgment of God. It is the fault of those pastors, the bible college teachers, because they are the ones that destroyed and scattered the sheep of His pasture.

We desired not to be unequally yoked, but these pastors destroyed our faith and the only option remaining is for us to live with them of the world. Now, the Lord God has taken His anger away from us that have been destroyed and scattered, this is what makes us the residue the army of God.

People are kicking me out of their midst, and yet I am still going to join them? There is no sense in joining the people that are kicking me out of their mist. I just need to remain in the world, since they have kicked me out of their midst and God saw that I wanted to dwell in the mist of the brethren and sisters only because of Him but they refused me "And from the days of John the Baptist until now the kingdom of heaven suffereth violence, and the violent take it by force" (Matthew 11:12.) Some may think that the kingdom of heaven is bread and meat. The bible revealed to you that, "narrow is the way, which leadeth unto life" (Matthew 7:14.)

The road is narrow. Many want to use all their efforts to pass this slim road, but they cannot make it.

If the God of heaven has taken His anger from you, systematically, you are faultless. English define the word faultless as, free from guilt or blame. Also, the word faultless means perfect, spotless, clean, immaculate. Because the wages of sin is death, God did not see any need to punish you again for the sins you committed. If God did not see any need to punish you, this defines you as perfect.

Anything that leads you to commit sin, God will search the root and the cause of the sin, this is from the pastors, and He will put the blame on them and as for you, you are faultless, God will chasten you, God Himself does not see any fault in you.

When Christ comes back a second time, before you shall be taken, there shall be no single fault found in your life. Not even one fault, not even half. The bible says, "And the very God of peace sanctify you wholly; and I pray God your whole spirit and soul and body be preserved blameless unto the coming of our Lord Jesus Christ" (1 Thessalonians 5:23.)

Be wise and do not let anyone hang his sin in your life, so mind your business do not betray anyone, if you do not want any person around you, just go your way in peace and let the other go his or her way in peace.

Example of Maria, if Maria had left me in peace, there were

many girls in the school who are daughters of God and at least I would have found one and lived in peace with her and had a holy marriage, now I cannot marry again.

There is no room for that. I have to live like this, any sin I committed, people made me to do this. Number (1) is Maria, (2) Cali Lilja, (3) Ingrd (4) My wife that broke our marriage.

They cannot say they are innocent, you don't axe a man from the bible school, a spiritual ground because of a small thing. Do not hurt my two witnesses. This what Maria has done, she sold me out without collecting money from the teachers. My wife, you do not have the right to break your marriage.

> "Rejoice not when thine enemy
> falleth, and let not thine heart be
> glad when he stumbleth: Lest
> the LORD see it, and it displease
> him, and he turn away his wrath
> from him" (Proverb 24:17, 18.)

People like Calle Lilja, Ingrid, Maria, these are the types of humans that have jubilations over the falling of other human beings and they are happy. Maria saw me crying on her step house and she refused to ask me what was going on. She locked her door against me.

Christianity is a race, like the 100 meters Olympic. Him who runs well wins the race.

"For I say unto you, That except your righteousness shall exceed the righteousness of the scribes and Pharisees, ye shall in no case enter into the kingdom of heaven" (Matthew 5:20.) The spoken word of Jesus here is very simple.

For a pastor to kick a flock of Christ from the bible college, this is not righteousness. This is evil. And this is a woe to that pastor. Your righteousness must exceed that of your own church pastor before you enter into the kingdom of heaven. People may think that the bible is child's play, but they are wrong. Every single word written in the bible must come to pass. None will be lost. If any word is lost from the bible, please do not ever call me a prophet.

What God will do now is to counsel this broken heart. Do you expect God to destroy such a soul that has been destroyed and damaged by these preachers? If you want God to destroy such a soul, then you are evil and God is holy.

The flock of Christ that has been scattered and destroyed, these are the stones the builder rejected. God will make them as a corner stone: these are the ones that will sit on the throne with God in white to judge the world in the last day.

For me to marry an unbeliever, this is prophetic, I went in a wrong direction, exactly what the bible says, there is no energy in me again and fall backward, and be broken, and snared, and taken." I had my calling and I enrolled in the bible college to be a minister, but I fell backward, broken, snared and taken.

If your faith is ruined, this can make you get married to a Jezebel. Married or have a relationship with a person that is a killer. We know what is happening in our world. A world of mystery. Some of the women will be pregnant, even a man will have a child with you, yet they are on mission to track you down. But a divine man is a divine man.

You cannot track a divine man, by appearance and behaviour you will misjudge him, and you may even call him a sinner. They that have been predestined, their body chemistry and the world is not the same. A divine man, anything you do with him, be honest and truthful, this is for your own safety.

If you play any kind of game with a divine man, that thing you have that makes you work on people will be taken from you. You will totally ruin your own life and you will never be the same again for ever, and at the end, you will not see any fault in the hands of a divine man, body chemistries are different. There is a mystery in the life of a divine man that you cannot tap into. And this mystery, the wisdom of Christ hidden in them. If you wish evil on a divine man, it turns to good, and you destroy yourself.

There is nothing like multiple repentance. Multiple repentance is not in the bible, repentance only happens once in your life time, if you repent twice or multiple times, this is an error. You do not know God. And the wages of sin is death.

Chastening happened to the prophets, their sufferings in captivity, God has taken away His anger from them and they will not face judgment. Then, for the ordinary believer, you will face the normal judgment because the scriptures will be fulfilled. Except God has chastened you.

God only recognises your first repentance; you cannot be born again twice or undergo water baptism twice. "And as it is appointed unto men once to die, but after this the judgment:" (Hebrews 9:27.) "behold, now is the accepted time; behold, now is the day of salvation" (2 Corinthians 6:2b.) Did you see twice here?

If you repent more than one time, you are classified as an unbeliever, there is no difference between you and him. Except you end up as a hypocrites. The unbeliever's case is black, one colour, these are sinners and they have already be condemned. And you cannot be black and white at same time.

The angels in heaven rejoice when a sinner repents and come to God and they do it once and not twice. You expect angels in heaven to be rejoicing for a single soul repenting every day? You repent today, tomorrow you repent, next tomorrow you repent, next coming week you repent, next month, next year you keep on repenting and repenting, please.

You see yourself hungry and thirsty after righteousness, but in surprise you see yourself committing a sin, you have to carefully check and ask why? With wisdom, you will see the fault. If you are snared by someone, God is holding such a soul responsible for any sin you have committed. What God will do is to chasten you because He loves you. And the chastening of God will strengthen you and yield good fruit.

Salvation has a process, when some received the word of God, they like it and they accept it and they rejoice over it, but did not put the word of God into practice, this capability is not in them. This is the reason why they repent continually.

Nonstop repentance. This category of human beings, what will come out of their mouth is that, no one is perfect, everybody is a sinner because they lack knowledge.

To say no one is perfect is unbiblical, the mystery of God does not work this way. There is no darkness in God. All the prophets in the bible from Genesis to Revelation, their message is, be established in righteousness, or do not let any fault be found in you when Christ comes back. Be unblameable. There was no single fault found in any of the apostles, their speeches were perfect and there was no fault in it. They were perfect, even the ancient prophets.

Not that the prophets did not sin, they sinned against God, but the bottom line is that they repented once and for all, there was no second repentance found in the lives of the prophets.

My life is truth and I do not believe in secrets. I do my things openly and you see with your naked eyes. Why should I hide myself?

Christ died once. He did not die twice. Like in my case, I repented once. After I repented, I heard the voices of angels in heaven as they were singing, it was amazing. After that, I moved to answer my calling by enrolling in the bible college Liverts ord, Uppsala, and they chased me from the house of God to end up in the night clubs and parties. In accordance to the prophecies of Jeremiah, "Woe be unto the pastors that destroy scatter the sheep of my pasture! saith the LORD". You can see clearly how I was destroyed.

For example, if you see me at night parties rolling and you say to me how can a prophet of God do these things? I will tell you that I was chased from the house of God. Period.

Get the understanding that devil will accuse you before our God in heaven, this is what he does. The prophets already revealed in the bible that the pastors will scatter the sheep of His pastures to a wrong direction, so when you see an elect of God as a scattered sheep rolling in nights parties with the girls you should remember the prophecies of Jeremiah, Isaiah and Daniel.

This is what that has been spoken. And Satan has no room

to accuse any of the elect. If you did not chase him from the bible college, there is no way he will be rolling, you kept him there. You cannot change prophecy. If you condemn any of His elect, you will be condemned.

In the bible, no single word shall be lost. When you ask somebody to leave a gathering in the name of God, where do you expect him to go? Thank God that he is still alive.

What do you understand by night parties, discos and much more? The people that go to these places are people that have no joy, they are searching for it, they go there if they can find. The greatest joy on earth is Christ.

When you have Christ, the joy is unspeakable. They that do not have Christ cannot understand what I am talking about. I have met dozens of girls in the night parties that live their normal life, they have one message: I am empty. If you begin to laugh at this ones, then, God will take away His anger from them and in the last day they will be established.

Many may quote that, "do not be unequally yoked with the unbelievers", but I will tell you that, that is what you have read, but you did not see anything.

Christ is Big, it is an error for anyone to think that is easy to find Him. Except Him or His Father called you, you cannot partake. Jesus is out to give to them who are thirsty, they that are empty, He will fill them with a joy that they cannot bear. Wealth does not give joy, technology does not give joy, is only Christ that can fill you up with that joy.

Some have their definition of their righteousness different from that of God. When I was in the bible college I did not steal, neither did I defraud any human being, I did not commit fornication when I was in the bible college, no man or woman will say I abused him or her and no underage girl will come out and say I, Thomas Bayo slept with her in Sweden and anywhere else in the world. I left all what I was doing to answer my calling, yet I was asked to leave the school. At a time in my life, I gave all what I had to the poor. As an African man in Europe, I woke up one morning and I saw that I had many properties, I saw myself rich in the midst of poor people who do not have. I gave everything I had in life to the poor, I was only left with my electronics and my belt, so that my trouser, what the American calls pant, does not fall off my waist.

Not because my belt was Fendi, because I normally use quality products and I needed the electronic radio to listen to news. Everybody marvelled at what I did, the people I gave all my things to thought maybe I was going back home, I told them no. To them, it was unbelievable; they were all shocked. I did not know what I had done, the news went far beyond what I thought.

The people that I did not even know told me what I had done, that I gave all what I had to the poor, I emptied my financial account and all went to the poor. I am not a liar, God is my witness and the Holy Ghost bears me witness, there are witnesses that saw this and they can stand for me at any time.

I left all what I was doing to answer my calling. And at the end I was axed from a spiritual ground.

Up to this day, I am still proud of that school in Uppsala, in the sense that I love them. I know that they did not allow me to graduate, but I still continue to love some of the students, especially Caroline, a native of Stockholm, Lilibro from Norway, Mike from Kenya, Flint both from Uppsala, Fred from Nigeria, Bradford from USA and many others. My heart is pure towards them. For the time I was in Livets ord, some of them that were in school with me shall be saved in the last day with the reward of a prophet. Both the English session and the Swedish session, including some of the teachers, like the teacher that taught us the course of righteousness and the founder of that church. This is the reward of a prophet.

The family I lived with at Uppsala, especially Michelle that has a great heart and her mother Elisabeth did comfort me. My heart is in tears of love for them, I never forget them and I know that God will not forget these wonderful souls. Elisabeth's brother and his wife, their faces always sweet with a positive heart, great people that have been blessed with eternal life, their sins are remitted and they shall be saved in the last day, the door of heaven shall not be shut against them, no matter the clock. Their houses and children and all their generation shall be blessed in the Lord of heaven that created all creatures.

"And before him shall be gathered all nations: and he shall separate them one from another, as a shepherd divideth his sheep from the goats:"

And he shall set the sheep on his right hand, but the goats on the left.

Then shall the King say unto them on his right hand, Come, ye blessed of my Father, inherit the kingdom prepared for you from the foundation of the world:

For I was an hungred, and ye gave me meat: I was thirsty, and ye gave me drink: I was a stranger, and ye took me in:

Naked, and ye clothed me: I was sick, and ye visited me: I was in prison, and ye came unto me.

Then shall the righteous answer him, saying, Lord, when saw we thee an hungred, and fed thee? or thirsty, and gave thee drink?

When saw we thee a stranger, and took thee in? or naked, and clothed thee?

Or when saw we thee sick, or in prison, and came unto thee?

And the King shall answer and say unto them, Verily I say unto you, Inasmuch as ye have done it unto one of the least of these my brethren, ye have done it unto me.

Then shall he say also unto them on the left hand, Depart from me, ye cursed, into everlasting fire, prepared for the devil and his angels:

For I was an hungred, and ye gave me no meat: I was thirsty, and ye gave me no drink:

I was a stranger, and ye took me not in: naked, and ye clothed me not: sick, and in prison, and ye visited me not.

Then shall they also answer him, saying, Lord, when saw we thee an hungred, or athirst, or a stranger, or naked, or sick, or in prison, and did not minister unto thee?

Then shall he answer them, saying, Verily I say unto you, Inasmuch as ye did it not to one of the least of these, ye did it not to me.

And these shall go away into everlasting punishment: but the righteous into life eternal" (Matthew 25:31-48.)

What God is asking Livets ord is, even if you say Thomas Bayo is a bad boy, which of these teachers will have an ox fall into a pit and will not straightaway take him out? Will any of these teachers ask any of their children to quit the school? God of heaven has already pronounced His judgment: He will not forgive these people.

Here in the holy bible, this is the case between me and Livets ord/Calle Lilja and Ingrid.

"Therefore is the kingdom of heaven likened unto a certain king, which would take account of his servants.

And when he had begun to reckon, one was brought unto him, which owed him ten thousand talents.

But forasmuch as he had not to pay, his lord commanded him to be sold, and his wife, and children, and all that he had, and payment to be made.

The servant therefore fell down, and worshipped him, saying, Lord, have patience with me, and I will pay thee all.

Then the lord of that servant was moved with compassion, and loosed him, and forgave him the debt.

But the same servant went out, and found one of his fellowservants, which owed him an hundred pence: and he laid hands on him, and took him by the throat, saying, Pay me that thou owest.

And his fellowservant fell down at his feet, and besought him, saying, Have patience with me, and I will pay thee all.

And he would not: but went and cast him into prison, till he should pay the debt.

So when his fellowservants saw what was done, they were very sorry, and came and told unto their lord all that was done.

Then his lord, after that he had called him, said unto him,

O thou wicked servant, I forgave thee all that debt, because thou desiredst me:

Shouldest not thou also have had compassion on thy fellowservant, even as I had pity on thee?

And his lord was wroth, and delivered him to the tormentors, till he should pay all that was due unto him.

So likewise shall my heavenly Father do also unto you, if ye from your hearts forgive not every one his brother their trespasses" (Matthew 18:23-35.)

This is how my little strength was destroyed. I trusted these pastors so much and I was ready to lay down my life in Christ to love them, but they did evil to me, up to this day I cannot recover myself. What God said to me was that, "I know your situation; what I will do for you is to comfort you." It is the Comforter that sustains me up to this hour.

I live on this earth like the wounded, and I know that I have been totally destroyed. I am not crying anymore. If I see the power that has been given to me by God, I am just okay. It is this power that has been given to me that makes my day. I am renewed every day, the Lord God of heaven has made me His vineyard planted on the river side.

Suicide was on my mind constantly because of what Calle Lilja and Ingrid, including Maria, did to me. The voice of suicide was hitting my heart and the voice would say: "Do it. It is better for you". I could not find anyone to explain this situation to. The only hope I have today is God, He continues to Comfort me physically, if not for the physical voice of God to me, I would had given up my faith. But He continues to Comfort me and He did not reduce His strength in me, He continues to reveal secret to me and He showed me mysteries, He even revealed the date the world will end to me, the Lord God is comforting me.

The Creator gave me the keys of hell, I can go inside hell and come out. The gods that are in hell (dragons) they know what the bible says about me. They have no power in me. They even tremble when they see the power of God. They know that in the world to come, God has created me for a purpose. They know the capacity. But the world does not know.

When you talk about salvation, if you boast with it, you are wrong, the testimony you hold is what you read, and you are only close to salvation. Your salvation will depend on the judgment of Christ and of His saints. Preachers may give you any kind of sweet talk about salvation, yet you must face judgment. Everything that I have written in this book is established in heaven.

The prophet Joshua knew that the citizens of Jericho would be destroyed and no one would be left out. God gave prophets power, and this power was designed for a purpose. "And Joshua saved Rahab the harlot alive, and her father's household, and all that she had; and she dwelleth in Israel even unto this day..." (Joshua 6:25.)

The salvation of Rahab and her family depended on the prophet of God, Joshua, he could still decide that Rahab and her family should perish, and Joshua had nothing to lose. After all, you are sinner and not only that; you are citizen of Jericho destined to perish due to your wickedness. But prophets are sweet people, they are not interested in any soul perishing that is why they persuade you to do good and live, to flee from evil. God gave me power to the capacity of Jericho on the end time as the spiritual Joshua.

The physical Joshua knew when Jericho would be destroyed so I am the spiritual Joshua that will give the date of the end. When Joshua told Rahab and her family that they will live they were saved based on the will of the prophet of God, the decision o f Joshua was the decision of God.

Today, this present world is Sodom and Gomorrah. But Christ's death saved you all. The entire world, this is why you need to rejoice. But when you rejoice, do it with understanding.

"And when he had opened the fifth seal, I saw under the altar the souls of them that were slain for the word of God, and for the testimony which they held: And they cried with a loud voice, saying, How long, O Lord, holy and true, dost thou not judge and avenge our blood on them that dwell on the earth?

And white robes were given unto every one of them; and it was said unto them, that they should rest yet for a little season, until their fellow servants also and their brethren, that should be killed as they were, should be fulfilled" (Revelation 6:9-11.)

The message in the above paragraph is PATIENCE. If you are a believer, you just need to wait, for the scripture to be fulfilled. Take any suffering that humans have caused to you and do not deny your faith. It may be a great pain, depending on the area yours manifested whether through your school, in marriage and relationship, work, government, church, victim of war, abused, humiliated, friends whatever way your tears manifested, you just need to have patience. God will not skip this message for anyone, the same message He gave to the first believers is the one He has given to you and me.

The message God has given to me is simple, this physically earth is just a temporary place but the next world to come is life eternal. It has no time and it has no age, the Lord God has showed me the promises face to face, I have seen His glory face to face. This is same message that I will also give to them that believe, because I am a prophet of the living God.

If I tell some people that they have been brainwashed, some say nobody can brainwash them. Do not make me laugh.

Before any can enter into the kingdom of heaven, first, he must be brainwashed, and if he or she is not brainwashed, such cannot inherit the kingdom of heaven. You have to accept that you have been brainwashed. And God will give you the wisdom to know that you have been brainwashed and you will testify it that you have been brainwashed. You will know this on earth here first, and you will accept that you have been brainwashed.

Those who insist that they have not been brainwashed, such souls shall perish in the last day. Because the bible told you that the saints or the elect with all possibility that we all must be seduced. "For false Christs and false prophets shall rise, and shall shew signs and wonders, to seduce, if it were possible, even the elect" (Mark 13:22.)

The word 'seduce' is to draw into a wrong or foolish course

of action. Or, lure or entice away from duty, principles, or proper conduct. This is exactly what happened to me; I was drawn into a wrong course of action, they tried to entice me with their theory so that I would deny my faith and harm myself.

But now, God is using a weak thing like me to confront those that are mighty. If you are dealing with me, you are dealing with the Holy Ghost, and remember that He has no power to forgive.

Many who insist that they have not been deceived, the holy bible revealed that these shall perish in the last day. God telling you the truth, that the people you are believing are false preachers and you refused to believe Him, instead you are believing in people who are telling you lies. A strong delusion will come to you and you shall perish in the last day. You have believed in lies. Many have been deceived in the entire world.

I have seen God the Father face to face, I have seen Jesus face to face. I know the face of God and I know His shape and I know His voice and I know His power. The bible says no man has seen God at anytime. To say no man has seen God at anytime, this word has a definition, because I know that all the prophets in the holy bible they all saw God the Father face to face which makes their testimony to be true.

The prophets, is what they saw and what they heard and what they touched with their two hands they gave to the world. Let us reason together on this statement: If the prophets in the holy bible spoke and wrote about God without seeing Him, their testimony is not true and to believe them is false hope. This is also means that all what they told us is fiction because there is no truth or assurance to talk of what you did not see, however, the holy prophets, they saw God the Father face to face and He spoke with them face to face, heaven and hell were revealed to these wise men and they saw these things face to face. Some were in the physical realm, while some were in the spirit but yet they all saw the shape of God and their testimony is true and on their side salvation belong to them.

My book is based on what I have seen that I wrote down. I saw God the Father face to face and I know His voice and

I know His shape. He spoke to me face to face and He has given to a mighty revelation that I will now give to the world. But the question is, will the world believe? Exactly the spoken word of Jesus, "Verily, verily, I say unto thee, We speak that we do know, and testify that we have seen; and ye receive not our witness" (John 3:11.)

The world was not able to believe Noah. The ability to believe Lot was not found in the people, not even a single soul believed Micaiah. Prophet Micaiah told the people, let everyman return to his own house in peace, but the ability to believe him was not found in the people.

It begins to amaze me! But how could God use me, a weak thing to give such a potent revelation to the entire world?

I have seen the Holy Ghost in the physical realm, and I have seen Lucifer in the physical realm. I have written a great book.

Satan wants me dead, because I have revealed him to the world.

When God appeared to me with His glory I was not willing to be a work man and many things happened.

God revealed to me that He has hidden the message of the end in my DNA and it is me that will reveal it to the world and tell the world, the end of age. This is amazing. The date of the end is with me. Can you believe this? God used my own DNA to convince me that I am the chosen one. My own body chemistry is amazing to me when I see it visually, such a wonder.

For example, it is what you know and what you have touched or seen face to face that should be your basic doctrine, so that your testimony will be based on a solid foundation of truth. This is the ministry of all the prophets and another example is that, if you are preaching the end of the world and you did not see when the world will end, such a testimony has no truth on it.

If you are preaching and saying that nobody will know when Christ will come back to this earth a second time, this kind of preaching is based on what you have read, but you did not see anything. Did you see anything? My friend, you did not see anything, the faith you have today is the foundation of what you have read. And even the salvation you believe you are holding, you have never seen heaven and you have never seen God the Father and you do not have any idea how the shape of God looks like.

You have never seen any of the heavenly angels, all what is coming from your mouth is what you have read and what you have been told, which means that your testimony is based on hope; you hope to receive, but you have never seen it. Open your ears wide and hear this, there are no guarantees for your salvation, that does not mean that you are not qualified for salvation, in this case your salvation will depend on the judgment of God and also by your own faith. This is the perfect definition of Christianity.

They that have guarantee into the kingdom of heaven are those who are born of water and born of the Spirit, and you should see the Spirit of God live, anything about the Spirit of God is based on truth, He is a Spirit of truth. If you say you know the Holy Ghost in this generation, then you have lied and you are saying what you do not know and testify of what you have not seen. Nobody in this generation has seen the Holy Ghost, anyone who tells you that he has seen the Holy Ghost in this generation has told you a lie.

If you say you have never seen the Holy Ghost live and you have only heard of Him as written in the bible, then you are a child of God and you have said the truth. But you have never seen Him and you do not know His appearance and continue to insist that He lives in you, you shall not inherit the kingdom of God, anyone that designs a lie, such a soul is unclean and no unclean soul shall inherit the kingdom of heaven. See the complete teaching of the Holy Ghost in the chapter of the Holy Ghost.

There are two types of salvation. First, the kingdom of heaven. Secondly, the kingdom of God on this earth. The kingdom of God on this earth and the kingdom of heaven, these are salvation. God says in the bible that He will create a new heaven and a new earth. The kingdom of God on this earth is symbol of beauty and paradise.

I, Thomas Bayo, my writing regarding the end of this world is what I have seen face to face and what I have touched with my two hands, both live and spiritual as what the God of heaven did to the past prophets that I wrote down. My testimony is not based on what I have read like what you have read, what you have read is the same information you are passing to people and teaching them what you did not see.

Chapter Seven

The Holy Ghost

You have read and heard about the Holy Ghost in the bible, but "you" have not seen Him at any time. It is biblically proven that the ancient Christians saw the Holy Ghost face to face, He sat on each of them on the day of Pentecost and they were not filled with the Holy Ghost and with fire exception of the apostles.

But today, everything you have heard about the Holy Ghost is based on what you have read. And no man has seen the Holy Ghost in this generation at anytime and anywhere. You do not know the Holy Ghost and you cannot describe His form. The big question is, who is the Holy Ghost?

The Lord God of heaven gave the true believers the promise of the Holy Ghost and He fulfilled this promise. The apostles the early Christians were filled with the anointing of God.

The people that first got the baptism of the Holy Ghost were the disciples. And later, some of the early Christians were filled. God fulfilled His promised. We have the evidence as written in the Holy bible.

Before sending down the Holy Ghost, one thing He did, was that He gave a warning of the Holy Ghost, that He has no power to forgive, in this earth and in the next one to come.

Before the Lord gave the teachings on the coming of the Holy Ghost to this earth, He said that He would go to heaven first, if He didn't leave, the Holy Ghost would not come, so, He ascended to heaven and later the Holy Ghost was given to the early apostles. Meaning the Holy Ghost was not in this world before Christ was born.

The Holy Ghost lives inside the man, He does not live outside a man. He lives inside the whole body, from the hair down to the feet, even in the body chemistry, the Holy Ghost is present. However, the world does not know the Holy Ghost.

The Holy Ghost occupies the entire human body system, the body of man is the temple of the living God. So, any man that is filled with the Holy Ghost, his preaching is not from him, those words that he speaks are from the Holy Ghost and they are true. The reason is that the Holy Ghost is a Spirit of truth and He is a God that cannot lie. And to say I do not believe the word of a man who is filled with Holy Ghost is as if you do not believe the Holy Ghost and you did not believe the Creator. Everything has a result and will yield a consequence.

After some years, when the apostles were filled with the Holy Ghost and they preached the gospel of salvation, they were killed, after this period, the Holy Ghost did not dwell with anyone for a specific reason. The God of heaven allows the gospel to move on like that. Allowing the gospel to move on like that is to say salvation was still available at that time, although there was no Holy Ghost. But God did accept the faith of man and gave salvation to the world. God has His own power to give salvation, just as the Holy Ghost has His own power to give salvation, same as the Lord Jesus. Three forms that make the Godhead.

The Holy Ghost returned to the earth after more than a thousand years; He came back to the earth because of the end time and is now living in only one person, which is me Thomas Bayo, the witness of the living God, the olive tree and the candle stick.

This teaching will give a perfect explanation of the Holy Ghost. Why was the Holy Ghost given?

Now, the Holy Ghost is Power. And He is a special anointing.

The Holy Ghost will specifically dwell only with the ones that will be in thrones. And this reason is fully explained as you read on.

When the apostles were filled with this Power, they were fully guaranteed heaven, their inheritance. They were given positions in heaven.

How does a believer know that he has this Power? To know that I have the Holy Ghost and fire, it is by physical manifestation and not by dreams or by feelings. The reason why God made it this way is so that the testimony of anyone that has the Holy Ghost and fire should be true, in the sense that such a soul knows exactly what he or she is saying. The Holy Ghost is not a God that you cannot see. In the Godhead, it is only the Holy Ghost that will manifest in the physical often. The Holy Ghost does not manifest in dreams. The ministry of the Holy Ghost is based on truth, because there are dreams and voices of vanity.

There are many preachers in this world who are writing about the Holy Ghost and their writings arrived at same argument; the Holy Ghost is a person. They do not know the Holy Ghost and the Holy Ghost is not a person. If they say the Holy Ghost is a person, how are they so sure? Have they seen the Holy Ghost?

Some will say the Holy Ghost lives in me and I do not see Him. This is a false witness and you are saying what you do not know and testify of what you have not seen. And your testimony is not true. The Holy Ghost is a Spirit of truth. Jesus said, "Verily, verily, I say unto thee, We speak that we do know, and testify that we have seen; and ye receive not our witness" (John 3:11.)

If your testimony is, I believe in God but I have not seen Him, this is a blessing. But the Holy Ghost is different.

When it comes to the subject of salvation, you need not to see before you believe and this is a great blessing. Faith is to hope for something that you have not seen. And the word believe is to see what you hope for according to the will of God, but not according to your own will. But when it comes to the subject of the Holy Ghost, you must have a testimony that you have seen Him face to face, and this means that you are saying that you have seen God. Like in my case, I have seen God the Father face to face and how the revelation manifested is written in my book titled, What Do You Want? When a man has seen the Father face to face, this is not the end; you need power to say such words.

Now, the world does not know the Holy Ghost and they cannot see Him, Satan himself cannot see the Holy Ghost. There is no way. This was exactly what Jesus said in the Holy bible. The Holy Ghost is just like the wind when its blows; you only hear the sound, but you do not know where it is coming from or where it is going. So are those that are born of the Spirit of God. Many do lie that they have the Holy Ghost, but believe me, they do not have the Holy Ghost. They do not know Him and have not seen Him at anywhere and at anytime.

"And I will pray the Father, and he
shall give you another Comforter,
that he may abide with you for ever;
Even the Spirit of truth; whom the
world cannot receive, because it
Seeth him not, neither knoweth him:
but ye know him; for he dwelleth
with you, and shall be in you"
(John 14: 16, 17.)

The world cannot receive the Holy Ghost and they cannot see Him and they will not know Him. The Holy Ghost is only for them that have been destined for heaven, not for them that are not destined for heaven. Any person can come to heaven if he or she is invited by the Lord, and any person who lives in heaven is greater than the greatest person on the planet. There are certain numbers chosen that will sit with God in heaven to rule the world; these are the chosen that are filled with the Holy Ghost.

If you do not have the Holy Ghost, that does not mean that you will not inherit the kingdom of heaven when you believe in Christ, it will be only by the judgment of God that you will inherit the kingdom of heaven. As you study the word of

Jesus as written above, it gives you all the truth about the Holy Ghost. The world cannot receive the Holy Ghost. And there is no way they can see Him.

Jesus said, "for he dwelleth with you, and shall be in you." If the Holy Ghost dwells in you, you will know Him and see Him face to face, not by dream. And you will be able to describe the shape of the Holy Ghost which you have seen.

Jesus said, "that he may abide with you forever." Jesus gave you a warning about the Holy Ghost also what the prophet already told you. But the people rebelled and vexed the Holy Ghost and He was turned to be their enemy and fought against them. He did not dwell with anyone anymore. This is the reason why the Holy Ghost refused to dwell with anyone after the first apostles were killed. Because He is the Spirit of truth.

"And I will pray the Father, and
he shall give you another Comforter…"

The Holy Ghost is a Comforter in this world of evil and pains for the righteous, the Holy Ghost is the joy of God in the life of the apostles.

At first, when the disciples had not gotten the Holy Ghost, sometimes they stopped following Jesus because there was no power in them, after the Lord gave them the Holy Ghost, it was that time in their lives when they were passing through heat. Many times, they were beaten, stoned and insulted, but the Holy Ghost was acting as a Comforter to them in physical manifestation. It was because of the Holy Ghost and fire that they were ready to lay down their lives for the love of Christ. If not for the Holy Ghost, they would had not preach the gospel.

After Christ was arrested, they all scattered and went in different directions. Christ Himself appeared to them face to face after His resurrection and let them to understand that He lives forever more. To the apostles, it was awesome.

Then He gave them this power Himself and they saw Him. The Holy Ghost comforted them and gave them strength and power to move on. The gospel was preached and the whole world heard the message with power, but not with sword.

The Holy Ghost is the power of God in a man. Among one of His fruits is love.

> "And I will pray the Father, and
> he shall give you another
> Comforter, that he may abide
> with you for ever;" (John 14:16.)

Jesus did promise believers on earth the Holy Ghost, that the believers would receive the Holy Ghost and it was not a tax that the Holy Ghost must be in the world forever. The Lord Jesus used the word "may". If you are a Christian and quote verses, you should know the word may. The word, may is used to indicate measure of likelihood or possibility.

The Holy Ghost is independent and He can act on His will, since He changed His mind that He will dwell with no one again, because the people coming to the church rebelled and vexed Him. He acted on His will, being as God.

Always remember that the Holy Ghost is not influenced or controlled by others in the matter of opinion or conduct. He is not influenced by the thoughts or actions of others. If He decides that He will dwell with only two people in the entire generation, no one will influence or control Him in matters of judgment and conduct, and stop Him. And He's not a God that will be influenced at any level. You cannot force the Holy Ghost to live in you when He already hates you because you are disgusting in facing evil.

Christ Himself warned you of the Holy Ghost, the prophets also gave you the ways of the Holy Ghost ahead of time. So, when the people committed abomination by facing the east position and many other evil, God was silent, waiting to take His action as proposed in His mind. No one can hurry God to end the world quickly or destroy those that worship the evil one by facing the east position. The Holy Ghost is instant in action, which was revealed in the holy nible. He takes action immediately.

<blockquote>
"But they rebelled, and vexed his
holy Spirit: therefore he was turned
to be their enemy, and he fought
against them" (Isaiah 63:10.)
</blockquote>

This is the reason why the world did not have the Holy Ghost and fire. They vexed Him. He has no power to forgive.

The Holy Ghost is the same Spirit that lives in God the Father, the same Spirit that lives in Jesus; this is not a person. It is the same Spirit He gave to His friends. The Holy Ghost is fire.

The Holy Ghost designed Himself only to dwell with believers that are potent, these are believers you see authority of Christ in their tongue, people that have a thrilling faith, although they do not have the Holy Ghost at present since the Holy Ghost will not change His mind. It is the former believers who were filled with the Holy Ghost and with fire. However, at present, God has not provided alternatives for the believers presently on earth, since the Holy Ghost is not with anyone, except me, Thomas Bayo on this earth.

Before I continue to write of the Holy Ghost in this chapter let me take a break and use this opportunity to explain, angels live in heaven and they were all created righteous. There was no sin found in them from the beginning of time, but along the line, sin was found in some of the angels in heaven. The ones found sinful, they corrupted themselves and they became wicked.

Their actions in this wicked ways were discovered by God. That sin crossed the threshold to other angels through a senior angel known as Lucifer. This Lucifer that was in heaven was at one time a great angel.

Lucifer was given great power in heaven that is greater than some of the other angels. He was given the keys of death, it would have been more dangerous for us if that particular key of death was still with him. After the death of Christ, His immediate action was to go to hell and collect that particular key from Lucifer. For three days, Christ the Saviour was in hell and He put Satan to shame and we all were saved.

Lucifer's power was so strong that when an angel did something wrong, he held the power and the office of disciplinary action (to explain.)

A prosecutor takes charge of investigation once a crime has been committed, presents evidence at a hearing before the grand jury, and questions witnesses during the trial. The power of a prosecutor is very strong, especially when he has evidence in any crime committed. In the case of Lucifer, when he was in heaven, his power was so strong that, he could drop any case at his own will, even though there is evidence. This is excellence of a high order, also he had the power of surveillance.

However, God the Father has the final say in heaven and His throne is surrounded by twenty-four elders and the holy angel. They work with the Almighty God to look at cases with the power of judgment. God remains the Supreme, Kings of kings and the Lords of Lords. In anything the Lord God will do, It will be according to His will to present it to His cabinet before any action, since He is a righteous Father.

The bible describes the devil as wiser than a prophet; there is no secret on earth with man that can be hid from the devil. It is that power he held in heaven that remains with him, a strong power of surveillance, he knows everything you are doing on earth. Even the message that other angels will take from heaven to a prophet, he knows.

In the beginning when Lucifer was created, he was described in the bible as blessed cherubim.

> "Thou art the anointed cherub
> that covereth; and I have
> set thee so: thou wast upon the
> holy mountain of God;
> thou hast walked up and down
> in the midst of the stones

of fire"(Ezekiel 28:14, 15.)

The word cherub here is symbolic. However, this royalty that was the model figure of Lucifer has already be stripped from him, and is now chained in this earth under darkness. Now, he is the prince of this world ruling the earth under darkness. The power he holds now is a dark one.

He was a great angel in heaven, Lucifer because of his power, if angels do any wrong in heaven and if Lucifer did not charge them, they may go for.

His duty was to discourage evil, but he did the opposite; he initiated other angels and they started worshiping him and they became his angels. Meanwhile, Lucifer was created holy from the beginning, and later, sin was found in him.

The devil was a trouble to the angels in heaven, so the angels in heaven needed a Saviour. Jesus delivered them in heaven same way He delivered us here on earth from the hand of this dragon and also a lion roaming about, looking for whom he may devour.

Since Lucifer became evil, he encouraged other angels to commit sin, and they were escaping cases and punishment with his influence in heaven as senior personnel. His sin was so strong that he started to deal with the junior angels, accusing them for nothing, and bringing these innocent angels to trial, the angels were all troubled and he took their freedom from them.

Lucifer collaborated with some other senior angels and junior ones, and they rebelled and planned a takeover in heaven to be in control, Lucifer's rebellion was so strong that he made war in heaven.

You can imagine when one, and some other beings stage a war against other angels in heaven This is the reason why the God of heaven gave a command to His army, led by Angel Michael, making sure they do something like Operation Sweep. The army of God is mighty, and all the wicked angels were swept out. Now in heaven, the angels left are the holy ones.

Lucifer and his angels were defeated and ejected from heaven and they were chained under darkness in this earth.

Lucifer came and continued to kill and to destroy in this earth. This is a man that troubled the holy angels in heaven. Many on this earth have been killed by him, and he brought diseases, confusion, death and much more into this earth. The mystification of this earth is so strong that many are in confusion, and some have questioned why the world is this way. In the book of Isaiah, it is written that Lucifer is that man that shakes kingdoms and him that makes this earth tremble.

"Yet thou (Lucifer) shalt be brought down to hell, to the sides of the pit. They that see thee (Satan) shall narrowly look upon thee, and consider thee, saying, Is this the man that made the earth to tremble, that did shake kingdoms;" (Isaiah 14:16.)

This earth has been heavily troubled by him, and people are in pains with a lot of tears. Many have lost their rights and happiness has been taken from them by this man; he brought sin into this world, he has ruined the entire heritage of people, destroyed races and their lands, nations have been made totally insolvent by him. Different kinds of calamity, and many other evils he has caused to mankind. Satan is destroying with wrath.

"And there was war in heaven: Michael and his angels fought against the dragon; and the dragon fought and his angels, and prevailed not; neither was their place found any more in heaven. And the great dragon was cast out, that old serpent, called the Devil, and Satan, which deceiveth the whole world: he was cast out into the earth, and his angels were cast out with him. And I heard a loud voice saying in heaven, Now is come salvation, and strength, and the kingdom of our God, and the power of his Christ: for the accuser of our brethren is cast down, which accused them before our God day and night" (Revelation 12: 7-10.) The word accuser here is to "make a charge of wrong-doing against another".

You can see clearly that Satan has the duty of bringing charges against other angels in heaven before God. But Lucifer was making a false charge. What did not happen, he would say it happened, his works were evil before God in heaven.

Look at what the bible says here "...for the accuser of our brethren is cast down," Who are these brethren? These are the angels in heaven. The English define accuser, as to charge formally with a wrongdoing. And the word formally is defined as, being or relating to essential form or constitution.

There are laws guiding the heavenly angels and they still have penalties when found guilty of sin. They will not just be punished, there are court proceedings, evidence is needed, and these angels, the proceeding court let them see and know why they were brought to trial. Their cases are read to their ears and they have the right to say their views. The cabinet of God in heaven still take their cases into consideration, the judgment of God is righteous, the angels in heaven have passions like we on earth. They know the difference between what is good and evil. But Satan brings lies against other angels in heaven.

All the angels that are left behind in heaven were created holy and they remain holy. Their joy is full, Satan is no more in their midst. GOOD FOR THEM.

The problem is the devil. All things in this world were created in peace and in love, even this earth was a paradise with abundance of life and of beauty. But this man came to destroy everything and still remains a problem to the earth. The ones in this earth are at war with the devil, but Jesus is our Saviour. Jesus is our testimony.

Jesus brought salvation to the earth, and according to the judgment of God the Father, some of the living beings on this earth will be taken to heaven to live with the Lord God forever, while some will still be left on the earth. Christ will come and rapture the true believers.

The believers that were filled with the Holy Ghost and with fire are the ones that will hold positions in the cabinet of God in heaven. They will be equal to the angels in heaven when the kingdom of Christ has been established. Other believers will also be rapture in lieu.

In heaven, when our government has been established by Christ, we shall have duties. The angels in heaven are greater than human so this earth, they are given the keys to the kingdom of heaven. The angels in heaven are righteous.

Heavenly angels will not commit sin, not that they cannot commit sin, they will not do it and they are in peace and in harmony with God the Father. Now, since man has been created and sin was found in man, the message of repentance and obedience was given to us by God, He gave us the ten commandments to follow. So do the angels have commandments given to them by God in heaven.

God decided to send down the Holy Ghost with fire from heaven to dwell inside the believers who have strong faith. These are the ones following biblical principles and living by it. When they get to heaven, there will be no story in their lives like what happened in the past in the case of Lucifer; he committed sin in heaven, and also deceived some of the angels into making war in heaven. So in this case, the pillar of this chapter is, the Holy Ghost and fire will be a complete guidance and helper to them that will rule with Christ. The saints that will be same as the heavenly angels, there will be no way they will commit sin, since the fire of the Holy Ghost is living inside them, this fire serves as blockage to sin.

To any act of evil thought, the Holy Ghost responds immediately with fire and manifests His righteousness in the life of the man He dwells in with great love.

If Satan did not sin there would be no way the other angels would have... If the first man, Adam, did not sin, there is no way mankind would have sinned. You can see how sin entered others; it came from the top. So, God decided to block all the avenues that will cause any more sin to His holy mountains, the Holy Ghost will do this work and there is no fear that sin will enter the saints to make them behave like Lucifer.

In the kingdom that will be established, there will be no more sin, no corruption or any kind of evil activities. God will continue to live as a righteous Father in heaven forever and His saints shall rule with Him in white. Any soul that sins shall die. This is an immediate action of destruction; there will be no more grace. Now, the earth lives by grace in Jesus name.

The present government of this world rule by the sword, but the world to come shall rule with the rod of iron, not by the sword. There are differences. That is why in this world to-day, when you see the police, army, and all kinds of people in military service, there is always a gun chained to their waste or held in hands, this is what they use in ruling this world. But in the world to come, our government is not by the sword; we are not going to be killers, that is why it is not the sword; the sword kills, but the rod is another system entirely.

The kingdom that shall be given to us in Christ, God will not allow sin to take place in it. This is a symbol of beauty and joy.

God promised to create a new heaven and a new earth, so those who have sinned against our God shall remain chained under the earth. If these evil ones are allowed to live in the world to come in the mist of the good ones, terror will continue to exist, meaning there will be no peace, same tears and suffering will still take place and plagues will continue.

No need to mention these sins, the world knows all the sins, because God wrote them in the hearts of mankind. Sins shall not be found in the world to come, according to what the Father in heaven has proposed to do in His mind.

I extended the teachings of the Holy Ghost to this book, I will still continue to persuade the entire world that the Holy Ghost and fire is with no one, but only me who is the end time witness of the living God that is filled with this special anointing, because I am one of the end time witnesses of the living God.

The Holy Ghost was only given for physical manifestation, and you must see Him and know what lives in you.

As a witness of the living God, the Holy Ghost communicates with me in the physical realm, every time, in the morning, afternoon, evening and night. But this generation does not have the Holy Ghost.

But Christ has His will and He loves His church. He will rapture them that are thirsty and hungry after righteousness. They shall be filled with righteousness.

You were warned by the prophets, the Lord Jesus warned you, of the Holy Trinity, the three that form the Godhead. One will not forgive, which is the Holy Ghost. All manners of sins will be forgiven, but to sin against the Holy Ghost, He has no power to forgive, He has not done it since creation and He will not do it.

The people vexed Him and He was turned to be their enemy and fought against them. For example, see what is going on in the church today? All the true messengers of God were killed they are in the church and evil is among the good in the church.

The Holy Ghost is the God of unity and love, not the God of division and separations. I have to confess that the world does not know the power of the Holy Ghost. If the Holy Ghost lives in you, to separate from the church will not even come to your mind. The thought of separating from the church of the living God, you will personally rule it out of your mind, because you are seeing the fire of God.

The fire of the Holy Ghost in the physical realm manifests in the body and stops any plan that comes into the heart, how much more will you separate from the church and form your own system different from the will of the Holy Ghost. He cannot dwell with people who cannot exercise the love of God.

The Holy Ghost uses His fire to stop any form of going in a wrong direction. His message will always be, "do not separate, do not condemn without evidence, and do not say you are superior, but live in peace, unity and love.

If the Holy Ghost lives in a man, He helps. The Holy Ghost reads the hearts of all, including the man He lives in, if the manifestation of separation is coming to his thoughts, the Holy Ghost will simply use His fire in physical manifestation to stop that thought. The Holy Ghost does not speak with an audible voice. The apostles in the bible saw this power and they all quivered. The apostles, they know the power of God, they were men filled with the Holy Ghost.

When the Holy Ghost manifested His power before the prophets which are the apostles, they knew the power of God. The Holy Ghost is the power of God and the prophets they warned "eat your bread with trembling and drink your water with carefulness". This is not fiction; this is what they have seen and what they were instructed to do. With fear and trembling, Noah did build that Ark. Knowing within himself and his family that all that dwelt on the face of earth would perish by flood.

But the people of the world did not believe that they would perish by flood in the time of Noah, within themselves, it was nonsense to them and they refused to repent and believe. If the people had believed and repented, God is good and faithful.

Meanwhile, all the people were doing their own thing, the false prophets and prophetesses were doing their own thing, scientists where doing their own thing, the killers were doing their own thing and much more of the people were doing their own thing but they all perished. The most important thing is that they were told what would happen to them. The word of God is true.

There are advantages and disadvantages in the human civilisation, the wise will carefully survey the disadvantage of modern civilisation; what shall it profit me? And flee from it. But the unwise will not survey. And the peril that is coming ahead as revealed and spoken by many prophets, the earth shall reel to and fro like a drunkard, and shall be removed like a cottage; and the transgression thereof shall be heavy upon it; and it shall fall, and not rise again.

Even I, Thomas Bayo whom God has ordained, the fire that will come upon this earth, I have personally seen it, I touched it in the physical realm and I wailed.

It was this fire that I touched and saw that made me fully repent. You should know that I saw something; they that know me understand perfectly that my repentance gave me a surprise wrap up and I glorify God that I gave up sin.

Words are not enough to explain the Holy Ghost in this book, but I did my best to write what I know, because the teaching of the Holy Ghost is beyond writing.

When I got the Holy Ghost, I told God in prayer that He will never see me again doing a wrong thing. And that I love Him. It is not by telling God that I will never, never do the wrong thing that I have been established to live without fault, it is the Holy Ghost in my life that is doing the work, that made me able not to commit evil again. I may say today that I will not sin, but tomorrow I may be seduced and tempted to commit sin, but this will not happen because the Holy Ghost has blocked all.

There is no way evil will pass into me. It is this ability that I have that makes me tell believers to be established in righteousness. This is the Holy Ghost power. Some pastors will say to you that nobody is perfect, because they do not know the power of God. God can establish you in righteousness and make you perfect as Himself when you are thirsty and hungry after righteousness; you shall be filled. But when you are not thirsty and hungry for it, there is no way you can be filled.

The Holy Ghost has made me above temptation and seduction. God knows right well that I have no power to stop sin, so He gave me the Holy Ghost as a helper and the Holy Ghost used His fire to block all future evil. This is the power of God. What God is interested in mostly is, be hungry and thirsty after righteousness and you shall be filled. He knows what to do, but you have to make the first move.

When the world hears the word 'repent' and they are not afraid. Because they have not seen the Holy Ghost at any time, neither do they know His power.

If you have not seen the Holy Ghost, it becomes a sin to

write a Christian book, because such a book has no truth. All those that say "I am an author" and have published a Christian book in their names will face a dreaded judgment, their works have made the works of God of non effect. This is how they transgressed the commandments of God with their tradition. All these commandments are written in the Holy Book. As for me, I praise our God in heaven for His love towards me and for giving me this power.

The apostles, they touched this power, they felt it, they saw it face to face and their message was: fear God. When Jesus Christ opened His mouth and spoke to the people that, "And if thine eye offend thee, pluck it out, and cast it from thee: it is better for thee to enter into life with one eye, rather than having two eyes to be cast into hell fire" (Matthew 18:9.)

If you survey the words of the apostles and study their lifestyle, some of them were dumbstruck, and from their bowels, they could not explain what they had seen.

Some of the prophets, when God instructed them to go and tell the people what they had seen, some did not even know what to say and what to do. Some, their response always was, "how can they believe me? How can these people believe me?" Some even ruled it out of their minds that the people would believe. God would always encourage His prophets with love to go forward and tell the people to repent or they would be destroyed. The prophets did not have their own private message for anyone, they acted on what the heavenly Father asked them to do. This takes my mind back to the Greatest Prophecy of all time spoken by Jesus in the chapter of this book.

After prophet Daniel saw a vision, the bible declared that he fainted and was sick for some certain days. "And I Daniel fainted, and was sick certain days; afterward I rose up, and did the king's business; and I was astonished at the vision, but none understood it" (Da:8:27.)

Even in my experience, when I saw only the seventh trumpet that sounded in a revelation given to m, I was shaking and I ran into cold in the midnight in the heart of Stockholm city.

I have witnesses; Theo was one of my witnesses and his wife. I ran outside into the cold directly from the bed. I ran out in my sleeping clothes in winter. Yet I was still shaking very mightily. This time, the Holy Ghost had not be given to me, I only feared God at this time in Stockholm. I had not even experienced that power of God.

The day the Holy Ghost was given to me directly from Jesus Himself, my mouth was opened wide and He put His breath inside me. I was filled, power given to me, and after some time this power started showing Himself to me. This power that is living inside me revealed Himself to me face to face, a wonder. I nearly told God that He should remove the Holy Ghost from me, that it is too mighty in me. It was fear that made me accept the Holy Ghost, because I had not known Him.

The Holy Ghost is a wise God; He knew that I was afraid and He started telling me that He would not consume me. That I am beloved. He is the anointing of God in me and I would soon be used to Him. After I got to understand the Holy Ghost, this power all the revelations revealed to me, this is the power that make this book and all my books. When the God of heaven gave me this power, I never knew what this power was all about, but later He lectured me slowly.

He told me that this power, which He has given to me, has the capability to destroy this earth with plagues. This power is given to me based on (Revelation 11: 3-6.)

But today, after many years, I am used to the Holy Ghost living in me and I know Him as the yummy lollies of all yummy lollies and the sweetest of any sweet. There is nothing sweeter than power, with this power everything created by the Creator is under this power, based on (Revelation 11: 3-6.) Keys of heaven have been given to me and the keys of hell have been given to me. Power is given to me to change water to blood, and it rained not in the days of our prophesies: when I see this power that lives in me, my thought is, my enemies' days are numbered. This is difficult to explain, but I pray for the saints on this earth.

With the message of a prophet, nations and people have repented when they heard the warning alarm of the prophets. An example is Nineveh; they repented and the Lord God of heaven did not destroy them. Sodom and Gomorrah did not repent and they were destroyed. If you obey the voice of the Lord God, you shall live and not see death.

The Holy Ghost, He only communicates with fire, but not with physical voice of any form, not in audio voice and His communication is clear to understand. A fire that you can touch and feel and you can also quench it, depending on the condition of the fire. This is why Paul told you "quench not the fire of the Holy Ghost". This is a fire that has been treated in the body of the apostles.

The people rebelled and vexed the Holy Ghost and He decided not to dwell with anyone. And God brought one alternative, however, He still continued to help His children, because The Lord said He will be with you even to the end.

As I have explained before, the Holy Ghost does not dwell with anyone anymore, and no one in this world knows the manifestation of the Holy Ghost because you have not seen Him at any time. That is why many preachers preach on the pulpit, telling you the Holy Ghost cannot be seen and you just believe them, some even say that they have seen the Holy Ghost and He is a person, but they say what they do not know and testify of what they have not seen.

Before the first brethren were filled with the Holy Ghost, they repented and were fully established in righteousness, they were pure in the heart and they chose to follow the perfect truth. Even though they were sinners, they repented and the Holy Ghost filled them and He will ever live with them.

The people rebelled and vexed Him and He has no power to change His mind, He was turned to be their enemy and He fought against them.

"Now when they had gone throughout Phrygia and the region

of Galatia, and were forbidden of the Holy Ghost to preach the word in Asia (Act 16:5.)

There is a language used in the bible here "forbidden". The word forbidden here is to refuse or prohibit. People do not know the mystery behind this verse.

The language used by the Holy Ghost here is very simple, forbidden meaning He refused to give salvation to Asians. If your ethnic origin is from Asia, the Holy Ghost does not have any business with you. The Holy Ghost hates these people.

The Holy Ghost will not give salvation to Asians in this world and the one to come. This is His decision and His decision is not hidden, it was boldly written in the holy bible that the Holy Ghost forbids preaching the word in Asia. This is hard talk. The mystery is revealed here in this book.

I believe that the Christians in the Asian continent of the world are predestined to have salvation through Christ, and I praise the Lord for their lives. The Holy Ghost spoke to apostle Paul not to go Asia to preach the gospel; this is His judgment.

The Asians may qualified for salvation. The salvation for the Asians is the normal salvation that is general for the whole world, that anyone can have in accordance to John 3:16, since they are among the population of this world. They are human beings like Africans, Europeans, and Americans. The Holy Ghost has seen ahead of time the faith of the Asians, and He made His judgment toward them.

Asia is located on the east side. The Holy Ghost will never live where there is confusion because His judgment is irrevocable; He is the God of consuming fire. Before apostle Paul could make any move on any mission trip, the Holy Ghost had seen ahead what was going to happen to him and he had seen the evil deeds of the people.

Even the Holy Ghost used another brother who was a prophet to inform Paul of what would happen to him in Jerusalem as he was going to celebrate the day of Pentecost.

"....were forbidden of the Holy Ghost to preach the word in Asia."

To command someone not to do something. Does it mean that the Holy Ghost does not like the Asians or He loves only the Europeans or the Africans? The basic principle or the fruit of the Holy Ghost is love and peace. The Holy Ghost loves all people, depending on if they vex Him or not, because He fights back and He makes enemies, forever.

The Holy Ghost will give salvation, Jesus will give salvation and God the Father will give salvation at their own will. The Holy Ghost has the power to cancel your salvation and will not forgive when you vex Him. When God gives, He does not take back. The salvation that has been cancelled by the Holy Ghost cannot come back again, His judgment cannot be cancel. This is why the Holy Ghost does not just fill people anyhow; the Holy Ghost is power, the special anointing of God.

When the Holy Ghost has spoken that one of His apostle should not preach the gospel in Asia, this judgment is eternal. Any person filled with Holy Ghost will not preach the gospel on the continents of Asia forever. The Holy Ghost has no power to change His mind.

The Holy Ghost has seen the error of the Asians and He commanded the apostles not go and preach His word in Asia. He will not reveal Himself to them in Asia, the people of Asia will not see Him face to face.

When you look at the world around today, Asia is located in the east position of the earth, among the mystification on this earth today are from these locations. The highest bomb blast on earth are from this location. Even a high number of suicide bombers on earth are from one region, the east position of the earth. War that threatens this world today is from that location. What relationship does the Holy Ghost have with suicide bombers? And what is special to Him in this location? The Holy Ghost does not make friends with people that have blood on their hands. God did make man His friend.

Any brutal bombing that has occurred in the north, south and west in this earth if you take time and trace the origin, you will find out that the easterners are involved or the ideology of the east has been planted. Every year, suicide bombers are born with same bloodline. Evildoers have no borders.

Jesus can go to Asia and give to them salvation, that is the power of the Lord Jesus since He controls the earth and heaven, and has the keys of hell. He will give to whom He wishes, but the Holy Ghost will not go to Asia and His apostles will not go to Asia to preach the word.

They that are filled with the Holy Ghost may pay visits to friends in Asia, go for holidays or any other activity, but to preach the word of God by a man filled with the Holy Ghost, this is forbidden.

You can go and preach the word of God in Asia, this is not a problem, but an apostle who is filled with this fire will not go and preach the word in Asia. The Holy Ghost has spoken and He has spoken.

The dove is a symbol of peace. And the dove remains the trademark or symbol of the Holy Ghost. Peace, Peace, Peace. The greatest love on earth is the fruit of the Holy Ghost. The fruit of the Holy Spirit is joy, love, peace, gentleness, goodness, long-suffering, faith, meekness, temperance.

If you sin against Jesus, you will be forgiven, sin against God you will be forgiven, Jesus will give salvation to the Asia, God will give salvation to Asia. But the Holy Ghost will not reveal Himself in Asia.

Asia is an example, the apostles were forbidden to preach the word in Asia. He did it to Asia and He has done it to the world now because, the people rebelled and vexed Him and He was turned to be their enemies and He fought against them. The Holy Ghost will reveal the truth to them, but man will not believe.

Human beings are executed in Asia on an industrial scale, this is in the east position of the earth. The only continent on earth where there is no human execution is Europe. The whole of Europe. The Holy Ghost is peace and cannot dwell in any other continent more than Europe. People may not know who the Holy Ghost is. The Holy Ghost filled me in Europe.

You have read of Him and but you have not seen Him in this generation at anytime. The Holy Ghost is God dwelling in man, and this is the presence of God on earth. The place the Holy Ghost will dwell must be a peaceful place.

Where there are religious riots and deaths, suicide, war, bombs, death penalties, unstable leadership, abuse of human rights, uneducated human beings, killing yourself in the name of God, (which He did not command you to do) and much more, the Holy Ghost will not dwell in such places. The Holy Ghost is a gentle Spirit. I did not come to Europe on my own; He brought me to Europe to live.

Even in Africa, the east position of this continent is hell. Human devastation, famine, war, drought, and many calamities have been in this area for ages. War never ends in this place, it continues raging for generations. The Holy Ghost will not dwell in such places, and He will not reveal Himself in such places.

Africa's severe problem today is the east position of this continent. The worst human catastrophe that has ever existed in Africa is linked to the east. Europe is not like this.

Zones that the Holy Ghost forbids are these type; can you establish peace there? Jesus will give to them salvation according to His will, and God the Father will give salvation to them according to His will. But when you come to the will of the Holy Ghost, He will not go to such places, like the way He commanded His apostles not to go to Asia.

History has shown that the west, north and south have not succeeded in establishing autonomy in Asia, and in the end, they all pulled out; who will break the record? And who will establish peace in hell? They refused to accept autonomy. Not that the Holy Ghost went there and later pulled out, He did not even go there at all and told His prophet not to go there to preach the gospel. Do not go to Asia, for it is forbidden.

But it is possible that the north, south and west will destroy massively in this east because hell is located in that zone. Study the four angels chained in river Euphrates, the holy bible is revealing to you that hell is there, and it will be there. Where there is prison, that is where offenders are kept and chained. Then, you want the Holy Ghost to go there to live? Reason twice. Please.

All the heavenly angels that sinned against God, they were dealt with and dropped in Asia. This is the east part of the earth. That area is reserved already. "And I hated Esau, and laid his mountain and his heritage waste for the dragon of the wilderness" (Malachi 1:3.) The word "dragon" here refers to the fallen angels. These are the old serpents.

You have to study the entire Europe. What the north Europe, south Europe and west Europe have to offer to east Europe. The East fell and they are trying to get up. Study the ways of the easterners; there are differences between the north, west and south.

This is what God Himself said very plainly. I will make the north courtiers great. Even if the east will rise, it is by the power of the north. If the east position is rising, this is because of the end.

The heavenly Father revealed Himself to me twice; the first time was when I was in Nigeria, and secondly when I was in Sweden. But there are differences; He gave me a divine visit in Nigeria and revealed Himself to me plainly and showed me His glory. In Sweden, it happened in Stockholm that heaven was opened and I saw the throne of God, the entrance of heaven is geographically located in Sweden. This is the place where I saw the Almighty. His body was like precious stones from His hair to His feet.

God did not appear to me just like that, it happened in the capital city of Nigeria, Lagos, this is for a specific reason. At this time, Lagos was the capital.

God did not speak to me in the place where I grew up. It happened in Lagos. With His sparkling garment down to the feet. The words that came out of His mouth were, "I appeared unto you" His voice is like a mighty sound of a roaring waterfall. Eyes like fire uniformed as a high voltage electronic.

Only God the Father has eyes like fire, no other being. That is His first identity, when you look at Him, you must fall down to the ground. Next, He speaks to you. This was what happened to all the prophets. This is because He is revealing Himself to a prophet to see Him face to face.

If the God of heaven is giving a message through anyone, what He does is that He wires the ear like a wireless telephone line, He speaks and he hears Him and no one else will hear him because the ear has been invisibly wired. This is how He spoke to all the prophets and they gave you the holy bible. So, He speaks to His prophet on earth from heaven and does not need to come down. But for Him to come down from His throne in heaven to visit a man, this is a divine visit.

In Sweden, I lived in Uppsala; all the time I lived in Uppsala I never heard the voice of God. One day, as I went to Stockholm, that was when He revealed His own throne for me to see. Heaven opened and I saw Him on His throne like a precious stone with the shape like a man, all surrounded with righteousness.

In reference to the Holy Ghost, I lived in Austria in the town of Suben, Krems, but the Holy Ghost revealed Himself to me in Vienna, not even Suben, or Krems, it happened in the capital city.

Jesus said to the apostles that they should not depart from Jerusalem, because they would receive power after the Holy Ghost is upon them, as promised by the Father. The capital city is the core when it comes in dealing with powers from heaven.

When God is revealing His glory to His prophets and speaking to them, He chooses to reveal Himself in the stronghold of that nation, the capital city. He will not come and reveal Himself and His glory in a non-stronghold city. The head of any nation is the capital city. God will dwell in the head but not the tail. If you know the meaning of Almighty, you will have a perfect understanding that God is Big. He remains the Biggest forever! As you read on, you will know the mystery of how God appeared to people in a specific places not just any place.

The Holy Ghost is the glory of God, the past brethren, they that have seen the Holy Ghost have seen God the Father. If you say you have seen the Holy Ghost, you are saying you have seen God the Father, but it is not good to lie. Tell the truth that you have not seen the Holy Ghost, and God knows how to take care of your salvation. Let your testimony be true. We have One God, not two.

When the Holy Ghost came to dwell with the apostles at the first time, Jesus explained more about the Holy Ghost to them, a very sound lesson, and His teachings were perfectly recorded in the bible, which was also written in the Acts of the apostles: "But ye shall receive power..."

"And, being assembled together
with them commanded them
that they should not depart
from Jerusalem, but wait for
the promise of the Father, which,
saith he, ye have heard of me.
For John truly baptized with
water; but ye shall be baptized
with the Holy Ghost not many
days hence. When they therefore
were come together, they asked
of him, saying, Lord, wilt thou at
this time restore again the kingdom
to Israel? And he said unto them,
It is not for you to know the times
or the seasons, which the Father
hath put in his own power. But ye
shall receive power, after that the
Holy Ghost is come upon you:
and ye shall be witnesses
unto me both in Jerusalem,

and in all Judaea, and in Samaria,
and unto the uttermost part of the earth"
(Act 1:4-8.)

The Lord commanded them not to depart from Jerusalem; this was the place where the Holy Ghost revealed Himself to the first Christians and they saw Him face to face and their testimonies were true. The Holy Ghost is not a Spirit of lie.

"commanded them that they should
not depart from Jerusalem."

Jerusalem was the capital city of Israel. If the Holy Ghost is coming from heaven to the earth in any nation, He is coming directly to the capital city.

There are certain sins a man may commit and God may over look it with His love and establish such a one in righteousness based on his repentance. But using the name of God in vain? What you did not see, saying you saw it.

The Holy Ghost's ministry is based on bodily manifestation. Christians who have strong faith the bible called them the elect, these are the saints and shall be as the heavenly angels to come. God has already protected them.

The first angels are the citizens of heaven and the old angels are now the fallen ones.

The Holy Ghost appeared and revealed Himself to the apostles in the stronghold of Israel Jerusalem. The initial Gentiles that had salvation were The Arabian Christians, Africans and Europeans, this is boldly written in the bible. This was a man that had tremendous faith, Cornelius.

Another place the Holy Ghost revealed Himself was in Europe, when you survey it with biblical knowledge. "And the night following the Lord stood by him, and said, Be of good cheer, Paul: for as thou hast testified of me in Jerusalem, so must thou bear witness also at Rome." (Acts 23:11.)

"To all that be in Rome, beloved of God, called to be Saints:

Grace to you and peace from God our Father, and the Lord Jesus Christ." While the Lord Jesus designed salvation for the Asians.

The Holy Ghost located peace in this zone and He dwelled with the saints in this place, this was in the time past but not at present.

You do not need to be afraid, when Jesus has given you salvation, you are saved indeed. There is song that says, there is nothing the Lord cannot do.

God Almighty, Jesus is God in flesh, Jesus will appear to a man anywhere and in any mood, because He is God the Son Omnipresent. While God the Father will chose a position to reveal Himself to His prophet.

In the past, when the Lord God of heaven revealed Himself to His prophets, He was on the top, not the bottom. Even Moses, God took him to Mount Sinai and spoke to him.

> "And Mount Sinai was altogether
> on a smoke, because the LORD
> descended upon it in fire: and the
> smoke thereof ascended as the
> smoke of a furnace, and the
> whole mount quaked greatly".
> (Exodus 19:18.)

God is a consuming fire. When God revealed Himself to Moses, it was in a special place, not just any place. God the Father will not go to the wilderness, such an ugly place and reveal Himself and His glory on a transit ground to women and men that were stripping naked.

The Holy Ghost is a mighty fire. When the Holy Ghost reveals Himself, His appearance is fire, and He is God. If any man sees the Holy Ghost physically, there is something that will happen immediately.

Unbelievers cannot see the Holy Ghost and live; in fact there is no way an unbeliever will see the Holy Ghost, to see the Holy Ghost is a great blessing.

He will not even show Himself to flesh and blood, so there is no way the world will see Him. When the people saw the Holy Ghost descending from heaven like the dove in river Jordan, they were baptised and they did repent.

They were not filled with this power, they only saw Him and they testified of it, and their witnesses are true. In River Jordan, the sermon of repentance was from a truthful mouth, it came from a genuine prophet and they were saved already because they believed the prophet of God who was John the Baptist.

Nobody was filled with the Holy Ghost and with fire in river Jordan when John baptised them. They only saw Him.

The Holy Ghost is not a person but a fire, and He is the glory and power of God, Moses saw the glory and the power of God. What did you think Moses saw? And Mount Sinai was altogether on a smoke, because the LORD descended upon it in fire: and the smoke thereof ascended as the smoke of a furnace, and the whole mount quaked greatly".

If Moses saw any shape of a human being, it must have been God or an angel. But the glory of God was revealed to him. Have you ever seen the glory of God? Can you imagine seeing fire on a smoke of furnace and the entire mount will quake greatly? You have only read of the Holy Ghost, but you have not seen Him.

It is only God the Father that has a unique voice, and no creature on earth and in heaven can replicate His voice. Secondly, no creature in heaven and on earth has the eyes of God and no one can replicate His eyes. His eyes are of light and fire. You can replicate colour in the eyes, but you cannot counterfeit fire in the eyes.

Angels do not have these eyes and voice like that of God. God has two voices as we humans have two voices. When a human being speaks in a normal mood, his voice is different from when he gets angry; the voice will change to another tune.

The normal voice of God is as the sound of roaring waterfall, and when God is speaking with His authority or gets angry, His voice will change to another melody and it is like the sound of many and great trumpets. The Lord God rebuked Satan in my presence when I was in jail in Austria. And His voice was like the sound of many trumpets.

The Voice of God is good; I love it so much. God rebuked Satan in my presence, the prison where I was kept was fenced round spiritually. He was trying to come in with a great force, but he was rebuked. Complete details of this is in my book titled, What Do You Want?

When God appeared to me the first time, His voice was like the sound of roaring waterfall. This is His normal voice. When God appeared to me in Nigeria, He spoke to me with His normal voice. In the book of Revelations in the bible, the tune of God was an action tune when He was speaking to John regarding the seven churches and regarding the end of the world. This is serious issue. His voice was recorded as the voice of a great trumpet.

God is protecting us the true believers every day from the hands of the enemy, but you cannot see it. He continues to guide His children spiritually.

God opened my eyes to see and I heard revelations, He has made me His servant, a chosen one in all the earth in the midst of billions of people. He has chosen me and saved me from the hands of the enemy.

The voice of angels, how does it sounds? When I gave my life to Christ, I was absent in the body and present in the spirit, this was when I heard voices of angels singing, and the tune of the song was like rejoicing, this was exactly what I heard:

Blessed be thy name,
Blessed by thy name,
Blessed be thy name
O' Lord, Alleluia!

The voice of angels has no filter, it is like the air. Their voice is glorious. Humans do not have voices compared to the ones of the angels I heard. I thought humans had voices, but after I heard the voice of angels, I changed my mind.

The greatest human voice on earth compared to the voice of an angel is sad. The voice of heavenly angels are golden and full of life and joy. This is exactly what the Lord says as written in the scriptures,

> "I say unto you, that likewise joy
> shall be in heaven over one sinner
> that repenteth, more than over ninety
> and nine just persons, which need no
> repentance"(Luke 15:7.)

Some people thought in their heart that I was bad boy, people like Calle Lilja and Ingrid, but I repented, the Lord had pity on me in the mist of multitudes of people who are just. When Calle Lilja and his wife Ingrid kicked me out of bible college thinking I was a bad guy, the faithful Father had favour on me and saved me from the pit. A missing sheep that fell into a gutter. However, I was a lost and found sheep and I am not ashamed of the gospel. Apostle Paul said,

> "For I am not ashamed of the gospel of Christ:
> for it is the power of God unto salvation
> to every one that believeth; to the Jew first,
> and also to the Greek" (Romans 1:16.)

It is what I know that I will say, this generation is a blessed generation that will see the return of Christ. This is what the world has been waiting for.

In the time of the early apostles, not all the Christians were filled with the Holy Ghost and with fire in the church.

"Then Peter said unto her, How is it that ye have agreed together to tempt the Spirit of the Lord?" This word came from one apostle of Jesus by name Peter, when he questioned a woman with her husband. These were Ananias and Sapphira, this account was recorded in the holy bible.

These were the kinds of people who were attending the church in the time of the early apostles, and the fact is that these categories of church attendants have not given up their evil desires, there are still many of them in the church up to this hour, they outwardly look like genuine believers, but inwardly they are not. In another case, these have increased rapidly in the church and this is one of the reasons why the Holy Ghost left their midst; the people refused to repent.

This was not the first time Ananias and Sapphira were in the church; they had been attending this church.

When I was studying the holy bible and vitally surveyed what happened between Ananias and Sapphira, I asked myself, did Ananias and Sapphira know what they were doing? To tempt the Spirit of the Lord?

And you have not sinned against the Holy Ghost. No man has sinned against the Holy Ghost in this world because he is not present.

"If my people, which are called by my name, shall humble themselves, and pray, and seek my face, and turn from their wicked ways; then will I hear from heaven, and will forgive their sin, and will heal their land" (2 Chronicle 7:14.)

Revelation is a very common thing that may even happen to a child. The big deal is, how authentic is the revelation you have seen? There are dreams and voices of vanities. Who will confirm your revelation as genuine and true? Satan is so equipped that he has the power to deceive; he can also give revelations to his children as a means to deceive.

Have you ever seen the Holy Ghost in the physical realm to verify those revelations? No.

This is the Holy Ghost that will authenticate all revelations as true, because He uses His fire to try it to know if what you have is false or not. He also uses His fire to purify revelations as seven times tried in the furnace of fire.

When you smell with the nose, you can sense how bright the smell is, the bible revealed that there are many false-christ in the world and we should try it to see if it is a true Spirit.

When Jesus appeared to me, I believed Him, meanwhile, at this time, the Holy Ghost had not be given to me to try the revelation with His fire, if it is false or not. Through hugging and feelings by scent of perfect righteousness in the body of the Lord, I was able to identify the truth. Since there are many voices and dream of vanities, I believe Jesus, coupled with the background and revelations given to me by the heavenly Father that involved Maria, which I saw ahead and what I was doing, seeing the revelation of the end and much more.

God revealed to me that I am His end time witness who will announce the coming of Jesus for the rapture. In accordance to what prophet Zechariah wrote in the Holy bible that it is I, (Thomas Bayo) who:

"shall bring forth the headstone thereof
with shoutings, crying Grace, grace unto it."

The truth is that in all my revelations, tears are always in my face. Without the power given to me, I cannot do anything, so, the power is the Holy Ghost that has been given to me. That is why this prophetic book is now available to the world.

And it is only close relations and friends that hug and kiss each other, not just anybody. I love Jesus very much and it resulted that my revelation was truth. After the Holy Ghost was given to me, all my revelations were tried with fire and it was confirmed as true.

Everyone has his own faith, but as for me, Thomas Bayo I cannot accept a revelation just like that without proper convincing and real authentication. So when God gave me the Holy Ghost, this was the time when I trembled and was deeply afraid and I believed. This was the time I knew that God is overlooking every human being; humans can be consumed within a twinkle of an eye by God and each individual on this earth is living by His grace.

Sometimes, when I see people making noise like a flood of mighty rushing waters, I just keep quiet and look at them. I stopped arguing with anyone and of any age. I just add people in my prayers. Because I know full well that they shall be rebuked by God in the last day.

Is easy to say "I have a revelation". The question is, do you have the Holy Ghost to authenticate it? Man needs to believe the Holy Ghost and if you do not believe the Holy Ghost, when the consequences of your wickedness will come, it is just like a person who could not finish the job he has started; if you believe God and maintain your faith, this is just like a man who stated a job and finished it.

The Lord Jesus called all His apostle friends, and they are not servants, because servants will not see what the master is doing. He allowed them touch Him. I did hug the Lord, However, we all are living in the time of grace, including the woman.

Folks should mind what they say regarding to revelations. When God visits a man, it is for a reason. The sins of man have reached an unbearable level. For God to pay a divine visit to the earth it has a great meaning.

God will not visit this earth for fun. When God the Father appeared to me and revealed His power and glory to me, God had a reason why He visited the earth. The reason is that we are at the end. The pure heart shall see God. The Scriptures are fulfilled.

God will never give a revelation to a man where there is no fire to try it if it is genuine one or not. Even when Jesus appeared to me, He only commanded me to search the bible very well because He in the bible I will find my biography. Everything He would tell me is there in the bible for me, my personal message were all encrypted and I got all information in the bible, protected and it was not stolen. The contents of this book is based on the Holy Ghost total information and all kinds of updates. Everything is in the holy bible for all of us. The Holy bible solved our questions and answers. If you do not have the Holy Ghost, that revelation remains illegal. There is no truth in it. Every information we need is all in the bible.

I am not giving a new prophecy and I do not specialised in giving prophecy is what that has been prophesied by the prophets that are here in this book. The things of God is by free will and by choice. He created life and He created death and the advice of a prophet is for good for anyone to chose life. That is why a true prophet will advice the people not to make a false testimony. And is not good to buy an evil power to cast spells on humans just because you want to have fame and money. Spell makes people to be out of their control — their thoughts and actions are dictated by that spell. Be genuine.

Anything that involves God the Father needs to be genuine and true. If it is found out on the judgment day that you made up stories yourself, saying "I have a revelation" when actually you do not, you just have to face the pit of hell. This will be implemented, because such a soul is a pestilent fellow and will not live in the mist of the righteous in the world to come.

When God appeared to me and gave me revelation, I did not write any book at the time immediately. To me, it was not merely important to the public. Because I did not know what they mean. It was in the prison that I came to myself and I remembered all the revelations, I remembered how the Father in heaven appeared to me face to face, and I saw when the world will end. I was not willing to answer my calling, and God arrested me and kept me in prison.

I told God that I am foolish; I deserved this prison because of my lukewarmness. I began to chasten myself and I wept. What I requested from the God of heaven was that He should please, give me the last chance. I will utilize this last chance.

When Jesus gave Peter a revelation of what was going to happen, Peter did not believe until the revelation was fulfilled at the appointed time, then he believed.

What made me really tremble in all these things is the Holy Ghost. I was shaken to the basc at first. When He entered me through the breath of God as my mouth was widely open physically and I took Him in, the Holy Ghost is a wise God.

He showed me Himself physically so that my testimony is true. All the revelations that were given to me, He tried all to be true. The Holy Ghost is the Spirit of truth. It was the Holy Ghost that made me know that Satan also gives revelations, the Devil can also counterfeit revelation and it may look like original, but what he cannot counterfeit is the Holy Ghost and fire.

Even the revelation that I was holding, I told God to let me investigate it, the Holy Ghost would always say "do not doubt, this is true and confirmed with fire ....purified seven times in the physical". He always let me to know this is something you have seen face to face and they are all written in the bible.

Sometimes, it will occur in my mind that, are these things true? Or are they just ordinary dreams? But seeing Holy Ghost in the physical manifestation day and night, not ordinarily but with fire, my faith is strengthened all day and I am joyful. I will always say I believe the Holy Ghost and I believe God and I believe all what is written in the holy bible, I cannot doubt the word of God. I will not doubt but believe. To me, this is wonderful and God is terrible.

Satan is a fallen angel and I have seen him in the physical realm. Satan said he moves alone and nobody is with him and if any person sees him, such a soul will die. He is going to kill any human being that sees him in the physical realm and use his blood to die his garment. But I saw Satan face to face, all the details I have written in the book titled, What Do You Want? It is not by my might nor by my power that I live today, but by the Spirit of the living God.

The Holy Ghost inspires me in all I have to say and all what I have written. If not for the Holy Ghost that lives in me, who I am to say I am a prophet? Who am I to say I have seen God the Father? The Holy Ghost made me today whom I am and He is my power.

We know that there are thousand of thousands of stories from people all over the world. There are people who confess and plead guilty to high profile crimes they never committed. This is called delusion. There is delusion in religion.

People will claim that they are sent by God and that they have seen Jesus, God and the Holy Spirit but actually, they have not. People testify of what they have not seen and say what they do not know.

Many will believe in lies and be filled with delusion. To believe in a lie is a grievous sin against the God of heaven.

There are some high profile crime cases that relate to rape, murder and many other crimes. Court judges have seen many of these cases. That is why most of these law enforcement agencies carry out DNA tests to be sure of their judgments. If your DNA does not match what you are talking about, they drop that case and ask you to get out of the detention canter or the prison. Can you believe that all prophets' DNA are in the bible? You don't know anything yet.

A truthful judge will not execute any judgment based on confession without DNA results, because there are billions of lies. They that have wisdom will not just believe any word. If God appeared to a man, if Jesus appeared to a man, if the Holy Ghost lives inside a man, it will show in his DNA. If you hug and touch Christ with your hands, if you have seen the God of heaven face to face and His eyes as a radiating fire or His gleaming-electric fire penetrates your eyes and gets into your system, it will be evident in the DNA of a man. If the Holy Ghost lives inside you, your biological body there must be an evidence of this in your DNA.

But in this end time, a man is revealing the end of the world like that of Noah.

Noah made a warning to all who dwelt on the face of the earth during his time. They saw Noah making the announcement and even saw him making an Ark, and the people did not survey the matter properly. They underestimated him.

When the voice of God began to hammer in my ear and His voice roar in my entire life, a voice like a fire that breaks the rocks in pieces. I stood alert, repented from my sins and prepared to do His will. This is the Holy Ghost and fire that makes me a complete witness of God.

On my side, God showed me more proof and convictions for His word to be established as a perfect truth, my DNA is in the bible. Zechariah mentioned my golden oil, this is DNA body chemistry. Another example of Maria, her DNA is written in the bible which is true, if a woman is raped, DNA does prove it. When the word 'apple' is used to illustrate a person biography, this is she that has been abused and must have DNA evidence. Her DNA proves that the bible does not lie.

Why will Maria's biography be in the bible? I have written in my first book titled, What Do You Want? A full chapter on her, to prove that the second witness is a woman. She was supposed to be the second witness, since the Creator needs two witnesses for His righteous judgment on the enemies, because God does not punish evil people without proper and truthful judgment and two witnesses must testify.

With all the revelations God gave to me in the north and south, west and east, God will not speak to anyone again, the bible has been written down for us. In it, we can search and find life.

A man can merely say "I am a prophet". But in reality, with a good sense of reasoning, this is not enough to execute a high profile revelation that brings message of the end to billion of humans in all the earth.

God knows that coming out of jail, I was going to face challenges, much temptations specifically designed to entice me so that I would continue to fall and find myself in a state of emotional injury. The Spirit that lives in Him is same Spirit He put in me and this Spirit is a consuming fire.

The Holy Ghost knows what will happen in five minutes, one hour, twenty four hours, the next day and in the future. This is why any man that is filled with the Holy Ghost will live a perfect life and no fault will be found in him.

I am no more under the law. I trust Him. Anything I want to do if He gives me the go ahead, I am satisfied and no have fear anymore, the Holy Ghost was given to me as a helper. If He says not to do it, I have great joy. Because He is saving me from death and destruction.

It is very easy for people to deceive me and even swindle me, because I have a soft heart. I trust people too much. After I have fallen into their net, that is when I will know.

But now, I only follow what the bible says. When we the remnant Christians follow the commandments as written in the bible, we are called fools, but we are not fools; we know what we are doing because Jesus commanded us what to do.

As for now, on this earth, we are peacemakers so that we can be called the children of God. I cannot even hold a gun, because of the Holy Ghost that is my power. If you hurt me, you have hurt this power.

Before the Holy Ghost was given to me, I was a Christian that believed in the law of Moses. If you hit me, I would hit you twice. In any situation, I was ready to die and I loved weapons, but not anymore.

But now, my understanding is opened by God, that what shall it profit a man to gain the whole world and lose his own soul? Your soul is very important any who is a peace marker shall have great reward from God. And my advice to people is, flee from trouble, if somebody hits you on the cheek, leave him and pray for him, follow the commandment of Christ.

I will continue to testify and testify as many times that the Holy Ghost is given for physical manifestation. The bible says the world did not know Him. No man has seen the Holy Ghost in this present generation at any time.

Whoever says the Holy Ghost is a person, such a soul has lied, because the Holy Ghost is a fire and the wonder of God that lives in man, the glory of God in man. He never departs from whom He dwells; no matter how bad is a human being is, the power is with the Holy Ghost to make such a man perfect.

To conclude, why a pastor is not qualified to preach the gospel in Asia on this chapter with examples, understanding and explanations. Apostle Paul's programme was to spread the gospel to the entire continent of Asia on an industrial scale, but the Holy Ghost gave him one simple message: do not go to Asia.

Apostle Paul's programme was so solid that he scheduled starting from the minor part of this continent. The Holy Ghost has seen ahead of time what would befall him in this mission.

"Now when they had gone throughout Phrygia and the region of Galatia, and were forbidden of the Holy Ghost to preach the word in Asia" (Acts 16:5.)

Paul was hardworking and he valued not his life for the sake of the gospel. He was ready to take anything, but, he was just a tool of God and it was the Holy Ghost that was doing the whole work. The Lord Jesus let Paul know that he needed to face Europe toward the north, but not to be proceeding deeply to the east position of the earth. Asia in the earth.

Apostle Paul was forbidden by the Holy Ghost to preach the word of God in Asia, and the Lord Jesus directed him on where to go.

Apostle Paul refused to hear the simple word of the Holy Ghost, instead, he went to Asia minor. As you read on, you will see what happened to him in Asia.

When Paul arrived in Asia, he was arrested and kept in jail with hard torture. Paul received stripes, was beaten up. The Holy Ghost had seen what would happen to him. Do not go to Asia.

It was in Asia minor that he received all these beatings. Meanwhile, he had not yet deeply involved himself with the Asian continent. But God did shake the prison with earthquake, and fear consumed the government of that nation. Paul was discharged and acquitted.

That fear of seeing the power of Almighty God, as the foundation of the prison was shaken to the base, the sudden quake was so strong that the prison warders requested salvation, for seeing the power of God in a physical experience.

They that have experienced the dread are the people who will tell you that God is dreadful. This is the place where I have seen in the bible that human beings were requesting for emergency salvation. This is the picture of the end, God will shake the heaven and the earth and many shall faint for fear. But there will be no emergency salvation in that day.

It shows here that by putting Paul in jail that they were foolish to have locked up a prophet of God, a prophet that has love enough to let them know the current news in the spiritual realm that would get them their salvation.

They would have missed this opportunity if apostle Paul had left. It was emergency water baptism. This will give you more understanding about these people that have experienced the power of God outside their physical body.

In the prison incident they trembled. What was the meaning of message they gave Paul? We are very sorry. The world does not know God because they have not seen the power of God.

On that last day, God has spoken; He will shake the heaven and the earth. If you are a wise man, then, meditate upon the word of God when He says He will shake the heaven and the earth. Only the foundation of a house that was shaken and people repented of their sins and they gave their lives to God without delay. They were baptised immediately.

Paul pulled out of the Asia mission. And ruled anything Asian out of his mind, not even to preach. He was born in Asia. And it was easy for him to travel all over Asia and still love these people enough to tell them the good news. This was exactly what the Holy Ghost explained to him, "Do not go to Asia."

However, the journey of Paul to Asia did not pose any serious risk or danger to his life; the Holy Ghost knew that He would save him from any death or serious danger. This is how the fire of the Holy Ghost works. The fire of the Holy Spirit, on a very minor cases that do not pose serious danger to the life of a prophet, the Holy Ghost will use His fire lightly to communicate.

But if such a prophet wants to proceed after experiencing the slight fire of the Holy Ghost, it is up to the prophet to either go ahead or do not. But at the end of it, the prophet will understand why the Holy Ghost has requested him not to proceed. But if it is something that will pose serious danger to the faith of a prophet, the Holy Ghost must use intensive fire to communicate and the prophet will understand fully that this is a no go zone, and that the Holy Ghost is serious about this matter.

The Holy Ghost will only use dense fire to speak on things that are extremely dangerous to a prophet, not to do it because it will cause harm to you. Even the words a prophet will speak out of his mouth that will implicate him, the Holy Ghost will always say "do not use such words, it will implicate you". If is too hard, He will give a prophet the right word to say and no one can resist that word. It is not all the time that the Holy Ghost will give a prophet a word to say. Normal things in every day daily life, we can use our common sense to do.

Brethren and sisters of the past in the early church who were filled with the Holy Ghost, Apostle Paul told them not to quench the Spirit.

For example, I may be walking toward a little problem, things like missing my way. I have to return. My return does not pose serious risk to my life. This is a small thing; the Holy Ghost may not use His fire to communicate about this.

Another example of how the fire of the Holy Ghost does His work; I may be writing something with the computer using Microsoft word program and the Holy Ghost will indicate to me with fire that I should look properly that the word I am writing there is a typographical error.

Maybe I wanted to write 'touch' and I missed one word and the computer automatically corrects and gives me 'torch' instead of 'touch'. If my eyes are not catching it, the Holy Ghost fire that has been programmed in my physical body will indicate to me to get this typographical error corrected, this fire that is switched on inside my physical body, I can quench it if I want without minding it. If I use my hand to touch that position in my body where the fire is, it will automatically quench. This is the reason why Apostle Paul said to the early Christians that they should not quench the Spirit. If He is telling you something, you should listen to Him. This fire is not harmful, it burns in the body because this is a healing fire and it is adjustable. This is how the Holy Ghost spoke to the early apostles. Not that He used an audible voice to speak. But sometimes when the Holy Ghost communicate with me in things that are little, I don't look at those things because they are small things but He always corrects me.

Anything that will pose a great danger to my life and the Holy Ghost has seen it ahead, He must use His dense fire to give me a sign of warning. This dense fire cannot be quenched by me, unless I stop the fire and the fire will stop. The more I stop earlier in response to the warning fire of the Spirit, the better for me, because this fire starts at a small level, telling me to stop and if I refuse to comply with this fire, then, it will increase its temperature to a high level.

There is no way I can proceed, I will definitely stop. God uses this fire to block evil. There is no way a prophet will do evil, a prophet that has Holy Ghost and with fire. It is the same Spirit that is in God that He gave to His prophets. This is same Spirit that is in Jesus Christ that He was not able to sin. Jesus is Lord God.

To save me from what I am don't see but is on the way, the Holy Spirit uses His fire to save depending on what is coming ahead. This is a refined fire that has been treated, it does not hurt. As I have said before, the Holy Ghost does not communicate with an audible voice. It gives great joy to see this fire radiating in the physical body and seeing it, the presence of the Almighty God in the life of a prophet, God is alive. The Holy Ghost is love.

One thing about me is that I am too slow to understand things; even when I receive lectures I hardly understand, but the Holy Ghost is such a patient God that He is never in hurry with me and He never gets angry with me despite the fact that my brain is too slow to understand. Sometimes I quench the fire, and sometimes I regret quenching it.

The Holy Ghost will always inform me of all things I do. He always says to me, 'do not be in a hurry." Even when I walk, He tells me to walk slowly. The things I am going to do, He is the one who will do it for me. Secondly, He put things into the memory; that is why the prophets were inspired to write.

Paul was baptized before many earlier Christians, and he experienced this anointing and the fire of the Holy Ghost. He gave the teaching of the Holy Ghost to the believers, based on his experience, just the way I am teaching the world now.

The Holy Ghost did not change His mind, "...and were forbidden of the Holy Ghost to preach the word in Asia."

Paul had great a experience in the prison and he gave a touching message to the people in Asia. The message was so strong that the people wept. If Paul had not been to Asia, there would have been no room for them to weep over his message, so the cause of such tears in Asia was not from the Holy Ghost, but was from Paul.

"And now, behold, I know that
yea all, among whom I have gone
preaching the kingdom of God,
shall see my face no more" (Acts 20:25.)

And they all wept sore, and fell
on Paul's neck, and kissed him,
Sorrowing most of all for the
words which he spake that they
should see his face no more.
And they accompanied him to the ship"
(Acts 20:38.)

The message the Holy Ghost gave to Paul was fulfilled. "You shall see my face no more."

Has the person you love ever said such a word to you? Seeing the person you love telling you that you will not see him or her again. The bible says they that heard this word, "you shall not see my face no more", wept sore. The word 'sore' here refers to a very painful experience.

This is as a physical pain, missing someone you love. But this is a place where Paul received beatings and lots of trouble. Paul never went to Asia again, his program of going deeply into Asia was cancelled by the Lord and he had to face the north, to Europe.

When I studied the mission of Apostle Paul to Asia, I came across a particular verse in the book of Acts. "All Asia and the whole world do worshipeth" (Acts 19:27.)

What kind of worship is this? This is an image, demonic, and a temple made with hands that is located in this continent that the entire world did worship. Asia has been known since the ancient times to be a source of demonic religion, which is still existing up to this day. The biggest image on earth, the greatest idol worshipers and false religion are located in that zone, which has spread to all parts of the earth today. This is the only continent that has the lowest population of Christians.

The salvation that goes to the eastern part of the earth is from God and Jesus Christ and whoever believes that Jesus is the Son of God, whether you are in the east, south, west, north, you have salvation already.

The Holy Ghost may not actually hate the Asians, He may loves the Asians, depending if they will not vex Him. The bible explains that they shouted and praised the idol they made with their hands. This voice is louder and the Holy Ghost has no pleasure in this.

An apostle that is filled with the Holy Ghost and with fire has no business in Asia regarding spreading the gospel. The Holy Ghost is gentle and peaceful, anywhere there is evil, He doesn't go there. Except on a special mission.

It is only God that has the power to spread the gospel in Asia, not man. And this "continued by the space of two years; so that all they which dwelt in Asia heard the word of the Lord Jesus, both Jews and Greeks."

Through the spirit that manifested physically, Jesus was able to spread the word of the gospel in Asia without an apostle preaching it. Can you believe this? Within the space of two years, the gospel went through all Asia.

The judgment of the Holy Ghost is perfect. The people of Asia all heard the gospel, which indicates that the gospel has already been preached in all Asia since as we all know as written in the scriptures, "And the gospel of the kingdom shall be preached in all the world for a witness unto all nations; and then shall the end come" (Matthew 24:14.)

You can witness what is happening in the world today. This is a great wonder that as mean as Muslim extremist there are, there are still Christian Arabs living in their midst. This is to tell you that God is Almighty.

Can you believe despite the hassles in Palestine, there are still humans that are Christian citizens of Palestine? And in other countries like Morocco, Libya, Turkey, Iran, Iraq, Afghanistan, and all part of Asia indigenes who are Christians living in their midst. Christ is the keeper of these ones living in the mist of wolves.

"If ye then, being evil, know how to give good gifts unto your children: how much more shall your heavenly Father give the Holy Spirit to them that ask him?" (Luke 11:13.)

God the Father did pour the anointing of the Holy Ghost out to the early Christians. The promise was fulfilled because He is a good God. But when the people that called themselves Christians, also called themselves born again when they did not know the definition of born again, this is going backward and they refuse to go forward.

They preferred to go back to Egypt, and refused to repent, by facing the east position to worship, when the bible has revealed to you that Satan the enemy is a spirit not a physical being and his mountain is located in Edom which is located on the east side.

Also, by refusing to face the north position to worship Him in spirit and in truth, facing the east position this is a spiritual focus to Edom in spirit and in lie. Then you want the God of heaven to give you the Holy Ghost do you worship in the East and face Edom?

You want God go give you the Holy Ghost while you worship Satan? It is a compulsory thing for the Moslems and the Buddhists to face east position to worship. You have rebelled against the Holy Ghost, you and your forefathers. This was exactly what God of heaven revealed to Ezekiel, "my anger is upon them."

The Holy Ghost has His own will and God has His own will. When the Holy Ghost has ruled it out from His mind to dwell with anyone, His judgment has been established. The Holy Ghost fought against the people by sending to them delusion, and He is now their enemy: "I am a jealous God."

Speaking in tongues is not evidence of having the Holy Ghost and fire. For example, you may see some people that have been deceived and are ignorant and there is no way you can convince them to turn back from their ignorance.

If you tell them to please turn, they will rebuke you and it will become a great fooling to you. Ignorance is a big threat to peace.

When the God of heaven takes away His anger from any group or any person, such a person or group will have no fault again, because he who laughs at them takes their sins. The Holy Ghost told the prophets to turn their laughter into mourning. "Be afflicted, and mourn, and weep: let your laughter be turned to mourning, and your joy to heaviness" (James 4:9.)

Do not even laugh at the Muslim, despite the fact that they are facing the east position and facing the pit. God may take away His anger from them and face you that are mocking them. You know that these people are perishing and this is giving you fun? All these things you see and hear, they are not fun.

I preached the gospel to a man that I know, I told him that he should turn his laughter into mourning; he rebuked me immediately. I nearly even burst into laughter, but I held it strong. If you cannot hold laughter, turn it to mourning. The most important thing is that you have to use wisdom.

The false prophets have great fun when dealing with people that have fallen into their nets. And deep inside their hearts, they do enjoy this power that has been given to them by the Devil. This is the reason why God will take away His anger away from many people because He knows that you have been seduced.

❧❧❧❧

"And when Paul had laid his hands upon them: the Holy Ghost came on them; and they spake with tongues, and proph-esied" (Act 19:6.)

Do not let anyone deceive you or give you an erroneous message; Speaking in tongues is not evidence of the Holy Ghost.

In this verse above, they were pastors. The people whom Apostle Paul laid his hands on were disciples, not just anyone. The Holy Ghost gave to them a gift of speaking in tongues, not that the Holy Ghost filled them or they had this power. Look at what the bible says here, "the Holy Ghost came on them." The word 'came' here is, 'draw closer'. Not that the Holy Ghost entered inside them.

The Holy Ghost gave to them the gift of prophecy. This happened in Ephesus, and this is part of Asia. Paul went there on his own to preach the gospel. You don't expect the Holy Ghost to instruct that it is forbidden to go to Asia, and at the same time fill the people in Asia.

So, speaking in tongues is not evidence of the baptism of the Holy Ghost. Many of the people in this world who say that they have the baptism of the Holy Ghost, they do not have the baptism of the Holy Ghost.

When the Holy Ghost lives in a man, he that is filled with the Holy Ghost cannot sin against the Holy Ghost and He will not depart from whom He lives. Remember that the Holy Ghost is fire.

The Holy Ghost suffered apostle Paul not to preach the word in Asia. Yet, Apostle Paul went to Asia. The Holy Ghost is a friend.

Consequently, do not use speaking in tongues to justify yourself that you are filled with the Holy Ghost; this is wrong to justify yourself.

The Holy Ghost is power and no power is greater than Him, this is the power that was given to the twelve apostles, you need power in this world to reveal secrets of any category, whether in this world or not. But revealing men in power and the secret that people refuse to say without power in you, you can be slaughtered, because the people that you are going to reveal are people that sit in power, both in the visible and the invisible world.

This is why the God of heaven gave me power to reveal great things. Without power to reveal a secret, your life remains in danger in this world and in the world to come. Humans can mastermind your death.

Professionals such as journalists, book authors, police, actors, musicians, artists, these people their lives mostly in danger; these are the people that deliver to the entire world messages depending on the area of field of expression. A message is a message, either it's put in a song or in a drawing, all is a message.

It is boldly written in the prison that you should look and close your mouth. The same message will also tell you, if you talk, you will see your death and no one on earth can challenge them. They used the picture of a monkey to illustrate the message; the monkey used his hand to close its mouth while looking. The same message will tell you face to face that you have no power. You cannot reveal people in power without power in your hands. It is not every news you hear that you need to believe.

Most of the news you hear have been sliced into pieces for

safety reasons and the main core cannot be heard.

Anyone that departs from this world without accepting Jesus as Lord and Saviour, such a person has no hope.

Do not take unnecessary risks, losing on earth and again in the world to come without salvation, because you refuse to take Christ as your anchor.

Power has been given to me by the Creator. So, when I see this power manifesting in my life in reality, then, I testify of what I see and say what I know. And I give my messages with the power that has been given to me. The words that comes from my mouth are not ordinary words, they are Holy Ghost blessed words.

God said, "I will give power to my two witnesses and do not hurt them." Who will put briars and thorns on the battle way of God? Who? God will gather them together and burn them up.

A man cannot just wake up in the morning and say the world will end in 2035; power is needed to reveal this.

Giving information to this world regarding the end of the world is as a threat to Satan. Telling the god of this earth that his days are almost over, this is the reason power is needed to reveal the date of the end.

When Satan hears that the world will end on any given date, he trembles because he knows that he will soon be going under the ground, chained in prison, hell.

If you call yourself a pastor or any kind of human being and give a date of the end, Satan will be interested in such a soul and he will find out who exactly is the person giving date of the end. And whether power is given to him or not. Satan has the power of surveillance, and he is known as the god of the whole earth.

As the author of this book, I know what I am talking about. You have only heard of Satan as written in the bible, but you have not seen him, he knows that time is running out for him.

Chapter Eight

Taken Up in the Rapture

What is rapture? And why is the rapture? The rapture was planned and designed by the Son of God that will place in the year 2035, meaning that He has specifically prepared places in heaven to accommodate humans that He has chosen. The mansions are so beautiful and well designed, and they more precious than gold and diamond which was confirmed to me by the Holy Ghost Himself as true. I personally saw it myself, the Holy City is beyond my explanation and the dance of the saints that I saw was amazing, a real joy which I have already explained in my book titled, What Do You Want?

Jesus coming back to the earth to take the chosen, granting them citizens of heaven and His coming back to the earth on His second time which is known as the rapture.

The basic fundamental plan of Jesus for the rapture is that, the qualified ones that are chosen and taken and granted citizenships of heaven, THEY SHALL NOT DIE, this is the eternal life. Death has not power over them. They will live forever with the Creator coupled with everlasting joy and they would not be subject to any kind of law, this is 100% liberty with no condition attached to it. The lowest citizen of heaven is greater than the greatest human being on this earth. This gives an idea of how important is the Christianity race. That is why some humans they go to any length to make sure they get their names listed in the book of life.

If there is anything that will deprived anyone not to make the rapture, the thing that will withdraw you, if it is your right hand, I will advice to cut it off, is better to have eternal life with one hand than to lose the rapture. Hope you understand?

You must be properly vetted by Christ before your name is listed on the list of rapturettees.   And the requirement is, a repenting heart. Is the repenting heart which Christ needed from anyone.

Christ do not need much requirement from anyone. If a repentance is in the heart, next leave the rest work for God because He that created you has the power to build you perfect like Himself, and no fault will be found in you. And what you will be seeing is unbearable joy. I have experienced people who knew God in their late age and regretted not knowing God since the day they were born to this earth. When they knew God they discovered joy and found peace and such people have the assurance of the rapture.

Another point is, one of the basic reason for the rapture is that, the heavenly Father who created the heaven and the earth has never be angry to the entire world after the flood of Noah, but due to the evil and wickedness of man including killings and sufferings of the prophets and the wise men. He has sworn that He will filter His wrath to the entire world. Which is 2035, but the day and the hour is not known, therefore Jesus does not want the chosen ones known as the saints or also called the biblical believers to experience this wrath of God because it will be very, very terrible. And you can see the reason why Jesus designed the rapture enable Him come back to the earth on His second time with His angels to take away the chosen from this earth, and at the end of the day the world would see the chosen that they are gone.

> "And if thine eye offend thee, pluck it out: it is
> better for thee to enter into the kingdom of
> God with one eye, than having two eyes to
> be cast into hell fire:" (Mark 9:47.)

You have been going to the Church for ages and the rapture comes and you are not taken and see that the biblical believers are gone. What will you do? This book is a great opportunity to the world and the reason why it's a great opportunity is because a spoken word came, "I Appeared Unto You". And the question is, who spoke this word? This is the Creator of the heaven and the earth, He Created mankind including all things in earth, things in heaven and things under the earth. He Created the angels, He is the Almighty God of heaven.

When His voice came to me like the sound of roaring water-fall it means that, His appearing is for the entire world because the Creator will speak through a single man and such message is for all the people of the entire world.

Why this book is a cutting edge, with common sense you should know that humans will never take any actions unless they are caught with their pants down.

Man is not always prepared, so this book is a great opportunity to as many that read it and pass the message on. And it really explains the rapture procedures enable anyone to meet up with the easy step by step measures. However, at present only what is available is the month and year of the coming of the Lord Jesus Christ, but I do not know the day and the hour because I was careless.

We still need to thank God that we have something (the month and the year) at least to watch and see the coming of the Lord Jesus.

Since man cannot take action in his life unless he is caught with his pants down here is a great opportunity for anyone who will humble himself, the rapture are of two dimensions. The first dimension is that Jesus will not rapture anyone slobbering in sleep, this is rule out.

"And what I say unto you I say unto all, Watch." (Mark 13:37.)

'Watch' is capitalised here, it shows the degree of the Lord speech regarding the rapture. Watch is define as, to look at or observe attentively over a period of time. So this is a length or portion of time. Nobody knows the day and the hour of the coming of the Lord Jesus. This is a period of time that is revealed on this book. I will continue to say sorry for the losing the accurate date, second, minute, hour, day.

So if you can keep your eyes open and watch His coming there are great chance for you to be taken, do your best to watch. But I may still go back to Turkey again in the city of Messina to the hotel that I logged including the customs police to check if I can get any record of my business transactions. As you know that this is not easy for Africans to acquire a visa to any country of the world. If the hotel can give to me the record of the few days that I was in the hotel room that the Lord God appeared to me. This will be nice. Because I remember that I only spent about three to four days or so in Messina.

I have checked my brain all over and over if I can remember the actual time I saw the date of the end on the tree either in the night or afternoon or early in the morning but there is no way I can remember it. But as from 10 AM to 1 PM I should be on the street and as from 5 PM to 9 PM I might had not slept.

And probably I should be at sleep as from 10 PM to 8 AM. At this time that I was awake those time that I was on the street or awake Jesus will not come because, the counting of the date starts at the exact seconds, minutes, hour, day, month and the year that I saw the date of the end on the tree. The coming of Jesus may be in the night, afternoon, morning and evening. So to calculate, anyone may use those time that I was on the street to have a rest in the Month of May, 2035 so that you don't go and sleep and slumber.

That is if you are alive. If Jesus is coming to pick anyone is only people that are awake that will be raptured.

The second dimension is this, please make sure in that month of May, 2035 remains holy in the body, soul and spirit. Do not let any single fault be found in you, be perfect, don't fight and do not keep enemy, keep away from anything evil, keep yourself from anything sexual intercourse, bless people that comes on your way. Give information to anyone that in the month of May they may not contact you, that you are on soul reflection. You may switch off all your contacts, to avoid distractions. Avoid any kinds of gatherings, flee from watching pornographic materials, flee from fornication and adultery. Do not watch any kind of TV programs that do not give glory to God if possible switch off your TV to avoid your soul be contaminated with worldly things. Evil people may discourage you and discredit the word of God because of their business in using you to make money.

Do not drink, anything such as drug avoid it, be truthful in conversation with anyone, anything computer games or telephone game from these things, anything such as gambling avoid it, anything stealing avoid it, make sure you forgive anyone and if you might have offended anyone make sure you should settle with them if necessary, anything that Jesus commanded you to do as written in the bible make sure you do all of them.

Make sure you are in good relationship with your father and mother and if there are any differences make sure you are in good spirit with them. Avoid excess smoking in this period of time that Jesus is arriving. Use your common sense to do the right thing.

You should remember that on this chapter we are talking about the rapture, this is not the judgment day. If anyone dies before the coming of Jesus or before 2035, it is appointed unto man to die once and after that comes the judgment. The commandment has been written before we were born into this earth and they must be broken but they shall be fulfilled.

Those whom are lucky to be alive shall see the coming of the Lord Jesus Christ, the Son of God. Since the sixth angel has sounded, the date when the sixth sounded is in the bible which is revealed in my book titled, What Do You Want? Now we are now wafting for the seventh angel to sound in 2035. Then the kingdom is given to Christ and His elects.

"And there shall be signs in the sun, and in
the moon, and in the stars; and upon the earth
distress of nations, with perplexity; the sea and
the waves roaring; Men's hearts failing them
for fear, and for looking after those things

which are coming on the earth: for the powers
of heaven shall be shaken. And then shall they
see the Son of man coming in a cloud with
power and great glory. And when these
things begin to come to pass, then look up,
and lift up your heads; for your redemption
draweth nigh" (Luke 21:25-28.)

The rapture is not something that will be hidden or it is something that will take place secretly. Let me describe the sound of the seventh angel here that I have seen, felt and heard. The sound will start like this Ggoooooo. Or Gguuuuuuuu. I use the best of my ability to explain it. When this seventh sound will boom, aircrafts falling, cars, trucks, trains, all kinds of vehicles will course a lot of accidents, buildings shaking, this will be very catastrophic. Night will change and turn to a bright day light, the day will change and turn to night immediately, every human being on the planet whether you are in Australia, Africa, America, Europe, Asia, Islands, Oceans all would see Jesus at same time. This will be kind of great wonder.

In the month of May, 2035 which I do not know the day and the hour, you will need to stay where you are, immediately as you begin to see signs such as the earth shaking and moving as if there is an earthquake, remain in the position you are, do not start running to anywhere either in your home or any place stay in that specific position that you found yourself. If you are at home do not move from your home, if you are in the church do not leave there, any location you are, as you see these terrible things happening remain in that specific position.

Mankind will be half dead because of the terrible thing that is coming ahead of time. Tears and great sorrows will send some looking for a place to hide, this is beyond my explanation. The reason why I am able to explain this to anyone is because I and God, we have rehearsed the end together. And I know how it is, despite the rehearsal that I underwent with the Creator, I was able to explain this experience in my book titled, What Do You Want? So I am not writing what I have read or what I was told, I write what I have seen and what I have touched and what I have experienced.

I do not know the inside of any human being is the Creator that can detect who is a nice person and who is fake because there are fake prophets around us, and any question anyone can ask himself or herself is that, who is me? What is my relationship with God of heaven? Everyone knows this answer to himself or herself.

Anyone who know his or her relationship with the Creator, then see what the bible says about him or her as a believer. The Creator singled you out as a believer and He knows your identity as a chosen generation, a royal priesthood, an holy nation, a peculiar people. This is where we should be prepared to be looking up to our salvation and be expecting our redeemer to reign with the King of kings and Lords of lords. As a peculiar person we are waiting for the bridegroom? Whosoever believe that, presently this is the time of pleasure and myth such person has deceived himself or herself. As the author of this book and as a prophet of God I can tell you that our salvation is in the time of trouble.

And for those that will be taken into rapture, the joy is unbearable and there is a great dance. I wish you happy eternity and we shall meet in the Lord's day by His power. Amen.

Chapter Nine

Tired And Exhausted

"And he shall speak great words against the most
High, and shall wear out the saints of the most High,
and think to change times and laws"
(Daniel 7:25a.)

The word wear out here in this verse is worn-out. This verse is talking about what exactly shall happen to them that will go into rapture with Christ since they still exist on this earth and the bible call them as the saints. This is also called the elects or also known as we the believers in Christ.

Prophet Daniel was able to illustrate the biographies of us the believers on this earth and as you can see as written in this verse above, the words of Daniel are unadulterated prophetic and it was the angel of God that brought this message to prophet Daniel.

The truth of the matter is that we the true believers are tired and exhausted in everything done by this world systems. Every day new laws are enacted and this making us go crazy every day in our daily live, sometimes we weep and sometimes it seems that there are no hope and looking at ourselves hopeless. Personally, when I see the harassment that the world do render to us the elects, sometimes I just don't know what to do. Unjust treatment makes the just goes crazy, I am talking of my experience in this book because all the saints have their own story exactly as what Daniel the prophet said, some cases may even be worst than mine and mine may be worst than some of the saints but they are of the same proportion.

We are not even allowed to get education on this earth but people cannot understand this: those beings that speak evil words against the most High refused to allow us the elects to get education on this earth. In the spiritual realm when they have decided that you cannot get a diploma, hand-work, university degree it is impossible that you will get education in the real world on this earth. This is the reason you see some of us that it will be impossible for us to complete our education because the source of this failure is from the spiritual realm. It is easy for Satan to enter any unbelief human being on this earth and use them to harass us and break our hearts into pieces, just like the way evil uses Judas. The way evil entered Judas to commit evil such craft of Satan still exist up to this hour. Satan controls this world economy, government, social system and much more. Some may ask why did God allow evil to befall the elects? Look at what the bible says here, "And he shall speak great words against the most High". The action of Satan is not only on us the elects but they also blaspheme the holy name of God, even our Father in heaven is also affected as you can see the prophey of Daniel.

My experience of this world injustice from the small to the top, is what the prophecy of Daniel is talking about here, from our neighbours, outside home, inside home, privates and to the law, this is not what I am making up this is what the bible is saying about us here.

The invisible seal of God is already on our forehead which the world know as written in the book of revelation and the manifestation of this seal has an impact in our lives as sheep of the most High that we are the genuine children of peace, and the issue is that the children of perdition can sense the manifestation of God seal on our forehead. And what next? That is the area the children of perdition wear us out which makes us get tired and frustrated in our lives.

The world in continuously to provoke us the elects so that

we can lose our temper, we are subjected to their demand or nothing for us as a way to contaminate us, we are pressed to the wall and much more. What the world will do to us the believers the world will not do it to the children of this world. People that are not in this class may not understand what I am talking about because they are not under the radar of the enemy. Every chosen knows what I am taking about. This is what makes us exhausted and tired of everything on this world system. We are afflicted so sore but we will continue to love our God.

This is a continual attack from the enemy. Is that sufferings that we undergo that create the partway for us to obtain heavenly citizenship, because the way to life is narrow and not all that have the power to walk through that road. This is why we need to pray all day.

The prophecy of Daniel made me to understand that in the time of pains and sufferings, I will not forsake my God instead I will show Him love despite my pains and sufferings in life as coursed by this world with their continues harassments, trap and injustice. We are tempted in every corner, we are snared in every corner, but God is holy and He is the Almighty.

The bible used the word wear-out the saint of the most high God, there is no where written here in the bible that the saints of the most High are in myth and laughter and what prophet Daniel wrote here is the simple truth and nothing but the truth.

They that gave us a single drop of water on our tongue in the time of our sufferings, tears in our hearts and pains and sometimes we are confused, or even a cup of water, they that visited us in prison, they that gave us the elects any little help of any kind, they are blessed, those that brought gift to us in the hospital when we are in sick bed for stomach pains, veins pains... they that had render any kind of help to us of any manner, these people have a guarantee to join the Lord in the air and it does not matter whom these people are of any kind of race and faith, because that cup of water you have given to any of us is like a great relief but you may not know and you may look at it as nothing, but to God it is a mighty relief to the elects and there is a great reward ahead of them that have done this to us.

> "And whosoever shall give to drink
> unto one of these little ones a cup
> of cold water only in the name of a
> disciple, verily I say unto you, he
> shall in no wise lose his reward"
> (Matthew 10:42.)

> Then shall the King say unto them
> on his right hand, Come, ye blessed
> of my Father, inherit the kingdom
> prepared for you from the foundation
> of the world: For I was an hungred,
> and ye gave me meat: I was thirsty,
> and ye gave me drink: I was a stranger,
> and ye took me in: Naked, and ye
> clothed me: I was sick, and ye visited
> me: I was in prison, and ye came
> unto me. Then shall the righteous
> answer him, saying, Lord, when saw
> we thee an hungred, and fed thee?
> or thirsty, and gave thee drink?
> When saw we thee a stranger,
> and took thee in? or naked, and
> clothed thee? Or when saw we thee
> sick, or in prison, and came unto thee?
> And the King shall answer and say unto
> them, Verily I say unto you, Inasmuch as
> ye have done it unto one of the least of
> these my brethren, ye have done it unto
> me. Then shall he say also unto them on
> the left hand, Depart from me, ye cursed,
> into everlasting fire, prepared for the devil
> and his angels: For I was an hungred,

and ye gave me no meat: I was thirsty, and ye gave me no drink: I was a stranger, and ye took me not in: naked, and ye clothed me not: sick, and in prison, and ye visited me not. Then shall they also answer him, saying, Lord, when saw we thee an hungred, or athirst, or a stranger, or naked, or sick, or in prison, and did not minister unto thee? Then shall he answer them, saying, Verily I say unto you, Inasmuch as ye did it not to one of the least of these, ye did it not to me. And these shall go away into everlasting punishment: but the righteous into life eternal. (Matthew 34:42-46.)

325

I Appeared Unto You

Thomas Bayo

I Appeared Unto You

9 788889 502426 4